VARIETIES OF VICTORIANISM

Varieties of Victorianism

The Uses of a Past

Edited by

Gary Day

First published in Great Britain 1998 by
MACMILLAN PRESS LTD
Houndmills, Basingstoke, Hampshire RG21 6XS and London
Companies and representatives throughout the world

A catalogue record for this book is available from the British Library.

ISBN 0–333–62901–9

First published in the United States of America 1998 by
ST. MARTIN'S PRESS, INC.,
Scholarly and Reference Division,
175 Fifth Avenue, New York, N.Y. 10010

ISBN 0–312–21719–6

Library of Congress Cataloging-in-Publication Data
Varieties of Victorianism : the uses of a past / edited by Gary Day.
p.   cm.
Includes bibliographical references and index.
ISBN 0–312–21719–6
1. English literature—19th century—History and criticism.
2. Great Britain—History—Victoria, 1837–1901—Historiography.
I. Day, Gary, 1956–   .
PR461.V37   1998
820.9'008—dc21   98–23532
                                                    CIP

This book is printed on paper suitable for recycling and made from fully managed and
sustained forest sources.

10   9   8   7   6   5   4   3   2   1
07   06   05   04   03   02   01   00   99   98

Printed and bound in Great Britain by
Antony Rowe Ltd, Chippenham, Wiltshire

For Charlotte, who loves the variousness of things

Contents

Acknowledgements

I would like to thank Clive Bloom and Charmian Hearne for their advice and support, and Margaret Griffiths and Charlotte Keating of De Montfort University Library for helping me to track down references.

Notes on the Contributors

Gary Day is a senior lecturer at De Montfort University, Bedford. He has edited a number of books in the Macmillan *Insights* series and is the author of *Re-Reading Leavis: 'Culture' and Literary Criticism* (1996).

Steven Earnshaw is a senior lecturer at Sheffield Hallam University. He is the author of *The Direction of Literary Theory* (1996) and the editor of *Postmodern Surroundings* (1994) and the co-editor of *Postmodern Subjects/Postmodern Texts* (1995). He is currently writing a book on literature and pubs.

Nadine Holdsworth is a lecturer in drama at De Montfort University, Bedford. She has written on popular political theatre and is currently researching into Joan Littlewood's Theatre Workshop.

Chris Hopkins is course leader of BA English Studies at Sheffield Hallam University. He has written on the British novel of the 1930s, Anglo-Welsh writing and representations of modernity in the nineteenth and twentieth centuries. He is currently writing *Thinking About Texts: an Introduction to English Studies*.

Simon Malpas is a lecturer in the department of English at Manchester Metropolitan University. He has recently completed his PhD at the Centre for Critical and Cultural Theory at the University of Wales, Cardiff and is currently working on constructions of subjectivity in postmodernism.

Jessica Maynard is a tutorial assistant at the University of Wales, Bangor. She has written on Henry James and Wilkie Collins as well as on representations of political violence. She is currently writing the poetry chapters for the Longman *Literature and Culture in Modern Britain* series.

Robert Mighall was recently a research fellow in English at Merton College, Oxford, and is now the editor of Penguin Classics. He has published an edition of Oscar Wilde's poems and is currently writing a book on Victorian Gothic fiction.

K.M. Newton is a professor of English at Dundee University. He is the author of a number of books among them *George Eliot: Romantic Humanist* (1981); *In Defence of Literary Interpretation* (1986) and *Interpreting the Text* (1990). He has also edited *Twentieth Century Literary Theory: a Reader* (1988), a new edition of which is forthcoming, and *George Eliot* (1992).

John Peck is a senior lecturer in English at the University of Wales, Cardiff. He is the joint general editor of *New Casebooks* and of the forthcoming series *Critical Issues* and the author of *War: The Army and Victorian Literature* (1998).

Carl Plasa is a lecturer in English at the University of Wales, Cardiff. He has written widely on nineteenth- and twentieth-century literature and has co-edited *The Discourse of Slavery: Aphra Behn to Toni Morrison*. He is currently writing a book on race and identification in colonial and postcolonial writing from Shakespeare to Tsitsi Dangarembga.

Nick Rance is a senior lecturer at Middlesex University. He is the author of *Wilkie Collins and Other Sensation Novelists* (1991) and has written introductions to Wilkie Collins's *The Woman in White* and Robert Louis Stevenson's *Dr Jekyll and Mr Hyde and Other Stories*. He is currently working on a book about the representation of serial killers.

Mary Angela Schwer is a lecturer at the University of Notre Dame. She is currently researching into nineteenth-century missionaries.

Peter R. Sedgwick is a lecturer in philosophy at the University of Wales, Cardiff. He has edited *Nietzsche: a Critical Reader* (1995) and is co-author of *Key Concepts in Cultural Theory* (1998).

Jonathan Skinner is a lecturer in sociology and anthropology at the University of Abertay, Dundee. He has written on the relationship between Victorian anthropology and contemporary Orientalism. He is currently researching into life in Britain's dependent territories, particularly the island of Montserrat.

Darryl Wadsworth is a lecturer at the University of Pennsylvania. He has written widely on Victorian melodrama and is currently researching into its connections with the conventions of soap opera.

Alistair Walker is a senior lecturer in English at De Montfort University, Bedford. He has written widely on twentieth-century fiction and is currently working on an anthology of British Romantic Poetry.

1

Introduction: Past and Present – the Case of Samuel Smiles' *Self Help*

Gary Day

In recent years politicians have extolled what they consider to be the virtues of Victorian values. They use the phrase as if the Victorian period were a smooth continuum from the ascension of the queen in 1837 to her death in 1901, but these years cover huge changes that make the early Victorian age quite different to the mid- or late Victorian one. We cannot therefore talk of Victorian values as if they were the same from the beginning to the end of the reign.

The Victorian value I want to concentrate on in this introduction is 'self help' but, before that, I want to suggest that that there are certain continuities between ourselves and the Victorians which seem to give Victorian values a contemporary relevance. I shall first outline some of these continuities before moving on to consider the historical specificity of self help as it appears in Samuel Smiles' book of the same name. I want to focus on the question of continuity because I believe that there has been too much emphasis over the past few years on the idea of history as rupture. Of course our age is different from the Victorian one, and this is something that those who urge a return to Victorian values fail to appreciate, but too great a stress on discontinuity obscures how the past inheres in the present and, if this is not recognised, we are doomed to repeat it. The task, if we are to move forward instead of marking time, is to understand both continuity and discontinuity.

The term 'Victorian values' has been part of popular and political rhetoric since 1983 when Mrs Thatcher and her ministers used it as both a diagnosis and a recommended cure for the ills of British society.[1] Briefly, these were a regulated economy, welfare dependency and the decline of the family. A return to *laissez faire*, individual charity and family discipline would revive Britain's

1

flagging fortunes and restore her place in the world. Even the election of a Labour government has not led to a questioning of these assumptions. On the contrary, the policies of Tony Blair have confirmed that the state should no longer provide cradle-to-grave welfare: henceforth the individual has to be responsible for him or herself.[2] The emphasis on the individual is thus at the expense of society and the most notorious expression of this doctrine is Mrs Thatcher's declaration that 'There is no such thing as society, only individuals and their families'.[3]

The idea of a return to Victorian values assumes that they have faded away into history, requiring a deliberate act to revive them. However, it is possible to argue that Victorian values have never ceased to be a shaping force throughout the twentieth century. The doctrine of state intervention is as Victorian as *laissez faire* and so too is the idea of poverty as a personal failing as well as a structural problem.[4] Victorian values have never gone away; different ones have merely been emphasised at different times. The continuity of Victorian values is partly explained by the continuity of the Victorian condition itself: what we understand as modernity and post-modernity can simply be seen as different facets of Victorianism. Thomas Richards has analysed how the Great Exhibition of 1851 ushered in a distinctively modernist mode of perception,[5] while Jurgen Habermas's characterisation of modernity as the division of substantive reason[6] into science, morality and art, each of which, as the province of an expert, excludes the 'larger public',[7] is equally a feature of the Victorian period where 'the consequence of reform in university and technical education was increasing specialisation, and specialisation undermined the synthesis of knowledge.'[8]

Jean François Lyotard uses the term modern 'to designate any science that legitimates itself with reference to a metadiscourse' while he defines the postmodern as 'incredulity toward metanarratives'.[9] Both these find a resonance in the Victorian period. Science derived a great deal of its cultural authority by linking technological development and the study of the natural world to the metanarrative of history as human progress, while Walter Pater could write that his age was distinguished from the ancient 'by its cultivation of the "relative" spirit in place of the absolute"'.[10] This view had been anticipated earlier in the century by Macaulay's mockery of James Mill for seeing history in terms of universal laws instead of events whose uniqueness made them impossible to systematise.[11] The exchange between Macaulay and Mills makes Linda Hutcheon's claim that what distinguishes postmodern historiography from traditional history is that '[t]he particular, the local and the specific replace the general, the universal and the eternal' seem positively anachronistic.[12] In the Victorian age, observes Robin Gilmour, there were 'no metaphysical absolutes to shore up self or society against the erosions of the relative spirit.'[13] We like, the Victorians, experience an ever-increasing stock of information beyond our ability to process it: the main difference is that we have not been traumatised, as they were, by the loss of a world view, Christianity, that had previously sustained them.

Aspects of modernism and postmodernism can also be found in Victorian art. The esoteric symbolism of the Pre-Raphaelites and the aesthetic movement's preoccupation with form look forward to the experiments of modernism while the description of postmodern art as one where 'no style pre-dominates'[14] can also be applied to the Victorian era where 'there was no canon of taste dominant enough to forge their [art] into a self sufficient contemporary style' hence the accent of the age was on 'revivalism'.[15]

Of course these broad similarities hide significant differences. In the case of art the Victorians used the past to critique the present. The Middle Ages, for example were used 'as a weapon against the mechanism, calculation, selfishness and ugliness of...industrial civilisation.'[16] Pugin's architecture, Ruskin's art criticism and Tennyson's *Idylls of the King* are all examples of the Victorian tendency 'of looking to pre-Reformation England for the socially responsible hierarchial community which modernisation had corrupted and dispersed.'[17] This is very different from postmodernism, where the past is problematised rather than appealed to as a standard by which to judge the present. According to Linda Hutcheon, postmodernism 'confronts and contests any...discarding or recuperating of the past in the name of the future' or indeed the present.[18] It does this by drawing attention to how the past is constructed through 'systems of signification' in which 'events' are selected, positioned and combined in historical or literary narratives.[19] Its characteristic relation to the past is parody, which both enshrines and questions it.[20]

Another difference between Victorian and postmodern art is that whereas the idiom of the former was realism that of the latter is irony; though this is not to say that irony could not be an important feature of nineteenth-century fiction, as a glance at the work of Charles Dickens or George Eliot quickly shows. The realism of the

Victorian novel was due, among other things, to omniscient narra-
tors, detached, detailed descriptions, and coherent plot. A postmodern novel like John Fowles's *The French Lieutenant's Woman*
(1969) deploys these conventions ironically to show how fiction is
less a reflection of reality than a construction of it. As Hutcheon puts
it, 'the nineteenth century structures of narrative closure (death,
marriage, neat conclusions) are undermined by those postmodern
epilogues that foreground how we *make* closure: Fowles's *A Maggot*,
Thomas's *The White Hotel*, Atwood's *The Handmaiden's Tale.*'[21]

In showing how literary fiction creates its imaginary worlds, postmodern novels 'help us to understand how the reality we live day
by day is similarly constructed, similarly written.'[22] The implication
here is that postmodern fiction, in comparison to Victorian fiction,
empowers its readers by making them aware that reality is a construct that they can change instead of a spectacle that they con-
template. This idea should be resisted, for one of the aims of
Victorian fiction, particularly the so-called condition of England
novels, was 'to publicise dreadful social conditions and . . . to stimu-
late a belief in the need for action.'[23] Victorian readers were asked
not to be passive spectators of their society but active agents in
changing it. The contrast that Hutcheon and others routinely make
between Victorian and postmodern novels not only cannot be sustained[24] it is also based on a binary opposition that belies the claim
that 'postmodern partakes of a logic "both/and," not "either/or." '[25]

A further difference between Victorian and postmodern art is that
between seriousness and playfulness, though again this is problematised as soon as we think of the work of Lewis Carroll and
Edward Lear. Generally speaking, however, the Victorians believed
that art had a moral purpose while postmodernists believe in art as
pleasure. Utilitarians saw 'literature as a seducer, almost a harlot',
distracting men from business, while Evangelicals argued that the
sensuous imaginings of art diverted people from the care of their
soul.[26] Given this attitude, it is not hard to see why there should
now be such an emphasis on art's libidinal intensities. We live in a
period, according to Steven Best and Douglas Kellner, where an
'erotics of art' is preferred to 'a hermeneutics of meaning'.[27] The
danger with this view is that it allies art with the gratifications of
popular culture, with the commodification of experience.

The Victorians were much more aware of this danger than
cultural commentators are today.[28] William Morris believed that
popular art, in the sense of representing 'the feelings and aspirations

of the people', could not exist as long as profit was the main consideration in artistic production.[29] Charles Kingsley, on the other hand, believed that art had an ennobling effect which countered the degradations of industrialisation. 'Picture galleries,' he wrote,

> should be the workman's paradise, and garden of pleasure, to which he goes to refresh his heart with beautiful shapes and sweet colouring, when they are wearied by dull bricks and mortar, and the ugly colourlessness which fill the workshop and factory.[30]

There they can be uplifted by 'high art pictures' which present their subject as 'a whole' as opposed to the characteristically partial treatment of a topic in 'low' art.[31]

Although Kingsley's argument seems naive it does recognise that art shows us alternative worlds and ways of living and that it is therefore a challenge to the existing order. Furthermore, despite the condescending tone, there is something democratic in the idea that the viewer can find a kinship with famous portraits. In Kingsley's words, '[t]hey may be noble and glorious men who are painted there; but they are still men of like passions with himself... and he begins, and rightly, to respect himself the more he finds that he too, has a fellow feeling with noble men and noble deeds.'[32] Such a view shows that a concept of 'high' art need not be incompatible with an idea of democracy.

Victor Burgin would argue that the above belongs to one of the 'master narratives of art theory' namely 'humanism's ascent of man'.[33] But how can we continue to believe in the constant moral and intellectual improvement of human beings when faced with the insights of Freud and the gas chambers of Auschwitz? Grand narratives have therefore given way to small ones which improvise rather than prescribe, are provisional rather than permanent. One consequence of this loss of 'master narratives' in art criticism is the dissolution of the boundaries between 'high' and 'low' art. Frederic Jameson sees in this 'the emergence of a new kind of flatness or depthlessness'.[34] The mingling of the two realms means that formal considerations are not as important as they were previously. One of the functions of artistic form was to differentiate art from reality and from the manifestations of popular culture. Now the line between high art and commercial forms 'seems increasingly difficult to draw'.[35] The experience of art becomes one of immersion rather than contemplation, critical commentary giving way to bodily pleasure. Art loses its transcendent power and affirms the here and now, thus fulfilling a quite different role to the one that Kingsley, and other Victorians – Matthew Arnold, William Makepeace Thackeray, John Stuart Mill and even Walter Pater – believed it should have.

The work of Tracey Emin may be taken as an example here. Her most notorious piece is a blanket on which she has embroidered the names of everyone she has ever slept with. She also commemorated the death of an uncle by exhibiting the squashed packet of Benson and Hedges supposedly in his hand when he died, which one commentator has interpreted as a sign of 'wit in play'.[36] Emin's artistic success – she was nominated for the Turner prize this year (1997) – would seem to bear out Burgin's comment that 'no special skills are necessary in order to make art today.'[37]

By Victorian and even modernist criteria, Emin's work appears tasteless and self-indulgent. Her happy admission that she is an 'egotist' is underlined by the existence of the Tracey Emin Museum, to which she hopes to add an 'Emin archive', and which is filled with photographs and video footage of the artist.[38] However, these criteria are inappropriate. It is better to see Emin's work in the context of women's traditional role in art as silent objects of the male gaze. Emin's vigorous egotism critiques this tradition, as does her presentation of herself as the subject rather than object of desire. Inevitably, this necessitates an attack on artistic form since this form embodied precisely the attitudes she criticises.

Emin's art shows that play can be serious in as much as it has a political point; in her case the representation of women. This again shows the difficulty of making hard and fast distinctions between Victorian and postmodern art. For example, it could be argued that the anarchic linguistic play of the nonsense poetry of Carroll and Lear asserts the uncontrollable nature of language in the face of authorities who would like to restrict its meanings to a particular view of self and society. It can therefore have just as much political point as a novel such as *Nicholas Nickleby* (1838–9), whose exposure of the conditions in Yorkshire schools paved the way for parliamentary legislation. The realism of the Victorian novel is as valid a political tool as the ironic play of the postmodern novel which criticises existing conventions, showing the desirability of extending or transforming them. As Patricia Waugh puts it: 'Fictional play...re-evaluates the traditional procedures of communication and allows release from established patterns.'[39]

This should not be taken to imply that play works according to a predetermined programme for, as Nicholas Zurbrugg notes, play is a 'creative commitment to innovative possibilities outside of the known universe'.[40] Perhaps this offers another perspective on the poses struck by the aesthetes whose preoccupation with form is matched by postmodernists such as Max Bense who stress 'the compositional rather than the existential qualities of work'.[41] Furthermore, as the example of Bense shows, postmodernism does not always preclude the issue of form; rather it experiments with different forms, mixing and juxtaposing but not integrating them. The resulting hybrid offers a different idea of wholeness from the sort espoused by Kingsley, but not perhaps from that found in Dickens, where a medley of styles – realism, melodrama, reportage, the picaresque and the fairy tale – jostle with one another unceasingly.

So far, my argument has been that there are similarities as well as differences between the Victorian period and our own. Like the Victorians, we are living through rapid change which constantly calls into question any belief system that seems to offer reassurance regarding the nature of truth, value and the foundation of behaviour. It is difficult to argue this case because our intellectual climate is dominated by the rhetoric of history as break or rupture rather than continuity, but I would counter by pointing out that what ensures a continuity of certain problematics of experience and art is the persistently self-renewing nature of the capitalist economy. The cluster of problems which constitute Victorianism, modernity and postmodernity cannot be separated from the nature of capitalism which, being in a constant state of development, is antithetical to stability except in the case of its own nature.

What is so frustrating about current thinking is that the emphasis on difference has made it difficult to perceive deep-rooted similarities of the kind I have described. The result is that the same problems keep being discovered as if they were new and so little progress is made in understanding them and even less in resolving them. Bearing this in mind, I would now like to consider Samuel Smiles' *Self Help*, the bible of those who advocate a return to Victorian Values. I will first make the point that this book can be used both to support and critique the idea of self help, at least as it has been portrayed by politicians and the press. I will then try to contextualise Smiles' work by comparing it with the Victorian novel and Charles Darwin's *The Origin of Species* (1859). In particular, I will suggest that the real aim of *Self Help* is not the creation of self. Finally, I will argue that this turns out to be an impossible project. My argument, in short, is that *Self Help* undermines the very idea of selfhood and for this reason it cannot be regarded as a solution to present day moral or economic crises; rather, it dramatises a problem which helps to perpetuate them.

Self Help was first published in 1859 and has never been out of print. It was reprinted with introductions by two Tories, Keith Joseph and Lord Harris, in 1986 and 1996 respectively.[42] However, the Tories do not have a monopoly on Smiles. Frank Field, the Labour minister for welfare, believes 'in the power of every human being, helped by example and encouragement, to do better and achieve more' and this idea 'lies at the heart of New Labour. Self Help is the doctrine of the moment. And Frank Field is its most committed Evangelist.'[43] Smiles is plundered for quotations that support the idea of personal responsibility; for example

> whatever is done for men or classes to a certain extent takes away the stimulus and necessity of doing for themselves; and where men are subjected to over-guidance and over-government, the inevitable tendency is to render them comparatively helpless.[44]

Taken at face value such remarks do indeed seem to support the idea that the individual should provide for him or herself rather than depend on the state but, taken in the context of the whole book, this reading becomes much more difficult to sustain. Indeed, if the passage is re-read, the phrase 'to a certain extent' stands out and implies that the existence of state provision is not entirely incompatible with the idea of self help. Smiles himself believed that the state should draw up measures to deal with the adulteration of food and that it should be responsible for a national system of education.[45] It is important to realise this since, as was pointed out earlier, the emphasis on the individual tends to elide the idea of society.[46]

Many of the examples in *Self Help* are not of self help at all but of helping others. The invention of the loom 'substitute[s] mechanical action for the irksome and toilsome labour of the workman' (p. 84) while entrepreneurs like William and Charles Grant, the originals for the Cheeryble brothers in *Nicholas Nickleby*, 'gave employment to a large population' (p. 370). Then there are the efforts of men such as Granville Sharp, who abolished the slave trade in England; Thomas Wright, who worked tirelessly for the rehabilitation of convicts, and

John Pounds, who founded The Ragged Schools. Smiles quotes with approval Humphry Davy, inventor of the miner's lamp, who wrote 'I have neither riches, nor power, nor birth to recommend me; yet...I trust I shall not be of less service to mankind' (p. 144), and Smiles himself speaks of 'the service of kindness which one human being owes another' (p. 296). These and other examples show that self help is not to be understood in the narrow sense given to it today of acquiring the skills necessary to survive in a competitive market. Rather, it is an integral part of Smiles' view that '[n]o individual in the universe stands alone; he [or she] is a component part of a system of mutual dependencies; and by his [or her] several acts he [or she] either increases or diminishes the sum of human good now and forever' (pp. 343–4). Hence we are all responsible for the kind of society we live in: 'every act we do or word we utter, as well as every act we witness or word we hear, carries with it an influence which extends over, and gives a colour, not only to the whole of our future life, but makes itself felt on the whole frame of society' (p. 345). It is because everyone has a part to play in the development of society that Smiles includes anecdotes and thumb-nail biographies of artists, scientists, philanthropists, missionaries, and the achievements of 'ordinary people'. This aspect of his work is not usually evident when politicians mention Smiles, and those who have not read him could be forgiven for thinking that his book is devoted to the achievements of entrepreneurs.

Given the awesome responsibility that 'there is not an act done or a word uttered but carries with it a train of consequences' (p. 343), it is incumbent on us to ensure that our influence on society is a beneficial one. Our starting point is ourselves; we must improve if society is to become more just and equitable. 'The most ordinary occasions' writes Smiles, 'will furnish a [person] with opportunities or suggestions for improvement, if he [or she] be but prompt to take advantage of them' (p. 142). Self help is thus self improvement and, again, this improvement should not be seen in narrow economic terms. Smiles' argument here is worth quoting at length.

> The highest object of life we take to be to form a manly character, and to work out the best development possible of body and spirit – of mind, conscience, heart and soul. This is the end: all else ought to be regarded as the means. Accordingly, that is not the most successful life in which a man gets the most pleasure, the most money, the most power, or place, honour or fame; but that in

which a man gets the most manhood, and performs the greatest amount of useful work and human duty.   (p. 300)[47]

The idea of self improvement and the awareness that we are all at least partially responsible for the kind of society we live in poses a challenge to the ethic of self gratification which informs consumer capitalism. Indeed, Smiles himself attacks the consumerism of his day, complaining of a middle class that lived beyond its income, criticising their 'taste for dress, style, luxuries and amusements which are inimical to the development of character' (p. 290).[48] The irony is that Smiles should have been evoked as a moral example by a conservative government whose deregulation of finance in the 1980s fuelled a consumer credit boom.

What Smiles has to say about scientific research is also applicable today where the criterion for funding is commercial success. This discriminates against pure research which cannot deliver measurable results within a stipulated period. Smiles notes that

> human knowledge is but an accumulation of small facts made by successive generations... the little bits of knowledge and experience carefully treasured up [and] growing at length into a mighty pyramid. Though many of these facts seemed in the first instance to have but slight significance, they are all found to have their eventual uses... Even many speculations, seemingly remote, turn out to be the basis of results the most obviously practical. (p. 139)

This sort of argument is not heard very often now, when scientists are expected to be the servants of industry and to justify their work in terms of company profit rather than of benefit to the community at large. For example, in 1992–3, the Medical Research Council funded all research projects that were awarded an alpha. This dropped to 70 per cent in 1995 and, when figures become available, they are expected to show a further fall through to 1997. This has meant that research into such matters as the sort of minerals and vitamins necessary to boost old people's resistance to infection has been scrapped. Overall, government research councils have received awards well below inflation while funds to projects with commercial links have increased substantially.[49]

However, to use Smiles, as politicians have, as a form of moral reproach and a means of moral regeneration not only ignores the historical specificity of his work but also the complexity of the social formation to which Smiles himself was oblivious. His belief 'that it is moral qualities which rule the world' (p. 360) is on a par with those Victorian novelists, like Mrs Gaskell, who believed that a recognition of common humanity between the classes would put an end to industrial conflict. Also like the Victorian novelists, Smiles relied on the conventions of the providential plot.[50] 'Accident' plays a key role in the success of many of the lives he describes. John Frederick Bottgher, the inventor of hard porcelain, spent years researching how to make white porcelain but without success 'until accident *again* stood his friend and helped him to a knowledge of the art' (p. 107, emphasis added). A belief in moral qualities and the role of providence combined to prevent both Smiles and the Victorian novelists from grasping the dynamism and complexity of their society. They failed to perceive how industrialism constrained individual freedom and how, in a society of two classes, there could be no basis for a common morality to which both Smiles and the Victorian novelists, in their different ways, appealed. What was needed was a theory of society; instead, there was an appeal to the individual. It says much that over a hundred years later the same remedy is applied to the same problem.

I have said that *Self Help* is related to the Victorian novel and this is nowhere clearer than in its concern with the creation of character which also, incidentally, anticipates the aesthetic project of continual self invention. In the words of Mary Poovey, the Victorian novel was

> a psychological narrative of individual development, which both provided readers with an imaginative image of what identity was and created a subject position that reproduced this kind of identity in the individual reader.[51]

This description applies to Smiles' book where '[t]he highest object of life' is 'to form a manly character' (p. 300), and where the reader is overwhelmed by examples of individuals whose development is measured by their determination to surmount the effects of poverty, lack of education and useful connections. Moreover, these individuals are offered as models which readers should use as their guide. 'The education of character' writes Smiles, 'is very much a question of models' (p. 347). The models that are offered in fiction are, however, different from those found in biography. 'The chief use of biography', Smiles asserts, 'consists in the noble models of character with which it abounds' (p. 350). It inspires others and 'never ceases to exercise an elevating and ennobling influence' (p. 351). By contrast, the novel reader is someone who 'indulges in fictitious feelings so much that there is a risk of sound and healthy [ones] becoming perverted or benumbed' (p. 318). And where biography stimulates the reader to action, fiction makes the reader insensible to reality, so that when he or she comes to 'face the work and duties of life, the result is usually aversion and disgust' (p. 318).

The distinction between literature and biography is by no means as clear cut as Smiles would have us believe. In the first place, *Self Help* is not just a series of biographical sketches, it also has certain literary features. We have seen that it shares with the novel the concern with the creation of model characters and a providential plot but it is also notable for its strong rhetoric, finely balanced sentences, clear theme and well worked contrasts. In short, the power of *Self Help* comes from the fusion of biography with litera- ture, 'true' stories told to good effect. In the second place, Smiles occasionally treats these two genres as if they were indistinguishable as when he writes, with characteristic briskness, that 'it is life rather than literature, action rather than study and character rather than biography, which tend perpetually to renovate mankind' (p. 39). The vigorous endorsement of 'life' and 'action' instead of books not only dissolves the distinction between literature and biography it also calls into question the value of reading and, by extension, the value of *Self Help* itself.

Self Help was published in the same year, 1859, as Darwin's *On the Origin of Species by Natural Selection* and the two books contrast and complement each other. To begin with, both share a common inter- est in the notion of origin; Darwin in natural origins, Smiles in social ones. Darwin's interest is in revealing human origins and his account of evolution 'put mankind back into nature, implicitly denying the distinction religion had traditionally set up between humans and the animals'.[52] According to Gilmour, one effect of this was 'a growing sense of the determining power of the environment over the individual'.[53] Smiles, on the other hand, only mentions origins as obstacles to be overcome and he cites numerous cases of those whose efforts lifted them from a humble background to posi- tions of eminence; men such as Richard Arkwright, inventor of the spinning jenny; the linguist Professor Alexander Murray, and Robert Thorburn, the painter. Another key idea in Smiles, 'it is not ease but effort – not facility but difficulty, that makes men' (p. 322), finds an echo in Darwin's notions of the 'great and complex battle of life' or the 'struggle for existence'.[54] Similarly, a case might be made for drawing a parallel between the role of accident in Smiles and random mutation in evolution; the one leading to new discoveries, the other to different lines of development.

My point is not, of course, that *Self Help* and *The Origin of Species* are equivalent – Smiles is talking about the development of the individual, Darwin of the evolution of species – but that the argument of each is organised around some common terms and images and this meant that each could be used to reinforce the other. Hence Herbert Spencer, perhaps the most prominent advocate of *laissez faire* individualism, could use evolution to support his idea that progress was 'the cumulative result of many individual acts of self improvement, not a preordained law imposed from on high'.[55] In order to do this, however, Spencer had to suppress the key element of Darwin's theory, namely that evolution had to be understood as tree rather than a ladder and so did not easily lend itself to a philosophy of 'progressionism'.[56]

The relationship of Smiles' book to the economic doctrine of *laissez faire* at first seems entirely complementary, particularly as he devotes a chapter to 'Men of Business', thereby strengthening the connection between self help and economic success. However, as mentioned earlier, the aim of self help is not the creation of wealth so much as the creation of character, though the two do not exclude each other. Central to both is work. In general, the Victorians shared Carlyle's view that work was 'the grand cure for all the maladies and miseries that ever beset mankind'.[57] Work was a refuge from the doubts that beset the age. Smiles sees work as a duty 'written on the thews and muscles of the limbs, the mechanism of the hand, [and] the nerves and lobes of the brain' (p. 59). This view was not shared by everybody. The same year in which *Self Help* was published also saw the appearance of Edward Fitzgerald's translation of the *Rubaiyat of Omar Khayyam*. Like Tennyson's 'The Lotos Eaters' (1832), this rejected the work ethic preferring instead a state of dreamy, sensual languor.

This dual attitude to work is discernible today. Government and employers demand more and more of those in work while others urge the need to savour 'the unrepeatable, precious moments borne on the back of idleness'.[58] Our notion of work is, however, different from the Victorians'. We do not place such a high value on it because we live in a society based on consumption rather than production.

Hence it is difficult to sympathise with the claims Smiles makes about the virtue of work. His first is that work has a social function since it imparts the ability to be useful (p. 59). By contrast, work is viewed in our society as a chore or a source of stress, rarely is it seen in terms of value to the individual or the community, except in the narrow sense of wealth creation or as a means of getting people off benefit. The idea that it is through work that we express ourselves (p. 264) also seems irrelevant in an age where identity is based on patterns of consumption. Finally, Smiles' claim that work forms a resistance to temptation (p. 270) is inapplicable to a secular society where temptation has, in any case, been institutionalised in the form of advertising. All our incitements are to leisure not work, to indulgence, not discipline.

Smiles' valuation of work is tied to a consciousness of time. J. H. Buckley is one of a number of critics who have drawn attention to how the Victorians were obsessed by time,[59] in particular how they felt diminished by the discovery of the immensity of geological time. There was therefore a need to make time significant.[60] Smiles proposes that '[t]ime should not be allowed to pass without yielding fruits, in the form of something learnt worthy of being known, some good principle cultivated, or some good habit strengthened' (p. 146). Not to 'use up the spare fragments of time which the idle permit to run to waste' (p. 307) means that we run the risk either of becoming victims of *ennui*, and so are exposed to temptation as a means of alleviating it, or of being crushed into nothing by the weight of the past. Since, in general, we are not so troubled by geological perspectives we have little need of the remedies Smiles proposes. Indeed, it can be argued that Smiles' solution has become, for at least some of those in work, a problem; it is no longer a question of using time, it is more a matter of not having enough time to do the things that have to be done. Smiles' idea that spare time can be used for self improvement seems quixotic in an age where there is little time to spare and where the idea of self improvement has been replaced by that of self gratification.

For Smiles, then, the proper use of time 'is self culture, self improvement and the growth of character' (p. 270). But the notion of character is problematic because it is neither articulate nor authentic. Throughout *Self Help*, Smiles lists what he considers to be important qualities such as: self control, self denial, self discipline, frugality, economy, prudence, forethought, industry, application, diligence, promptitude, perseverance, self reverence, chastity, cleanliness, morality, sobriety, honesty, patience, virtue, wisdom, understanding and cheerfulness. These qualities define the Protestant work ethic and Max Weber has shown how important this is to the development of capitalism.[61]

However, while Smiles acknowledges that '[t]rade tries character perhaps more severely than any other pursuit in life' (pp. 278–9) and that 'some of the finest qualities of human nature are intimately related to the right use of money' (p. 281), it is also the case that the kind of character he has in mind is not best expressed by economic considerations. 'There are' writes Smiles, 'nobler aspirations than the accumulation of wealth' (p. 241). These aspirations are to do with self improvement and being of service to others, and the pursuit of wealth is seen as inimical to these: '[h]e who recognises no higher logic than that of a shilling, may become a very rich man, and yet remain all the while an exceedingly poor creature' (p. 298), an idea that is encountered repeatedly in the Victorian novel where '[a]gain and again plots . . . are arranged to demonstrate that the craving for money . . . simply corrupts.'[62] Smiles would not have approved of the government view in the 1980s that to become rich was an expression of moral worth. That idea was crucial to early Protestantism, which stressed that the entrepreneur was a steward of God's gifts whose duty was to increase them and whose subsequent wealth was a sign of election. However, this view could not be sustained once religious faith began to be undermined in the nineteenth century.

The characteristics that fuelled the development of capitalism could not be wholly expressed in economic activity to which they could even act as a reproach. 'It is one of the defects of business,' writes Smiles, 'that it insensibly tends to a mechanism of character' (p. 298). Ultimately, character is incompatible with trade, though Smiles never ceases to describe it in monetary terms; a good character is 'of sterling worth' (p. 360) and 'character is itself a fortune' (p. 280). This tension describes a problem that is still with us today: how to value ourselves and others without recourse to an economic idiom. Smiles tried to resolve that problem by invoking the figure of the gentleman. But 'gentleness', which 'is indeed the best test of gentlemanliness' (p. 380), is the very antithesis of those qualities that Smiles has previously extolled. This split between an active, energetic character and a passive, mild one is, of course, found in Dickens, as is the ambition to be a gentleman, further allying *Self Help* with the Victorian novel.

The gentleman does not provide an answer to the problem of the valuation of character because his character does not exemplify that 'resolute determination in the pursuit of worthy objects' which alone 'is the foundation of all true greatness of character' (p. 228). The qualities of which Smiles approves are therefore split between two types, the man of energy and the gentleman. Consequently, there is no coherent notion of character in a book devoted to the importance of character. There is neither an idiom that synthesises all the different qualities into a whole character nor a language with which to evaluate it. The notion of character remains fundamentally unarticulated.

There is also a question surrounding the authenticity of character. Smiles believes that '[t]here are many counterfeits of character, but the genuine article is difficult to be mistaken' (p. 362). But then he immediately relates the following anecdote which undermines this claim.

> Colonel Charteris said to a man distinguished for his honesty, 'I would give a thousand pounds for your good name.' 'Why?' 'Because I could make ten thousand by it', was the knave's reply.
> (ibid.)

It is possible, then, to counterfeit character. But to counterfeit implies that there is such a thing as the genuine article which one looks for in vain since, as was mentioned earlier, character is 'very much a question of models' (p. 347). Character, that is to say, is imitation. Moreover, this imitation is barely a conscious matter in as much as a person 'cannot help gradually assimilating' him or herself to 'a model' (p. 348). The existence of models means that character is neither genuine nor an expression of individuality, but a copy. In this, *Self Help* testifies not to the creation of character but to its reproduction from a limited series of templates: promoting individuality, it endorses the manufacture of types.

It is evident from this that the idea of the self is in crisis and so it is not surprising to find that its characteristic pose is defensive; Smiles talks of the 'outworks of habit' (p. 291), recalling a castle under siege. He does not analyse the social nature of this threat but sees it in terms of unruly instincts requiring that a person 'study' and 'watch' himself continually so that he is not deflected from his goal (p. 293). But the self is disintegrating because of external, not internal pressures. The fact is that Smiles was writing at a point where the philosophy of *laissez faire* individualism was beginning to give way to state intervention: the visions of the poet, the painter, the inventor, the scientist and the entrepreneur would soon be eclipsed by the bureaucrat's classifications, necessitating a profound change in the representation of character and the human self.

With the tension in his work between the individual and the model, Smiles dramatises a complex shift from valuing individuals to slotting them into categories that neutralise their unique qualities. This is most evident in the classifications of the poor in the latter part of the century. Gone is Henry Mayhew's mixture of statistics, minute social observation and individual portraits, 'written up as though he were directly transcribing their speech in answer to his questions',[63] instead the poor are placed in categories – the unemployed, the old age pensioner, the widow and so on – which take no account of how they see themselves. Classification renders them silent and static.[64]

This contrasts with Smiles' subjects who exemplify his maxim that '[i]n study, as in business, energy is the great thing' (p. 307). He sees energy 'as the very central power of character in man – in a word, it is the man himself' (p. 229). The equation of energy with character suggests a conceptualisation of the human in terms of the dynamism associated with the power of machines or market forces. The appearance of Freudian psychoanalysis at the end of the century also means that Smiles' notion of a driving energy that either exceeds or resists its representations – the entrepreneur and the gentleman – can now be interpreted in terms of the libido. I have already mentioned that Smiles cautions his readers against the disruptions of instincts but instinct is also what compels the characters he describes: .'What mainly impelled him was the irrepressible instinct of the inventor, who no sooner has a mechanical problem set before him than he feels impelled to undertake its solution' (p. 90). This driven quality not only prohibits any simple moral valuation or political appropriation of self help, it also looks forward to postmodern conceptions of subjectivity in terms of desires and schizoid intensities.

I have tried to show that the historical specificity of *Self Help* means that it cannot be applied, either as a diagnosis or a remedy, to our society. This is not to say that *Self Help* is simply a historical document that can no longer speak to us. My claim is that *Self Help* describes a problem that is still with us today. That problem is how we imagine character and, ultimately, the idea of the human. Smiles places the creation of character at the centre of his book, yet it is an unachievable goal – Smiles mentions that 'we must labour on; for the work of self culture is never finished' (p. 311). The emphasis Smiles gives to character may be a reaction to the revelations of evolution or the absorption of the individual into the anonymity of the industrial mass. Whatever the case, it is clear that Smiles is ultimately bereft of the resources for representing or evaluating character. Character is finally an energy that resists representation except in terms of market forces; hence, although it is presented as a quality, it is never quite separate from economic quantification.

The absence of these resources together with the close association between character and money has meant that the notion of the human can, and indeed has been, appropriated by business. The human is now the province of company directives, market surveys and personnel management. An alternative view of the human used to be found in traditional literary criticism, but this was skewed by the same problems that are found in Smiles. F. R. Leavis, for example, was acutely and painfully conscious that he could never quite escape economic metaphors in his evaluation of literary works.[65] These economic metaphors have now become the unquestioned basis of theory which celebrates the 'free play' of meaning and the circulation of desire within a 'libidinal economy'.[66] The market analogies of theory therefore make it more supportive of the existing order than traditional literary criticism ever was.

What Smiles offers, then, is not a solution to moral decay or economic inefficiency; rather, *Self Help* dramatises the problem of how to imagine and value the human without recourse to economics. His work represents a moment, also found in traditional literary criticism, where the human exists in some tension with the economic. The absence of that tension now, when the human has been absorbed into the economic, defines one difference between ourselves and the Victorians. However, Smiles' need to find a language for thinking about and valuing the human that breaks free of the terminology of market forces is still relevant. That, and that only, is the challenge that Smiles poses for us today.

As well as testifying to a variety of Victorianisms, the essays in this volume all engage with the question of how the concerns of our culture were anticipated in the nineteenth century. In their different ways they trace how the Victorian formulation of these problems determine, in part, how we think of them today. Mary Angela Schwer's discussion of Thomas Hughes's biography of David Livingstone (1889) follows on from this introduction by considering another model of selfhood, muscular Christianity. The next four essays raise wider issues. Chris Hopkins and Jessica Maynard consider the relation between the Victorians and modernity. Hopkins's essay describes how the Great Exhibition at once promoted the idea of change yet sought to contain it within traditional categories, while Maynard shows how the heroine of Wilkie Collins's *Armadale* (1866) anticipates our attitudes to the commodity. Simon Malpas shows how Lewis Carroll's writings prefigure postmodernist critiques of totalising reason, while Peter Sedgwick finds parallels between Lyotard's *The Differend* (1988) and John Stuart Mills's essay *On Liberty*, which appeared at the same time as *Self Help*.

Then there are essays which look at the literature and painting of the period. K. M. Newton challenges the traditional view of *Silas Marner* (1861) as a novel that presents the ideology of work as a compensation for the loss of religious faith, showing, among other things, how it is more of an obsession. John Peck discusses Thackeray's novel *The Adventures of Philip* (1861–2) and argues that it rejects the conventional notion of character development, concentrating instead on issues of class, race and gender, but he warns against seeing the novel as anticipating too closely our understanding of these terms today. Steven Earnshaw questions the view that whereas the Victorians cultivated abstinence, we celebrate consumption. His reading of *The Mayor of Casterbridge* (1886) shows how an apparently critical attitude towards alcohol gives way to one that shows it first, as expressive of authentic selfhood in contrast to the artifice of the self-made man and, second, as cementing rather than disrupting the social bond. Carl Plasa looks at Robert Browning's *Pauline* (1833) showing how its reading of Wordsworth's 'Tintern Abbey' (1798) anticipates how it itself will come to be read by theory, thereby deconstructing not just itself but criticism of it too. Alistair Walker looks at Lawrence Alama-Tadema's painting, *The Roses of Heliogabalus*, and discusses what it meant to the Victorians and what it meant to Rover, who used a part of it to advertise their new 400 saloon series in 1996. His argument is that while the Victorians used the past to explore certain moral ambiguities of their own period, we use the past merely for commercial ends.

A number of essays concentrate on different aspects of Victorian popular culture. Nadine Holdsworth argues that while melodrama is a distinctive Victorian form it also has features common to post-modern theatre, such as spectacle, an emphasis on the body and an awareness of artifice. Darryl Wadsworth, focusing on various melodramatic adaptations of Dickens's *Bleak House* (1852–3), makes the point that Victorian melodrama promoted a sense of class awareness while reinforcing a sense of class impotence by telling its audience to trust to providence rather than their own efforts; nevertheless, he claims, at least melodrama raised the issue of class unlike popular entertainment today.

Nick Rance looks at how popular fiction, by drawing on the trial of Madeleine Smith in 1857 for murdering her lover, Emile L'Angelier, presented a view of women that not only challenged the ideology of the angel in the house but also gave rise to a tradition of representation that is still evident today in, for example, the novels of Ruth Rendell. Robert Mighall takes issue with critical and cinematic representations of Dracula as an agent of sexual liberation against Victorian repression, claiming that this ignores the historical specificity of the novel. Finally, Jonathan Skinner's discussion of the Elephant Man raises, among other things, the relation between the Victorian attitude to 'freaks' and our own. More generally, these last two essays perhaps suggest that in exceeding its models – the entrepreneur, the gentleman and the missionary – the self can only configure itself as other; the monstrous outsider or the freak exhibited for spectacle.

In dealing with different facets of Victorian culture, these essays show how difficult it is to make generalisations about the period. As a corrective to the facile demand for a return to Victorian values, they insist on the historical gap between ourselves and the Victorians. But, at the same time, they acknowledge the existence of continuities which reveal the otherness of our culture to itself, and which must be confronted if we are not to keep reinventing the past as if we were simply discovering the present. Only then can we begin to talk properly about the problems to which Samuel Smiles is supposed to have the solution.

Notes

1. See Raphael Samuel, 'Mrs Thatcher's Return to Victorian Values' in T. C. Smout (ed.), *Victorian Values: Proceedings of the British Academy 78* (Oxford: Oxford University Press, 1992), pp. 9–29. For a general view of Victorian values, see the other essays in this collection and also James Walvin, *Victorian Values* (London: Cardinal, 1988) and Gordon Marsden (ed.), *Victorian Values: Personalities and Perspectives in Nineteenth Century Society* (London & New York: Longman, 1992). See also Ralph Harris, 'How Victorians Helped Themselves', *The Times*, 6 June 1996; David Marquand, 'Victorian Values, Modern Strife', *Guardian*, 28 October 1996 and Joan McAlpine, 'Reforming Energy, the great Victorian Value', *The Times*, 29 December 1996.
2. See John Lloyd, 'More Equal Than Ever', *New Statesman*, 24 January 1997, pp. 21–3.
3. Quoted in Samuel, op. cit., p. 27.
4. See Jose Harris, 'Victorian Values and the Founders of the Welfare State' in Smout, op. cit. pp. 165–82. See also Martin Loney et al. (eds), *The State or the Market: Politics and Welfare in Contemporary Britain* (London: Sage, 1987).
5. Thomas Richards, *The Commodity Culture of Victorian England: Advertising and Spectacle* (London & New York: Verso, 1990), p. 71.
6. Substantive reason is concerned with values, ends and possible attitudes to life and is contrasted with instrumental reason where what matters are rules, process and expediency.
7. Jurgen Habermas, 'Modernity – an Incomplete Project' in Peter Brooker (ed.), *Modernism / Postmodernism* (London & New York: Longman, 1992), pp. 125–38; p. 132.
8. Robin Gilmour, *The Victorian Period: The Intellectual and Cultural Context of English Literature 1830–1890* (London & New York: Longman, 1993), p. 136.
9. Jean François Lyotard, *The Postmodern Condition: A Report on Knowledge*, trans. Geoff Benington and Brian Massumi (Manchester: Manchester University Press, 1984), pp. xiii–xiv.
10. Walter Pater, quoted Gilmour, op. cit., p. 239.
11. See Gilmour, op. cit., pp. 157–8, 179.
12. Linda Hutcheon, *A Poetics of Postmodernism: History, Theory, Fiction* (London & New York: Routledge, 1988), p. 99.
13. Gilmour, op. cit., p. 230.
14. Walter Truett Anderson, 'What's Going on Here?' in Walter Truett Anderson (ed.), *The Fontana Postmodernism Reader* (London: Fontana, 1996), pp. 1–11; p. 10.
15. Gilmour, op. cit., p. 20.
16. Ibid., p. 47.
17. Ibid., p. 48.
18. Hutcheon, op. cit., p. 19.
19. Ibid., p. 97.
20. Ibid., p. 124.
21. Ibid., p. 59.

22.   Patricia Waugh, *Metafiction: The Theory and Practice of Self Conscious Fiction* (London & New York: Routledge, 1984), p. 18.
23.   Kate Flint, 'Introduction' in Kate Flint (ed.), *The Victorian Novelist: Social Problems and Social Change* (London & New York: Croom Helm, 1987), pp. 1–13; p. 7.
24.   On this point see Robert Kiely, *Postmodern Fictions and the Nineteenth Century Novel* (Cambridge, MA: Harvard University Press, 1993). Among other things he argues that the nineteenth-century novel 'reads' postmodern fiction in the same way that postmodern fiction reads the nineteenth-century novel and this reveals unexpected affinities between them.
25.   Hutcheon, op. cit., p. 49.
26.   See Richard Altick, *Victorian People and Ideas* (New York & London: Norton, 1973), pp. 270–3.
27.   Steven Best and Douglas Kellner, *Postmodern Theory: Critical Interrogations* (Basingstoke: Macmillan, 1991), p. 10.
28.   Cultural studies has eroded the distinction between 'high' and popular art. Since the dominant discourse for discussing texts – gender, sexuality and so on – precludes questions of value discriminations even while it assumes them, it is extremely difficult to even raise the issue without exciting accusations of élitism. The assumption seems to be that if you want to make an argument about the value of 'high' culture you must despise popular culture and by implication democracy itself. For views on the relation between the two spheres see John Frow, *Cultural Studies and Cultural Value* (Oxford: Clarendon Press, 1995). See also Richard Hoggart and Barbara Cartland, 'Head to Head', *Guardian*, 22 February 1997. For an expressions of the view that the traditions of 'high' culture are atrophying see Melanie Phillips, 'The Videotic Age of the Philistine', *Observer*, 13 August 1995 and Henry Porter, 'Trivial Pursuit', *Guardian*, 1 February 1996. For the opposite view see *Cultural Trends* 1985/95 (London: BECB, 1997).
29.   William Morris, 'Art and the People' in Robert Peters (ed.), *Victorians on Art and Literature* (London: Peter Owen, 1964), pp. 279–89; p. 287.
30.   Charles Kingsley, 'The Worker in the National Gallery' in Peters, op. cit., pp. 183–90; p. 183.
31.   Ibid., p. 187.
32.   Ibid., p. 185.
33.   Victor Burgin, *The End of Art Theory: Criticism and Postmodernity* (Basingstoke: Macmillan, 1986), p. 200.
34.   Frederic Jameson, *Postmodernism or, the Cultural Logic of Late Capitalism* (London & New York: Verso, 1991), p. 9.
35.   Ibid., p. 18.
36.   Robert Yates, 'First Person Singular', *Observer*, 17 December 1995.
37.   Burgin, op. cit., p. 201.
38.   Yates, op. cit.
39.   Waugh, op. cit., p. 36.
40.   Nicholas Zurbrugg, *The Parameters of Postmodernism* (London: Routledge, 1993), p. 65.
41.   Ibid., p. 70.

42. Samuel Smiles, *Self Help* with an introduction by Keith Joseph and Samuel Smiles, *Self Help* with an introduction by Lord Harris (London: Institute of Economic Affairs Publication, 1996). For a review of the latter see Dave Hill, 'Self Help Comes Up Smiling', *Observer*, 28 August 1996.
43. Roy Hattersley, 'Frank Field: What about the shirkers?', *Observer*, Review Section, 10 August 1997. See also Mark Seddon, 'Bank cashes in on Victorian Values', *Guardian*, 25 August 1997.
44. Samuel Smiles, *Self Help: The Art of Achievement Illustrated by Accounts of the Lives of Great Men* with a Centenary Introduction by Asa Briggs (London: John Murray, 1958), p. 35. Page references given in the text.
45. See Asa Briggs, 'Samuel Smiles: the Gospel of Self Help' in Marsden, op. cit., pp. 85–96.
46. On this point see Ralph Dahrendorf, 'Changing Social Values under Mrs Thatcher' in Robert Skidelski (ed.), *Thatcherism* (Oxford: Basil Blackwell, 1989), pp. 191–201.
47. It is clear from this that, for Smiles, character is masculine. There are no women in his book except in a subordinate role. The whole culture of self help is therefore rooted in patriarchy.
48. Warren Susman has argued that where the nineteenth century was concerned with character, the twentieth century is concerned with personality. Mike Featherstone has claimed that this represents a change from discipline and self denial to self gratification. See Warren Susman, 'Personality and the Making of Twentieth Century Culture' in J. Higham and P.K. Conkin (eds), *New Directions in American Intellectual History* (Baltimore: Johns Hopkins University Press, 1979), pp. 212–16 and Mike Featherstone, 'The Body in Consumer Culture' in Mike Featherstone et al. (eds), *The Body: Social Process and Social Theory* (London: Sage Publications, 1991), pp. 170–96.
49. Natasha Narayan and Stephen Court, 'Research hit by funding squeeze', *Observer*, 25 February 1996.
50. For a full discussion of this and related issues see Catherine Gallagher, *The Industrial Reformation of English Fiction 1832–1867* (Chicago: The University of Chicago Press, 1985), esp. Chapter 2.
51. Mary Poovey, *Uneven Developments: The Ideological Work of Gender in Mid-Victorian Fiction* (London: Virago, 1989), p. 89.
52. Gilmour, op. cit., p. 131.
53. Ibid.
54. Quoted in Gilmour, pp. 126–7.
55. Peter J. Bowler, 'Darwinism and Victorian Values: Threat or Opportunity?', in Smout, op. cit., pp. 129–47; p. 133.
56. Ibid., p. 136.
57. Quoted in Altick, op. cit., p. 169.
58. Natasha Walter, 'Get a life or get job', *Observer*, 20 July 1997.
59. J.H. Buckley, *The Triumph of Time: A Study of the Victorian Concepts of Time, History, Progress and Decadence* (Cambridge: Mass., 1966). See also S. Toulmin and J. Goodfield, *The Discovery of Time* (Chicago: Chicago University Press, 1965) and P. J. Bowler, *The Invention of*

Progress: The Victorians and the Past (Oxford: Oxford University Press, 1987).

60. Autobiography was perhaps the key way in which many Victorians came to terms with the problem of time. See J.H. Buckley, *The Turning Key: Autobiography and Subjective Impulse since 1880* (Cambridge: Mass, 1984) and G.P. Landow (ed.), *Approaches to Victorian Autobiography* (Athens: Ohio, 1979).

61. Max Weber, *The Protestant Ethic and the Spirit of Capitalism* (London: Allen and Unwin, 1974). See also R.H. Tawney, *Religion and the Rise of Capitalism* (Harmondsworth: Penguin, 1994).

62. Valentine Cunningham, 'Goodness and Goods: Victorian Literature and Values for the Middle Class Reader' in Smout, op. cit., pp. 109–29; p. 113.

63. Flint, op. cit., p. 163.

64. See Stuart Hall and Bill Schwarz, 'State and Society' in Mary Langan and Bill Schwarz (eds), *Crises in the British State 1880–1930* (London: Hutchinson, 1985), pp. 7–32.

65. For a full discussion of these issues, see my *Re-Reading Leavis: 'Culture' and Literary Criticism* (Basingstoke and New York: Macmillan, 1996).

66. Jameson, op. cit., p. 274.

2

Imperial Muscular Christianity: Thomas Hughes's Biography of David Livingstone

Mary Angela Schwer

Although use of the term 'muscular Christianity' was derisive when it was first coined in the 1850s, by the end of the century it perfectly characterised popular British attitudes towards imperialism. Originally an exhortation to British boys to develop their manhood and their piety simultaneously, it was almost always associated with what J.A. Mangan has termed 'the games ethic',[1] and public schools. Beginning with Thomas Hughes's interpretation of Rugby School under Dr Arnold in *Tom Brown's Schooldays* (1857), various works of juvenile fiction and numerous periodicals elaborated on Hughes's fictional paradigm. A number of critics have noted what a good fit the central tenets of 'muscular Christianity' were to the needs of colonial administration; in *Sinews of the Spirit*,[2] Norman Vance characterises the tradition of Christian manliness which Hughes and his friend and fellow 'muscular Christian' Charles Kingsley draw upon in their writing as composed of three elements: physical manliness, chivalry and the ethic of service, and moral manliness. In *True Manliness*, Hughes draws these three aspects together in his discussion of courage.

> 'Manliness and manfulness' are synonymous, but they embrace more than we ordinarily mean by the word 'courage'; for instance, tenderness and thoughtfulness for others. They include that courage which lies at the root of all manliness, but is, in fact, only its lowest or rudest form. Indeed, we must admit that it is not exclusively a human quality at all, but one which we share with other animals, and which some of them – for instance the bulldog

and weasel – exhibit with a certainty and a thoroughness, which is very rare amongst mankind.[3]

What humanises this animal courage, Hughes goes on to explain, is moral courage, which may even be the prerogative of the invalid, who, though infirm of body, is willing to fight for the truth. Loyalty to truth, for Hughes, along with devotion to duty are the supreme virtues, but the only way to prove devotion to truth and duty is by fighting for it.

'Muscular Christianity' brought together Broad Church theology with other earlier conceptions of Christian manliness. As Catherine Hall and Leonore Davidoff[4] point out, evangelical masculinity during the early years of the nineteenth century was based on the assumption of male rational superiority. The popular stereotypes of masculinity of this time included that of the spendthrift aristocratic gambler, a sportsman who followed race meetings in the hope of winning back his family fortunes. In contrast, evangelical manhood was connected with ordering of both the domestic and business spheres. Man was both the head of his own household, responsible for the piety of all living under his roof, including servants, and responsible for the Christian stewardship of his business affairs. To the extent that his prosperity was seen as flowing from his religious fidelity, he was also expected to share that prosperity with the poor and unfortunate, but this social assistance was usually in the form of tracts or Bibles designed to convert the morals of the lower class, consonant with the evangelical belief that conversion of morals must precede the eradication of poverty.

In *Godliness and Good Learning*, David Newsome traces the background of ideal Christian masculinity through the reform movement in public schools.[5] Originally Hughes's beloved Thomas Arnold, pioneering headmaster of Rugby, used the term 'manliness' not in opposition to effeminacy, but to 'childishness'. Only later were proponents of 'Christian pugnacity' such as Kingsley and Hughes to emphasise the importance of athleticism and social outreach in opposition to what Kingsley characterised as the effeminacy of Roman Catholicism in his infamous denunciation of Newman on the one hand, and the popular repudiation of Christianity as weakness by the working class on the other. Addressing the latter prejudice, Hughes in his defence of the YMCA at the beginning of *The Manliness of Christ*[6] states:

If you pursue the inquiry [into opinions about YMCA] you will often come upon a distinct belief that this weakness is inherent in our English religion; that our Christianity does appeal and must appeal habitually and mainly to men's fears – to that in them which is timid and shrinking, rather than to that which is coura- geous and outspoken. This strange delusion is often alleged as the cause of the want of power and attraction in these associations.

(*MC*, p. 5)

To counteract this prevailing popular sentiment, Hughes suggests his own particular interpretation of the life of Christ, interpreting 'Christ's whole life upon earth' as 'the assertion and example of true manliness ... one long campaign, in which "the temptation" stands out as the first great battle and victory' (*MC*, pp. 80–1). Hughes casts Christ in the role of successful military commander, even though his final campaign cost him his life. Not only was Christ's physical example manly and his chivalrous concern for women and the poor evident, but he was the exemplar of Hughes's trinity of moral virtues: Truth, Purity and Courage.

Courage will nerve a man to fight against the outward adversaries that may beset his path; truth is a still but forceful weapon, of resistance rather than of attack, though in the end it must prevail; purity is a shield against the weaknesses of a man's own human nature, enemies who assume the garb of friends, but whose attacks are deadlier than the open onslaught of the declared antagonist.[7]

But the public schools were not the only source of ideas about Christian manliness in mid-century. Olive Anderson carefully traces the development of evangelical acceptance of the idea of the Chris- tian soldier from early to mid-nineteenth century.[8] Initially, the army was perceived as a hotbed of vice, a haven for rakish younger sons of the aristocracy, and therefore as a potential field for evangel- isation. The work of the Bible societies began to bear fruit in popular literature around the time of the Crimean War through the explo- sion of necrologies of pious Christian soldiers, including that of General Henry Havelock, who died in the Rebellion in India in 1857. These Christian soldier-martyrs came to closely resemble mis- sionary martyrs, and were largely described in the same terms of pious lives spent in prayer and witness to non-believers, followed by agonising death, sometimes in battle, sometimes simply in the throes of some inexplicable disease. For there to be such a close correspondence between missionary and military virtues, ideas about Christian masculinity must have undergone considerable change. While missionaries did not overtly share the militaristic programme of athleticism championed both by the military and by the domestic proponents of 'muscular Christianity' such as Charles Kingsley, the rigours of life in the bush meant that only hardy, physically fit missionaries could, in fact, survive.

Neither Kingsley nor Hughes were directly connected with missionary work, though both were concerned with the patriotic progress of empire.[9] They were probably not particularly interested in missionary work because the evangelical tenor of much of the missionary discourse before 1860 championed a Manichean contempt for things of this world, which Kingsley abhorred in both evangelical and Roman Catholic writing. However, Kingsley was very interested in the development of the idea of the Christian soldier, and in 1856, the London Missionary Society's agent David Livingstone enjoyed a triumphant return to England, very much in the mode of a triumph for a victorious soldier.

Livingstone's subsequent published account of his adventures in Africa, *Missionary Travels and Researches in Southern Africa* (1857), was an overnight success, and altered missionary discourse for good, winning the approval of secular and religious critics alike for his hardy, manly construction of himself as a chivalrous, moral actor on the stage of Africa. However, when Livingstone's next expedition up the Zambezi River ended in acrimonious failure, Livingstone himself sank from public view until the early 1870s, when, during a period of intensely jingoistic sentiment, Stanley organised one of the earliest 'media events' to find Livingstone. However, Stanley was not the only one to construct a posthumous persona for Livingstone. In her book *Livingstone's Legacy*,[10] Dorothy O. Helly recounts how Horace Waller's hagiographical shaping of 'the Livingstone legend' through his editing of Livingstone's *Last Journals* portrays Livingstone as the patron saint of the 'White Man's Burden', thereby priming the British public for a patriotic response to the Berlin Conference partition of Africa in 1884.

While Livingstone's own account of his adventures, as well as Stanley's and Waller's constructions of him as the lonely patron saint of Africa, were aimed primarily at an adult audience, Thomas Hughes published a biography of Livingstone in the English Men of

Action series aimed primarily at juvenile readers.[11] If children's literature is one way that adult popular values are conveyed and represents a reasonable measure of cultural consensus in a given period, then Hughes's *David Livingstone* is proof of the impact of 'muscular Christianity' upon popular thinking about imperialism.

One of the chief problems which Hughes faced in his juvenile writing was that of how to keep manliness Christian, and Christianity manly at the same time. As Vance notes,

> The secular hero is captain of his fate and master of his soul, confidently dominating the action. But sooner or later the Christian hero must acknowledge Christ as captain and master. The literary and social antecedents of the notion of 'manliness' could make such allegiance difficult.[12]

In his writing of the Livingstone biography, however, Hughes is aided by Livingstone's own conception of his mission, which was essentially 'muscularly Christian' on the pattern of Hughes's own beliefs. Physical toughness, a chivalrous concern for social inferiors and women, as well as an ethic of service and confident moral courage are easily traced in *Missionary Travels*; Hughes's chief contribution to the Livingstone legend is to interpret the missionary–explorer as though he were a public-school product.

In Hughes's life of Christ, childhood is a time 'in which the weapons must have been forged, and the character formed and matured, for the mighty war' (*MC*, p. 44).

> In the time of preparation for the battle of life [patience] is the true touchstone. Haste and distrust are the sure signs of weakness, if not of cowardice. Just in so far as they prevail in any life, and his work will have to be done over again. In Christ's life up to the age of thirty there is not the slightest trace of such weakness or cowardice. From all that we are told, and from all we can infer, He made no haste, and gave way to no doubt, waiting for God's mind, and patiently preparing Himself for whatever His work might be. And so His work from the first was perfect, and through His whole public life He never faltered or wavered, never had to withdraw or modify a word once spoken. And thus He stands, and will stand to the end of time, the true model of the courage and manliness of boyhood, and youth, and early manhood.
>
> (*MC*, pp. 62–3)

This model of juvenile perfection is one that Hughes endeavours to make Livingstone fit as well, though Hughes is careful to keep the 'rough and tumble' elements prominent in Livingstone's case. While Hughes acknowledges that young David was a lover of books and was devoted to learning and natural history, he also is careful to point out that he also loved 'rough play, ducking his comrades in fun as he swam past them in the Clyde'. Lest hagiography cloy the spirit of juvenile exuberance which Hughes has in mind, he adds a brief picture of Livingstone, on at least one occasion, as a youthful salmon poacher! (*DL*, p. 5).

Unlike the earlier missionary biographies which would have focused upon Livingstone's conversion from such worldliness to a more serious turn of mind, Hughes includes these details to demonstrate Livingstone's early and essentially masculine propensity to fight for what he wanted, a quality which Hughes considers essential to the integrity of the Christian life, as he explains in a much quoted passage from *Tom Brown's Schooldays*:

> After all, what would life be without fighting, I should like to know? From the cradle to the grave, fighting rightly understood, is the business, the real, highest, honestest business of every son of man. Every one who is worth his salt has his enemies, who must be beaten, be they evil thoughts and habits in himself, or spiritual wickedness in high places, or Russians or border-ruffians.
>
> It is not good for Quakers, or any other body of men to uplift their voices against fighting. Human nature is too strong for them, and they don't follow their own precepts. Every soul of them is doing his own piece of fighting, somehow and somewhere. The world might be a better world without fighting, for anything I know, but it wouldn't be our world; and therefore I am dead against crying peace, when there is no peace, and isn't meant to be. I am as sorry as any man to see folks fighting the wrong people and the wrong things, but I'd a deal sooner see them doing that, than that they should have no fight in them.[13]

In Africa, Hughes sees this disposition towards pugnacity first in Livingstone's determination to quell rumours among his African bearers who were describing him as puny. After overhearing them saying 'He is not strong, he is quite slim, and only seems stout because he puts himself into those bags [trousers]; he will soon knock up' (*DL*, p. 18), Livingstone decides that in order to gain proper respect he must impress them with his superior physical prowess. He does this immediately by walking as fast as he possibly can, and the Africans are suitably impressed. Later, he swims the river along with his men, another physical feat they did not expect of the 'soft' European, according to Hughes, and Livingstone expresses pride in their adulation.

The wisdom of this means of gaining the respect of the natives is transparent to any old Rugby boy, Hughes implies, by trying hard to see a parallel between Livingstone's athleticism and Dr Arnold's dictums. Since Livingstone's own hard-won education took place after work in the cotton factory, the closest Hughes can bring him to Dr Arnold is to highlight the fact that Livingstone's friend and fellow explorer, Oswell, was trained at Rugby under Arnold, and therefore, 'One could see his training in always doing what was brave, and true, and right' (*DL*, p. 32). Friends though they were, however, Hughes is at pains to dispel any doubts about the manliness of their relationship. Hughes notes that Livingstone was proud of the fact that he and Oswell never showed affection. Later Hughes continues his praise of Rugby by noting that the game of football is single-handedly responsible for winning African children's interest in European education (as it certainly won the young Tom Brown's!) (*DL*, p. 197).

But the narrative would be dull if the natives were simply cowed by Livingstone's physical prowess. Instead, he must show himself master of the situation as an adult among rowdy African schoolboys, invoking the already established precedent of the childishness of subject peoples. Hughes constructs Livingstone as the master in charge, staring down a rebellious class of Chiboque with his double-barrelled shotgun.

> I then said that as everything had failed to satisfy them they evidently meant to fight, and if so, they must begin, and bear the blame before God. I then sat silent for some time. It was certainly rather trying, but I was careful not to seem flurried; and having four barrels ready for instant action, looked quietly at the savage scene around.   (*DL*, p. 58)

The crisis passed, only to recur again, when Hughes recounts how Livingstone, wild with fever, threatens his men with his shotgun for making noise while he tries to sleep (*DL*, p. 60). Instead of

Livingstone appearing a bully, Hughes again paints him as the schoolmaster who knows best how to tame the restless energy of his boys, only because he himself has matured beyond their level. Proof of Livingstone's physical mastery of himself is even more pronounced in Hughes's depiction of his illness than in the rude health of his physical prowess. When Hughes mentions Livingstone's illnesses, he tries to show Livingstone's mastery over his body through this time of testing. In one case, Livingstone holds himself upright long enough to be able to have an important audience with Shinte; in a second instance, he is shaking so badly that he cannot take a sextant reading of the moon (*DL*, pp. 56 and 59). Although Livingstone fails to live up to his reputation as superior to all physical weakness, Hughes's paradigm of the old boy/schoolmaster still resonates. In order for the old boy to become a successful schoolmaster, he must remember what being under authority feels like. Illness is just such a reminder for Livingstone, in Hughes's account, keeping him humble and human, but successful enough in his own self-discipline to make his anger against those he considers laggards arresting. When Livingstone hears that Bishop Tozer is moving the Universities Christian Mission from the interior to the coast because of the high death rate in the former, his missionary toughness bristles.[14] Later, Hughes reports his exhortation to brother missionaries recorded from a diary note written on 23 May 1872:

> I would say to missionaries, 'Come on, brethren, to the real heathen. You have no idea how brave you are till you try. Leaving the coast tribes and devoting yourselves heartily to the savages, as they are called, you will find, with some drawbacks and wickednesses, a very great deal to admire and love.' (*DL*, p. 168)

Even in the last years of his life, Livingstone tried to live this example of physical toughness. Hughes cites Stanley's report of Livingstone's stamina in walking eighteen miles back to camp, even though he had been badly bee-stung.

> He had been stung dreadfully in the head and face; the bees had settled in handfuls in his hair; but, after a cup of warm tea and some food, he was as cheerful as if he had never travelled a mile...Under that way-worn exterior lay a fund of high spirits and inexhaustible humour; that rugged frame enclosed a young and most excellent soul. (*DL*, p. 159)

Livingstone's physical stamina was material proof of the unself-ish, chivalrous nature of his soul. In his manual for boys, Thomas Hughes puts the virtue of unselfishness first among the virtues, since 'the great pattern and type of unselfishness is Jesus Christ Himself, who went about doing good, and the supreme act of whose life was a deed of utter self-sacrifice'.[15] For Hughes, chivalry is composed both of unselfish concern for others, and unfailing courtesy both to peers and inferiors. As Hughes notes, the highest social classes tend to be the most courteous to inferiors.

> The reason is not far to seek. The prince or the great noble is too well assured of his position to fear lest he should compromise it, – and besides, *Noblesse oblige*. But the small official, or the parvenu, or the 'gentleman's gentleman' tottering on the verge of gentility, feels his own status so insecure that he dares not risk it by permitting in persons of a supposed lower grade any approach to familiarity.[16]

Nevertheless, Hughes throughout his work emphasises that poverty is no bar to gentility. 'You may be a crossing-sweeper, or a cobbler, and yet be a gentleman, if you preserve your own self-respect and your regard for the feelings of others',[17] and Hughes takes pride in pointing out that Livingstone was proud of 'my own order, the honest poor' while no stranger to gentility either. Hughes describes Livingstone's refusal to alter the inscription he had graven upon his parents' tombstone:

> To show the resting-place of Neil Livingstone
> and Agnes Hunter, his wife,
> and to express the thankfulness to God of their
> children John, David, Janet, Charles and Agnes,
> for poor and pious parents

even though other family members with social pretensions urged him to change it to read 'poor but honest' (*DL*, p. 5). Livingstone's early poverty made his subsequent rise to fame all the more remark-able, proof that capitalism was a boon to the individual who was willing to seize the main chance, and could operate in conjunction with the positive effects of religion. Indeed, the humble circum-stances of Livingstone's birth make him an ideal candidate for pres-entation as one of Hughes's authoritarian but just natural leaders, whose authority comes not from birth but from his survival in the school of hard knocks.[18]

Hughes feels that from this position of confident leadership, Livingstone is then able to act chivalrously toward women, beginning, in proper hagiographical fashion, with his attitude toward his mother. In this case, his masculine authority is not yet confident, for Hughes quotes the young David as saying, 'Mother, if you'll bar the door, I'll scrub the floor for you,' a concession to the male prejudices of Blantyre which Hughes significantly says he would not have made later in life (*DL*, p. 3). Livingstone's chivalry toward women matures by the time he reaches Africa, however. Hughes reports that David Livingstone's first recorded interaction with the Africans on his way to his first mission in Kuruman was to protect a girl about to be given in marriage against her will (*DL*, p. 15). Though Gayatri Spivak's point that 'White men are saving brown women from brown men' effectively silences the colonised woman in the text,[19] the real purpose of this anecdote is to show how fundamental the patriotic paternalism favoured by Hughes is to Livingstone's character.

Like a chivalrous knight errant, Hughes describes Livingstone as possessing a great 'love of home', despite his absence. This regard for the domestic sphere, an acknowledgement by the masculine of a need for the feminine, Hughes asserts, is characteristic of all 'true men' (*DL*, p. 10). To make the point even further, Hughes includes a sentimental poem written by Mrs Livingstone during her husband's five-year absence:[20]

> You'll never leave me, darling – there's a promise in your eye;
> I may tend you while I'm living, you will watch me die.
> How did I live without you through those long, long years
> of woe?
> It seems as tho' twould kill me to be parted from you now.
> And if death but kindly lead me to the blessed home on high,
> What a hundred thousand welcomes will await you in the sky!
>
> (*DL*, p. 80)

The Celtic peroration ('a hundred thousand welcomes') suggests not only the sentimentality popularly associated with the Celts, but an ideal feminised response to Livingstone's knight errantry. Carol Christ suggests that the discourse of the 'angel in the house' trapped men to an even greater degree than women, since the purity demanded of a fit partner for an 'angel' ruled out many masculine activities beyond the domestic sphere.[21] The effusive character of Mary Livingstone's poem neatly positions itself as sentimental and passive against Livingstone's prosaic narrative of action. In fact, Livingstone himself and Hughes generally refer to Livingstone's Celtic (Highland) ancestors to suggest a precedent for Livingstone's hardy masculinity rather than to imply sentimentality of any kind.

Even though Hughes and Livingstone himself are constantly asserting that shows of emotion are unmanly, Livingstone's reaction to his wife's death must be represented differently. Hughes does his best, as we have noted, to present Livingstone as a devoted family man despite the fact that the missionary explorer sent his growing family back to England after the death of his youngest child and his wife's partial paralysis. This is no easy task, given Livingstone's virtual abandonment of his wife and children for five years, but Hughes's paradigm of Christian masculinity demands the effort. Hughes is at least able to depict Livingstone as breaking down and crying bitterly after Mary's death during his second tour of Africa, on board ship, sailing up the Zambezi in 1862 (*DL*, pp. 108–9).

Besides a relationship to the poor and women, chivalry suggests an element of military prowess, of triumphant authority. Livingstone's reputation for physical stamina offset his many bouts of fever, but Hughes needed to depict him as a soldier, on the model of Christ, his captain (*MC*, part VII). After leaving the London Missionary Society to serve the British Consulate, Livingstone's soldierly bearing reflected itself more and more in his dress. Hughes reports that on Livingstone's return to India in 1865 to sell the *Lady Nyssa* after the disastrous Zambezi expedition, he scandalised the missionaries he addressed by his clothing.

'He dressed more like a post captain or admiral', wrote one of his brother missionaries. 'At the communion on Sunday (he sat on Dr. Wilson's right hand) he wore a blue surtout with Government gilt buttons, shepard tartan trousers, and a gold band round his cap.'
(*DL*, p. 120)

Later, Stanley was to comment on Livingstone's appearance in the bush by saying, 'He is accustomed to wear a naval cap, by which he has been identified throughout Africa' (*DL*, p. 144). This identification, then, was with the forces of empire, not the forces of the Cross.

What was never in doubt, however, at least to Hughes, was Livingstone's moral courage in the face of hostility to his Christian teaching. In *The Manliness of Christ*, Hughes cites the Sermon on the Mount as one of the most courageous statements of all time, outlining how God's Kingdom was to be enacted upon earth – more wonderful than a miracle. Hughes characterises Jesus as 'a peasant repudiated by His own neighbours and kinsfolk, and suspected by the national rulers and teachers', and therefore, Hughes concludes that Jesus' candid speech to the poorest was nothing less than heroic. Like Christ, David Livingstone fits Hughes's paradigm for moral heroism. A peasant like Christ himself, Livingstone preached Christianity to those oppressed by the slave trade and ignorant superstition. Hughes was particularly impressed by the kind of Christianity which Livingstone preached to his African audience, which was Broad enough to satisfy Hughes' own leanings. Hughes quotes Stanley as saying of Livingstone:

> His religion is a constant, earnest, sincere practice. It is neither demonstrative nor loud, but manifests itself in a quiet practical way, and is always at work. In him religion exhibits its loveliest features: it governs his conduct not only towards his servants, but towards the natives, the bigoted Mahomedans, and all who come in contact with him. Without it, Livingstone, with his ardent temperament, his enthusiasm, his high spirit and courage, must have become uncompanionable and a hard task master. Religion has tamed him and made him a Christian gentleman, the most companionable of men and indulgent of masters
>
> (*DL*, pp. 152–3)

Presumably the religion which tamed the wild explorer is also the best means of taming the wild and superstitious people among whom he worked. So wrapped up in his activities of geographical and commercial enterprise for the sake of the gospel was Livingstone that when he reached London in 1856, according to Hughes, 'the "well-done" of a proud and grateful nation broke on the simple pious missionary with bewildering force and unanimity' (*DL*, p. 80). Livingstone's most recent biographer, Tim Jeal, suggests that Livingstone delighted in his notoriety,[22] but the Victorian discourse of moral authority prohibits Hughes from allowing Livingstone to bask overlong in the sunlight of his overnight popularity. Instead, Hughes strives to portray Livingstone's virtues as the marriage of manliness and patriotism. In his study of *Tom Brown's Schooldays*, Ian Watson notes the collusion between capitalism and the virtues of Christian manliness.

> The ideology of the industrialist capitalist class (or rather, the class compromise of which we have spoken) after mid-century welded what we may call 'capitalist' values of competition, individual achievement, the survival of the fittest and social mobility; with older, loosely 'feudal' ideas of honour, social obligation to the less well-off and social hierarchy.[23]

Livingstone's character, as constructed by Hughes, is the epitome of what Hughes elsewhere calls the British national virtue: perseverance. In his inspirational compilation of Hughes's writings on masculinity, *True Manliness*, Brown reprints a quote from Emerson:

> 'I find Englishmen', says Emerson, 'to be them of all men who stand firmest in their shoes. They have in themselves what they value in their horses – mettle and bottom...The one thing the English value is pluck'. It is this pluck that has borne the British flag from one end of India to the other, and planted us there, the rulers of two hundred and fifty millions of human beings; it was pluck that carried Livingstone across the torrid plains and trackless wilds of Central Africa; it is pluck that has made the fairest and broadest lands of both hemispheres British colonies. When things are at their worst, thinks the Englishman, they must mend. 'Curse those English! cried Napoleon; 'they never know when they are beaten.'[24]

Hughes goes on to underline the moral:

> I want you, my boy, to carry this thoroughly British quality into your life, – and not only into your highest efforts, but into the smaller matters also, and even into your amusements. Disappointments you must discount beforehand. Failures daunt a dastard, but make a man.[25]

Hughes justifies Livingstone's final depression and lonely death by romanticising him as a martyr as well as a Christ-figure.

Has not the experience of every martyr been the same? The more perfect the self-sacrifice in life, the more surely would this shadow seem to have hung over the last hours of the world's best and bravest, the only perfect life being not only no exception, but the greatest exemplar of the law. *(DL,* p. 193)

The comparison with Christ is an apt one. Like Christ, Livingstone died questioning the efficacy of his life and work. But also like Christ, his memory was used to sanction a variety of imperialist actions which he himself would have abhorred. The Livingstone legend, as shaped by Hughes and others, went on to define the boundaries of the White Man's Burden among a coming generation of imperialists.

Notes

1. J.A. Mangan, *The Games Ethic and Imperialism: Aspects of the Diffusion of an Ideal* (New York: Viking, 1986), pp. 168–92.
2. Norman Vance, *The Sinews of the Spirit: The Ideal of Christian Manliness in Victorian Literature and Religious Thought* (Cambridge: Cambridge University Press, 1985).
3. E.E. Brown (ed.), *True Manliness: From the Writings of Thomas Hughes* (Boston: D. Lothrop, 1880), p. 14.
4. Catherine Hall and Leonore Davidoff, *Family Fortunes: Men and Women of the English Middle Class 1780–1850* (Chicago: University of Chicago Press, 1987).
5. David Newsome, *Godliness and Good Learning: Four Studies on a Victorian Ideal* (London: John Murray, 1961).
6. Thomas Hughes, *The Manliness of Christ* (London: Macmillan, 1894), hereafter referred to as *MC* with page references given in the text.
7. Thomas Hughes, *Notes for Boys (and their Fathers) on Morals, Mind and Manners* (London: Elliot Stock, 1885), p. 62.
8. Olive Anderson, 'The Growth of Christian Militarism in Mid-Victorian Britain', *English Historical Review* LXXXVI (1971), pp. 46–72.
9. Hughes was involved briefly in a scheme of colonial settlement in Rugby, Tennessee, while Kingsley wrote extensively on colonial management in *Two Years Ago* and in other works.
10. Dorothy O. Helly, *Livingstone's Legacy: Horace Waller and Victorian Mythmaking* (Athens, OH: Ohio University Press, 1987).
11. Thomas Hughes, *David Livingstone*, English Men of Action Series (London: Macmillan, 1889), hereafter referred to as *DL* with page references given in the text.
12. Norman Vance, *The Sinews of the Spirit*, p. 7.
13. E.E. Brown (ed.), *True Manliness*, pp. 22–3.

14. Despite Livingstone's annoyance Tim Jeal, Livingstone's biographer, contends that Livingstone helped to cause this through his own neglect of the inland missions before transferring to government service in 1858. See Tim Jeal, *Livingstone* (New York: G.P. Putnam's Sons, 1973).
15. Thomas Hughes, *Notes for Boys (and their Fathers) on Morals, Mind and Manners*, p. 1.
16. Ibid., p. 45.
17. Ibid., p. 44.
18. See Ian Watson's 'Victorian England, Colonialism and the Ideology of *Tom Brown's Schooldays*', *Zeitschrift für Anglistik und Amerikanistik* 29.2 (1981), pp. 116–129.
19. Gayatri C. Spivak, 'Can the Subaltern Speak?', in C. Nelson and L. Grossberg (eds), *Marxism and the Interpretation of Culture* (University of Illinois, 1988), pp. 271–313.
20. This is exactly the kind of poem that would have made Livingstone cringe. Early in his career, he roundly scolds one of his sisters for wasting her time on making a verse about his exploits. This quotation, then, is clearly tied ideologically to Hughes's need to depict Livingstone's masculinity as chivalrous concern for the foolishness of women.
21. Carol Christ, 'The Angel in the House and Victorian Masculinity', in Martha Vicinus (ed.), *A Widening Sphere: Changing Roles of Victorian Women* (Bloomington: Indiana University Press, 1977).
22. Tim Jeal, *Livingstone*, op. cit.
23. Ian Watson, 'Victorian England, Colonialism and the Ideology of *Tom Brown's Schooldays*', p. 123.
24. E.E. Brown (ed.), *True Manliness*, pp. 34–5.
25. Ibid., p. 35.

3

Victorian Modernity?
Writing the Great Exhibition

Chris Hopkins

There is no question that for Victorian Britain the Great Exhibition became a defining event for mapping not just 'The Progress of the Nation',[1] but the whole progress of mankind into a modern age. Account after account among the enormous quantity of writing inspired by the Exhibition represented it as an unprecedented experience, a landmark of the extent of human self-transformation, and a starting point for yet further development. Prince Albert's characterisation of the aims of the Exhibition at his Mansion House Banquet speech of 1850 makes these points forcefully:

> Nobody... who had paid any attention to the peculiar features of our present era, will doubt for a moment that we are living at a period of most wonderful transition...
>
> Gentlemen – the Exhibition of 1851 is to give us a true test and a living picture of the point of development at which the whole of mankind has arrived in this great task, and a new starting point from which all nations will be able to direct their further exertions.[2]

Other accounts gave, with varying emphases, a similar sense of the Exhibition's uniqueness and promise. Henry Cole, prime mover with Albert of the Exhibition, wrote in comparatively restrained terms that 'for the first time in the world's history, the men of Arts, Science, and Commerce were permitted by their respective governments to meet together to discuss and promote those objects for which civilised nations exist'.[3] The popular poet Martin Tupper (less restrainedly) saw the Exhibition as marking a universally beneficent increase in the pace of history itself:

These twenty years – how full of gain to us,
To common humble multitudinous Man;
How swiftly Providence advances thus
Our flag of progress flaming in the van!
This double decade of the world's short span
Is richer than two centuries of old.
[...]
All wonders of the world gladden the sight
In that world's wonder-house the Crystal Palace;
And everywhere is Might enslaved to Right.[4]

The Times in its account of the opening ceremony became positively mystical in the attempt to represent the significance of the experience: 'They who were so fortunate as to see it hardly knew what most to admire, or in what form to clothe the sense of wonder and even of mystery which struggled within them'.[5]

For cultural commentators and historians, then and since, the Exhibition and its year have retained this capacity to mark a period – usually, as for Asa Briggs, that of 'high Victorianism'. Thus, as Briggs says of his book *Victorian People*: 'the year 1851 is an obvious point to start.... The symbol of the Crystal Palace...dominates the whole period from 1851 to 1867'.[6] Other historians have given different closing dates for this period, and different names – for W.L. Burn 'the Age of Equipoise' lasted from 1850 to 1865, while for Geoffrey Best the years 1851–1875 represent 'mid-Victorian Britain'.[7] However, there has been a general consensus of a distinctive era beginning in the middle of the century. G.M. Young even traces the first uses of the word 'Victorian' to 1851 (in E.P. Hood's book *The Age and its Architects*).[8] For most historians writing about the Great Exhibition the questions raised by the periodisation are mainly concerned with the 'character of the age', with a sense that 1851 and the Great Exhibition really do mark a turning point. The location of difference between what came before 1851 and what came after is usually explicitly linked to the development of a distinctively modern industrial society. In this sense modern historians have rarely disputed the central terms which Victorians themselves used to represent this marked sense of *change*. It is not surprising to find a modern historian seeing change as principally stemming from economic development, as Best does: 'the character of British society in the mid-Victorian period was more or less conditioned by its remarkable economic development'.[9] Nor does it seem that strange to find *The Economist* in 1851 similarly focusing on economic development and its consequences:

> perhaps the best way of realising... the actual progress of the last half-century would be to fancy ourselves suddenly transferred to the year 1800, with all our habits, expectations, requirements, and standards of living formed upon the luxuries and appliances collected around us in 1850.

However, it should be noted that the similarity may signal some shared sense of a modernising model of historical change – a secular model driven by social and economic activity. Likewise, Briggs sees the period as in many respects authentically characterised through the terms deployed in its own public discourses: 'the key words of the times were "thought", "work" and "progress" '.[10]

Despite this general agreement about the period as marking a transition towards a modern society, however, there has been little discussion of how the Great Exhibition represented, and focused representations of, modernity. Many historians discuss Victorian concepts of 'progress' – an important component of discourses of modernity – but relatively little has been said about how Victorians variously used language to figure the ideas, debates, tensions, hopes and experiences of modernity which the Great Exhibition came to represent. For that matter, there has been little work on what *kind* of modernity is represented by writings about the Great Exhibition, or even whether modernity is really a suitable terminology for Victorian attitudes to progress and change ('Victorian modernity' still sounds paradoxical). This essay will, therefore, explore ways in which a variety of Victorian texts represent the modernity of the Great Exhibition.

The nearest anyone comes to approaching the Great Exhibition specifically in terms of modernity is Marshall Berman in his classic discussion of modernity: *All That is Solid Melts into Air – The Experience of Modernity* (1983).[11] However, he touches on the Crystal Palace mainly as it is perceived by foreign visitors, in the course of a discussion of Continental attitudes to modernity in the 1860s.[12] Berman contrasts Dostoievsky's fantasy of the Crystal Palace as symbol of repressive, alienating modernity with his own sense of its general reception as a liberating image of the modern. 'We are likely,' Berman says, 'to wonder if Dostoievsky ever saw the real thing at all' (though, in fact, he did, in its Sydenham version, in 1862).[13]

Dostoievsky's hero, in *Notes From the Underground*, talks of a building which is 'all ready made and computed with mathematical exactitude...every possible question will vanish, simply because every possible answer will be provided.' The building will force any spectator to 'become silent forever'.[14] Berman supplies a different response based on his sense of the actual impact of the building, partly based on the reactions of the German Lothar Bucher,[15] partly on surviving photographs:

> What we see is a glass structure supported by barely perceptible slender iron beams...light almost to the point of weightlessness ...its colour alternates between the colour of the sky through the transparent glass, which covers most of the building's volume, and the sky blue of its narrow iron beams...
>
> In its relationship to nature, it envelops rather than obliterates: great old trees...are contained within the building...Moreover, far from being designed by arid mechanical calculation, the Crystal Palace is in fact the most visionary and adventurous building of the whole nineteenth century...We can appreciate it even more if we compare the Palace with the ponderous neo-Gothic, neo-Renaissance and neo-Baroque enormities that were going up all round it. In addition, the Palace's builders, far from presenting the building as final and indestructible [i.e. as Dostoievsky does], prided themselves on its transience:...it was built in six months ...disassembled in three months...and then put together again in an enlarged version halfway across the city.[16]

This vision of the Palace as symbol of liberating modernity develops its possibilities in ways which suggest both technological modernisation (the use of prefabrication, the most recent materials, the speed of construction and capacity for mobility and flexibility) and an associated modernist architectural aesthetic (the lightness of construction, the play of light through glass, functionality, inventiveness and freedom from exhausted traditions). There certainly *are* nineteenth-century representations of the Crystal Palace in (partly) analogous terms to these,[17] but it should be noted that Berman's account is heavily involved in a modernist and modernising aesthetic, which does not altogether spring from Victorian responses to the Great Exhibition building. Thus, his opposition of the Crystal Palace to the 'ponderous neo-Gothic' and so on does not wholly reproduce a Victorian perception. Though there was an appreciation of the lightness of the building, this was not put in sharp opposition to more conventional architecture as evidently superior. Indeed, as Berman himself points out, the Crystal Palace remained more or less alone as an example of Victorian modernist building: 'the building was not a grand consummation...but a courageous and lonely beginning that lay underdeveloped for many decades...no more genuinely modern buildings would be built in England for another fifty years'.[18]

Others of his characterisations of the Crystal Palace can also be queried as Victorian responses – though there was much pride in the rapidity of the building's construction, its 'transience' may not have been seen as centrally valuable in the way he suggests. In fact, its designer Henry Paxton fought hard to have the building retained permanently on its original site in Hyde Park as a 'winter garden' for Londoners to enjoy in poor weather.[19] He was also a founder of the Crystal Palace Company, which undertook to move the building to Sydenham, where it was quite extensively (and relatively slowly) remodelled in an enormously expensive landscaped park which was intended to be anything but 'transient'.[20] It is true that from the very beginning, Paxton intended the construction materials to be re-usable (in the original contract the engineering company Fox and Henderson were made the owners of the whole material used in the Crystal Palace after the Exhibition had finished – Paxton's Crystal Palace company had to buy it back from them).[21] But this plan may not express the modernist virtue of transience so much as a more Victorian one of thrift, and a preference for private enterprise. The prefabricated parts *could* be re-used (though many new parts had to be made and the Sydenham Palace was much less 'light' both visually and in construction than the Hyde Park version[22]), but this was not necessarily part of a modernist scheme in the way that Berman suggests. To explore Victorian notions about the modernity of the Great Exhibition we need to go back to Victorian accounts of it, with a sense that their modernity may not be quite our modernity.

The Great Exhibition generated an enormous amount of writing – indeed, its status as something like a mass media event may be one of its modern features. Anthony Bird observes that:

> Between 1 May and 15 October 1851 rather more than six million people visited the Great Exhibition...and it sometimes seems that this total is equalled or even exceeded, by the number of words

written about the Crystal Palace in which the Exhibition was staged.[23]

If this is true of the Crystal Palace alone, it is equally true of the whole Exhibition. Such writing ranged from a speech by Prince Albert, via Parliamentary discussion, daily newspaper reports, a critique by Ruskin, poetry, through various guides, catalogues and handbooks, to cartoons in *Punch* and even verses printed on silk handkerchiefs![24] Some of this writing was openly anti-Exhibition, some was more subtle in its reservations, but the great majority was avowedly positive about the whole event, though not thoughtlessly so. Both negative and positive reactions can, of course, tell us things about the nature of 'Victorian modernity'. The texts I have chosen to examine are picked from among a mass of available material. I have tried to give a range of kinds of writing and of different opinions, without underrepresenting the mainstream consensus.

Prince Albert's Mansion House Banquet speech, briefly referred to at the beginning of this essay, seems a good place to start, for it contains a vision which helped to originate the actual event, and one which became widely shared. The speech was delivered at the end of a lavish meal hosted by the Lord Mayor of London to an audience composed of 'Her Majesty's Ministers, Foreign Ambassadors, Royal Commissioners of the Exhibition...and the Mayors of one hundred and eighty towns'.[25] The speech is in many ways closely tied to this occasion (as was the visual environment, since the Mansion Hall was specially decorated with models symbolising the industrial production of Great Britain[26]), and its rhetorical strategies actively try to create a version of the modern ethos which it envisages. As an immediate aim Albert needed to unify public opinion in favour of the Exhibition because there had, in fact, been considerable initial opposition to the project. His speech asserts and applauds the unity displayed by the collected dignitaries, who are regarded as a representative assembly not only of England, but also of Europe and the world. In concert with this strategy, Albert develops a complex theory of unity as an effect and condition of modernity. The keynote of the whole speech is 'unity'. Albert is delighted to observe that his proposal for the first ever 'International Exhibition' has met with 'such universal concurrence and approbation'. This should in principle be expected, because chief among the 'peculiar features of our present era' are forces which lead towards 'that great end to which ... all history points – the realisation of the unity of mankind'.

The reasons for this growth of unity are material, technological ones:

> The distances which separated the different nations and parts of the globe are rapidly vanishing before the achievements of modern invention, and we can traverse them with incredible ease; the languages of all nations are known ... thought is communicated with the rapidity, and even by the power of lightning.   (p. 1)

One notes the resemblance to some more recent ideas of the effects of 'globalisation' and communications revolutions. Technologies of steam and the telegraph dissolve problems of distance, leading to the transformation of communication in terms of both speed and ease. This 'unification' of the world leads to the unity of mankind for two reasons. Firstly, knowledge circulates more freely, so that closer knowledge of elsewhere is unavoidable. Secondly, another mechanism is associated by Albert with his version of 'the information highway' – the principle of peaceful competition. Everyone wishes to acquire further knowledge because there is a *free market* in knowledge, and because this knowledge allows competition in order best to benefit your self, city, nation and so on:

> Knowledge acquired becomes at once the property of the community at large ... the publicity of the present day causes that no sooner is a discovery or invention made than it is already improved upon and surpassed by competing efforts.   (p. 2)

It is noticeable that the unity which is Albert's central value results not from any static identification of common interests, but from a dynamic system of competition which ensures a forward movement that necessarily unifies the world and its peoples. Similarly, knowledge itself has not through ease of distribution become 'universal' in the sense that a stable and comprehensive world view is shared by a mass of individuals. Instead, progression towards unity is sustained by greater specialisation of knowledge in particular fields, and by the continual revision of knowledge. Indeed, for Albert, the modernising social organisation of 'the division of labour' is the key to all kinds of production, especially that of the production of knowledge: 'the great principle of the division of labour, which may be called the moving power of civilisation, is being extended to all branches of science, industry and art' (p. 1).

Albert is, in fact, quite clear that his speech figures a system which produces unity from difference and, even, from increasing differentiation. He predicts 'not a unity which breaks down … the peculiar characteristics of the different nations of the earth, but rather a unity, the result and product of those very national varieties and antagonistic qualities' (p. 1). His representation of the age is very much a totalising one – a complete system which explains how the world works for humankind, and what the human place in that system is. Thus, it is not only different nations which are – ultimately – unified, but also differing fields of knowledge ('science, industry, and art').

The system can even accommodate religious knowledge – or rather, God is the ultimate originator of the system:

> So man is approaching a more complete fulfilment of that great and sacred mission which he has to perform in this world. His reason being created after the image of God, he has to use it to discover the laws by which the Almighty governs His creation, and, by making these laws his standards of action, to conquer nature to his use; himself a divine instrument.   (p. 2)

In some ways this is a traditional version of the relation between God, Man and Reason – reason is a divine quality bestowed upon Man, enabling him to discover the order in the world which God originally instituted. This ties in with a 'grand narrative' of progress in which humans by their own efforts journey forward ever closer to perfection. However, the essential place of competition in Albert's progressive world order seems less clearly traditional, and gives it modernising powers of ever accelerating transformation. Here, competition is not, for example, a failing of mankind, but a positive quality leading to improvement on earth. Equally, the order which human reason discovers is not so much a divinely established set of laws which remain constant, as a transforming power which is constantly subject to further transformation through competition, specialisation and the rapid circulation of knowledge. The speech tries in some respects to suggest a stable order which contains and transcends the dynamism in the system, but this runs counter to a strong sense of comprehensive mobility and transformation. Thus God appears to have created a finite order which Science can discover, Art has 'immutable laws of beauty and symmetry', and the universal Christian virtues of 'peace' and 'love' are consistent with and basic to both national and individual behaviour. However, the capacity of these still points to resist the speech's general rhetoric of constant movement seems doubtful, when 'no sooner is a discovery . . . made than it is already improved upon and surpassed by competing efforts' (p. 2).

Though the speech is markedly positive about the potential of the modern world, it attempts to see the kind of transformation which progress brings about as none the less containable within traditional systems of value. The speech compares interestingly in this respect with Marx and Engels' representations of modernity, which have a similar sense of transforming mobility, but are also certain of the utter transformation of social value that will accompany technological and economic change. Thus, famously, for them 'all that is solid melts into air, all that is sacred is profaned'.[27]

An important part of the context for texts about the Great Exhibition was, indeed, an explicit national debate about the relation of Britain to the wider world, free communication with which Albert saw as so inevitable and progressive. The issue of 'Free Trade' was, as Asa Briggs points out, still a live one, and the Great Exhibition was seen as a celebration of the correctness of a free trade policy.[28] Free Trade lies behind the pioneering role of the Great Exhibition as the first *International* exhibition: it was to celebrate and promote not only national progress, but also to celebrate the progress that all (European) nations had made in co-operating in unrestricted and peaceful competition. Many opponents of the Exhibition were also well aware of its role in representing a new world order. The next group of texts I will discuss are by the most vociferous of the Exhibition's opponents, the Tory MP for Lincoln, Colonel Sibthorpe.

Sibthorpe was a notable reactionary, opposing many reforms. His opinions were often eccentrically expressed, but the oddities arise precisely from a wholesale distaste for a progressive world-vision. He opposed a Parliamentary Act concerned with the opening of new public libraries on the grounds that he 'did not care much for reading at all'.[29] His immediate concern may have been any increase in public expenditure (often an early source of opposition to the Great Exhibition itself), but beyond that he seems to fear exactly the free circulation of knowledge, and indeed of people, which inspired Prince Albert. He had successfully opposed the granting of £50,000 a year to Albert as Consort on the grounds that 'he, the Colonel, did not like foreigners',[30] and gave the same pseudo-rationale for his opposition to Catholic Emancipation and to legislation allowing further development of the railways. He was, needless to say, a bitter opponent of Free Trade. The common theme between all the things Sibthorpe disliked seems to be a fear of the kind of mobility which Albert saw as the key to the modern world.

In numerous speeches in the Commons, Sibthorpe raged against the Exhibition. His topics included protesting against the felling of any trees on the proposed site in Hyde Park (in fact this was his most effective argument, causing much grief to the organisers, and answerable only because Paxton was able rapidly to modify his design so that a number of trees could remain in their place within the Crystal Palace itself[31]), economic loss to the government and the country, and the international nature of the event. On 18 June 1850 he referred to both trees and foreigners: 'Are the elms to be sacrificed for one of the greatest frauds, greatest humbugs... ever known?... I will do nothing to encourage foreigners – nothing to give secret service money to them in the shape of premiums'.[32] Sibthorpe assumes that far from everyone co-operating in the free trade rationale of the Exhibition, Europeans will only come if paid to do so. The Great Exhibition is thus a great fraud on the public. His speeches over the next year continued to develop these fears:

> Who will pay?... The foreigner? Why, he has no money... The House has been told that labourers throughout the country will save their shillings, that they might be enabled to visit the exhibition. Who will take care of their families whilst they are away in London? The poor labourers are to come up to London, helter-skelter, where they will suddenly find themselves amidst the temptations of the great metropolis... What will become of the chastity and modesty of those who might become the victims of those temptations?

For Sibthorpe, naturally, the Foreigner will have no money – if people come from abroad, it can only be to steal from the solid and stable mass of British money. For the Colonel, movement can only result in crime – earlier in this speech he gives an account of a gentleman who, living near Hyde Park, woke up one morning to find some of its trees missing. The gentleman, claims Sibthorpe, 'thought that some thieves had *run* away with them, for it did not occur to him to suspect the Commissioners of Woods and Forests' [my emphasis].[33] Working men – Sibthorpe assumes, incorrectly, that working class *families* will not attend – who come to see the Exhibition on railway excursions will be subject to a sudden ('helter-skelter') and probably fatal urbanisation. Being used to the traditional chastity and stability of the country, the sheer variety of the city will entrap them, particularly, he implies, through its prostitutes. Free trade leads not so much to free love as to unregulated sex, and that apparently inevitable aspect of instant urbanisation leads inexorably to the circulation of venereal disease.

Sibthorpe strongly associates many aspects of widespread Victorian anxieties about the city with the Great Exhibition. It will promote movement to London, the decay of virtue and self-restraint, an influx of gimcrack foreign goods, a 'mixed' cosmopolitan population, crime, corruption and disease. If free trade, national and international unity and prosperity were envisaged by Prince Albert as a complete system, Sibthorpe's speeches constitute a no less total system. All his objections fit together to oppose the greater circulation of *anything*. First of all, 'the promoters wish to introduce amongst us foreign stuff of every description without regard to quality or quantity', paving 'the way for the establishment of cheap and nasty trumpery'. The use of the word 'establishment' interestingly suggests that Sibthorpe sees this change as liable to be a permanent loss of quality – the market and public taste, once exposed to 'trumpery', will be for ever debased. Then, even more frighteningly, will come actual foreign invasion. Sibthorpe on 4 February 1851, hoping that lightning will destroy the Crystal Palace before it is completed, warned: 'Your property, your wives and your families will be at the mercy of pickpockets and whoremongers from every part of the earth'. Once England's boundaries are breached, the more private boundaries of property and even bodies will be invaded. In a grand finale reserved for the period when it had become clear that the Exhibition certainly would go ahead, Sibthorpe recapitulated all his favourite themes:

> That miserable Crystal Palace ... Let them beware of man-traps and spring-guns. They will have their food robbed – they will have a piebald generation, half black and half white; but I can assure them that my arm will be raised to prevent such a violation. They might look for assassinations, for being stabbed in the dark; but careless of that, I am determined to pursue an even, straightforward course.[34]

Here his horrified fears leave behind any attempt at literal plaus-
ibility and become metaphorical – the fear of unrestrained foreign
sexual behaviour has now become a prophecy of a whole generation
of mixed race, and the focus has shifted from European visitors to
(wholly imaginary) black sexual intruders. Once allowed in, the
corruption will be long lasting, and eventually will catch up with
those responsible for the Exhibition. At times, here, Sibthorpe's
language becomes confusing, perhaps sign of his increasing distur-
bance at the inexorable approach of the Exhibition's opening. The
metaphorical spring-guns and man-traps are not immediately comprehensible – it may be significant that these anti-poaching devices
which a country land-owner might use against intruders on his
property are here being set against the 'rightful' owners of England
through their willingness to welcome 'foreigners'. The last sentence
also seems a little confused. The assassinations were predicted by
those worried that the Exhibition would become the focus for
attacks by European anarchists (at one time both government Ministers and the Exhibition Commissioners did plan to advise the
Queen against going to the opening ceremony lest she be attacked,
or mobbed[35]). In Sibthorpe's sentence this anxiety is turned from
attempts to disrupt the Exhibition to an armed attempt to stop him
from opposing it!

Sibthorpe's vision of the Great Exhibition does, in its own way,
share a common vision with Prince Albert's: both see the Exhibition
in terms of the collapsing of rigid boundaries and the opening up of
new possibilities of movement. But while Albert sees England as
benefiting from this mobility by gaining whatever it needs from the
free market, he has no fear of any corresponding addition or flux in
terms of individual or national identity. Oddly, Sibthorpe may be
closer than Albert to one part of Marx and Engel's thoughts about
modernity in his hysterical fears about the loss of England's bodily
integrity. For they too could see that the social order itself would be
transformed and previous notions of stability overturned (their
attitude to the international nature of modernity was ultimately
very different, of course).

Sibthorpe's fears about the Great Exhibition may seem eccentric,
but they not only pick up common anxieties about the City, they
were also, at first, part of a mainstream reaction to the proposal. For
the year before the building of the Crystal Palace, *The Times*'s warn-
ings against the Exhibition were not much less hysterical
than Sibthorpe's: 'the whole of Hyde Park and ... the whole of

Kensington Gardens will be turned into a bivouac of all the vaga-bonds in London.'[36] The paper reported that 'foreigners' were rent-ing houses near the proposed Exhibition site to use as brothels. The letter pages of the paper hosted many who also objected, often on grounds which we have already met in Sibthorpe's speeches. Patrick Beaver comments that:

> Before long the Great Exhibition became one of the main topics of letters to the Editor... doctors warned that the expected influx of foreign visitors would bring with it an epidemic of the plague, while others saw in the threatened invasion a spreading of vener-eal disease throughout Britain. Clergymen wrote that the scheme was arrogant and, in flying in the face of God, was likely to call forth his wrath. The main and most virulent objectors were man-ufacturers who feared ruin if England were flooded with cheap foreign goods.[37]

Once the Crystal Palace itself came near to completion, however, *The Times* began to change tack. It had to face the now undoubted fact that the Exhibition was wildly popular in England. 'The whole nation', says Beaver, 'was Exhibition mad'.[38] Twenty-five thousand season tickets had been sold, London was packed with visitors, and *The Morning Chronicle* even began printing parallel articles in Eng-lish, French and German to aid European co-operation and under-standing.[39] By the time of the opening ceremony on 1 May 1851, *The Times* had moved to the position which was now dominant: the Exhibition was the chief modern wonder of the world. Its report of the ceremony gives another way of representing the experience of the first 'Exhibition of the Industry of All Nations'.

The *Times* correspondent used a markedly religious language in his account of the opening, not only in noting that some present read the spectacle in explicitly religious terms, but also in his own willingness to render the inexpressible nature of the experience. He notes the uniqueness of the event ('the like of which has never happened before and which in the nature of things can never be repeated'[40]) and the difficulty of framing responses: 'they... hardly knew... in what form to clothe the sense of wonder and even of mystery which struggled within them'. He returns repeatedly to phrases based on Paul's First Epistle to the Corinthians, 2: 9 ('Eye hath not seen, nor ear heard'): 'all conspired to suggest something even more than sense could scan, or imagination attain', 'it was felt to be more than what was seen, or what had been intended', 'there was so much that seemed accidental, and yet had a meaning, that no one could be content with simply what he saw'. The correspondent does suggest three more specific readings of the experience, but none seems finally sufficient (including perhaps even the third alternative!): 'Some saw in it the second and more glorious inauguration of their Sovereign; some a solemn dedication to art and its stores; some were most reminded of that day when all ages and climes shall be gathered round the Throne of their Maker'. The sense of the inexpressible is striking, and indeed, is not entirely unique to this account (Queen Victoria's own diary entry for the day has a related sense of the multiplicity of the experience, though she assigns it more readily to the religious role of inspiring devotional thoughts[41]).

The biblical language and reference is no doubt in one way an obvious resource for a Victorian writer wishing to give a sense of experience beyond the mundane, but they are not used in this account as a merely convenient shorthand for approval. St Paul's phrase (and its context in the whole Epistle) is used to suggest ways of thinking about a genuinely new experience. The experience is that of an awareness of a modern multiplicity beyond simple mastery or summary ('they... hardly knew what most to admire'), inspired by the enormous range and size of the Exhibition, as well perhaps as by the glass building's radically new sense of light and spaciousness. The approach to this shock of the new through religion seems in one way to offer an ordering discourse. Indeed, the sense of the Exhibition as devotional has some relation to Albert's idea that Science and Progress are fulfilling God's idea of humanity. However, the comforting order thus offered is made more difficult of simple attainment within the *Times* account by the use of this particular biblical text. St Paul's Epistle discusses the limitations of human knowledge and the unknowability of divine order (except, as the final words of the letter point out, through the earthly ministry of Christ). Applying this text to a description of the Great Exhibition is, to say the least, interesting. For the Exhibition is essentially a celebration of the achievements of human knowledge, of what could be termed in Pauline words 'the wisdom of this world... of the princes of this world, that come to nought' (6).[42] The *Times* passage neither asserts that the Exhibition is to be connected straightforwardly to divine wisdom, nor suggests the superiority of a different order of wisdom beyond the Exhibition, but instead transfers the unknowability of the divine to the experience of the Exhibition itself. This may suggest that the Exhibition is a reflection of divine qualities (and undoubtedly partly does function in that way), but it is not quite a traditional religious procedure. The indescribable novelty of the Exhibition remains important in its own terms (rather than in a religious world order), and that overwhelming experience is, I think, one of modernity.[43] This text gives a sense not so much of Albert's abstract system of the modern world as of being in the midst of a human creation which, though wonderful, seems beyond the human capacity to master. Though the modernising world order may promise universal improvement, here an individual is represented as pondering not the system, but the experience of multiplicity. The text significantly represents the new through a traditional source of authority which both orders the unprecedented event, and leaves it unorderable.

The next text represents one of the many (unofficial) kinds of writing about the Exhibition which visitors were invited to buy as souvenirs. It is a small satirical booklet of fifteen pages entitled *Mr Goggleyes's Visit to the Exhibition* (1851), said on the final page to be 'A new work! invented and designed for the Exhibition...by Tim[othy] Takemin'.[44] Among other things, that final signature marks the booklet's role as a mock exhibit in the exhibition itself – an impression reinforced by the illustration on the last page which shows a catalogue-like book clearly labelled as exhibit 'no. 90000000000 and last', which on closer inspection turns out to be a drawing of the cover page of...*Mr Goggleye's Visit to the Great Exhibition*! Each of the other pages is similar in general design, the space being occupied mainly by a cartoon drawing (or more usually two separate drawings) accompanied by a caption, and, for pages 5–12, an (alleged) Exhibition number for the object or scene illustrated. The first four pages show Mr Goggleye's progress from the country to the Exhibition, with page four showing his acquisition of the Catalogue from which the booklet's remaining pages are said to be extracts. The booklet's satirical jokes about the Exhibition have some things in common with Colonel Sibthorpe's objections. Thus there are references to taxation and to theft (p. 5 shows in its bottom half a screw labelled 'income tax', captioned 'a screw that was made to last about three years, but it is now supposed will never wear out'; p. 12 shows in its lower half a hand withdrawing a handkerchief from a coat pocket, captioned 'British Industry! – Silk drawn and spun by hand'). On the final page, the booklet even echoes

(coincidentally or otherwise) one of Colonel Sibthorpe's speeches –
it exhibits a nutshell labelled 'Common Sense', above the caption 'a
nut shell, in which is contained an infallible specific for the cure of
Cant, and Humbug'. However, these similarities are only partial.
Against Sibthorpe's horror of any change this booklet presents a
more rational and, indeed, dynamic critique of the Exhibition, on
grounds which neither assume that change is undesirable nor accept
that the Exhibition is really about significant change. Its conclusion
with its nutshell of common sense suggests the kinship of its criti-
cisms of the Exhibition with older Enlightenment debates between
common sense and rationalism run riot. So too, does its reference to
Swift's *Gulliver's Travels* on page 9, where the lower drawing shows
exhibit 'no. 2708717', consisting of a machine and two cucumbers
with rays emanating, with the caption 'a Machine for extracting
SUNBEAMS from Cucumbers'. The original of this idea comes in
Gulliver's Travels, Book III, where it is one of the improving ideas of
the academicians of Lagado (unfortunately, they have not yet made
the process actually *work*). Above the sunbeam-extracting machine is
another clearly connected exhibit, captioned 'a project for building
Castles in the air'. Other pages show a variety of exhibits which
satirically show the things which should engage national attention,
or the distractions which are offered instead. Thus there is the
picture of a scarecrow with the caption 'Irish Industry! specimen
of Irish manufactured wearing apparel' (p. 6) and a drawing of the
London river-front, complete with labelled sewers, soap factory and
bone boilers, with the words 'fever, typhus, cholera, filth and death'
floating on the river surface, and the caption: 'a plan showing that
the present system is the best for draining London – of its population!' (p. 13). Significantly, there seems to be a reference to Prince
Albert's Mansion House speech and its call for unity, in a drawing of
spectacles and binoculars captioned 'Glasses, for enabling everybody to take the same view of everything, so that there will never
be no disagreement on nothing!' (p. 7). This, presumably, is one of
the distracting functions of the Exhibition – to promote apparent
progress and consensus with mere gimmicks. The name of the
booklet's hero, Mr Goggleye, may suggest that his wonder at the
exhibition is part of an indiscriminate and deluding love of spectacle, rather than a realistically progressive attitude.

The booklet's satire aims, then, not so much at the transforming
project of the Exhibition, but at its actual failure to engage with
reality, let alone to change it. It suggests a critique of grandiloquent

rhetoric and schemes of progress in favour of attention to problems which may not be new, but which are as yet unsolved. Overall, the booklet implies that the whole exciting discourse of modernisation and scientific progress as presented at the Exhibition may not be the key issue of the age at all. The key problems do need progress, but remain unengaged by the abstractions of the Great Exhibition.

The final text I will examine is, mainly, as positive as Prince Albert and *The Times* in its view of the Exhibition. However, it introduces a classic question about the nature of the exhibits which none of the other texts so far considered have raised, and one which is important in terms of Victorian responses to modernity. The text is *The Art-Journal Illustrated Catalogue of the Industries of All Nations* (1851),[45] a large format and copiously illustrated work, sponsored by a periodical whose 'project' (their word!) was an attempt 'to connect the FINE ARTS with the INDUSTRIAL ARTS'.[46] The classic question concerns the relationship of the *design* of exhibits at the Crystal Palace to the ideas of progress which the Exhibition was meant to celebrate, and thus to the whole issue of Victorian taste and modernity. Asa Briggs raises the issue in *Victorian Things*:

> In 1851 at the Great Exhibition Alexander Bain had displayed his electrically powered clock in a richly scrolled rococo French-styled case ... 'Our age is retrospective' Emerson had complained in the 1840s. Why, he asked ponderously, should it not proclaim 'an original relation to the universe?', a question not very different from the favourite Victorian question posed by architects, why should they not have 'an architecture of our period, a distinct, individual, palpable style of the nineteenth century?'.[47]

It was certainly a matter of contemporary concern that the age had not developed a clearly recognisable style of its own, and/or that English taste in design in particular was eclectic and uneducated. Indeed, an essay on taste was selected as the Exhibition Prize Essay (*The Art-Journal* contributed the one-hundred guinea prize, and printed the essay, by Ralph Wornum, as the last item in their *Illustrated Catalogue of the Industries of All Nations*).

Wornum in his Essay, 'The Exhibition as a Lesson in Taste', notes that:

> there is nothing new in the Exhibition in ornamental design; not a scheme, not a detail that has not been treated over and over again

in ages that are gone; that the taste of the producers generally is uneducated and that...the influence of France is paramount... bearing exclusively in the two most popular traditional styles of that country – the Renaissance and the Louis Quinze...[48]

His attitude to this derivative or historical style is not uniformly disapproving, and in the end he cannot imagine any real possibility of a distinctively 'modern' design. Nevertheless, he makes distinctions between different ways of using the past. Thus he is critical of copying unrelated to modern needs:

> The Medieval court is open to much the same objection... We have in this collection not an evidence of the application of a peculiar [i.e. specific] taste to modern and ordinary wants or purposes, but simply the copy of an old ideas; old things in an old taste.[49]

And he is also anxious that a generalised and eclectic design aesthetic should not mix the differing historical styles indiscriminately.

> The time has perhaps now gone by... for the development of any particular or national style, and for this reason it is necessary to distinguish the various tastes that have prevailed throughout past ages, and preserve them as distinct expressions; or otherwise, by using indiscriminately all materials, we should lose all expression... For if all objects in a room were of the same shape and details... the mind would soon be utterly disgusted. This is, however, exactly what must happen on a large scale; if all our decoration is to degenerate into a uniform mixture of all elements, nothing will be beautiful, for nothing will present a new or varied image to the mind.[50]

The passage makes it clear that for this Victorian, at least (and, in fact, this was a dominant and widespread feeling), the only imaginable 'modern' style is one based on past styles. *The Illustrated Art-Journal Catalogue* reinforces this impression, praising many exhibits whose style is unquestionably not 'modern' in the twentieth-century (modernist?) sense of being in a distinctively modern style. Thus, it engraves an exhibit called 'the Chatelaine':

it is an excellent example of steel-manufacture, displaying considerable taste...the modern chatelaine is but a reproduction of
an article of decorative ornament, worn by ladies in our own
country more than a century and a half ago...The elegant and
ornamental character of the object may again ensure its favourable reception; and the beauty of such as that we now engrave
must recommend it even to the most fastidious utilitarian.[51]

This commentary sees no contradiction between the most modern
production processes – 'steel manufacture' – and its application to
a decorative object derived from the past. Indeed, it suggests
that the beauty of the steel design will bring the chatelaine back
into favour as an item of costume. There is certainly no sense – as
there might be in the twentieth century – of steel as a modern
material requiring a modern[ist] style. There is, though, an odd
conclusion about the 'most fastidious utilitarian', which does seem
to half point towards a conception of a modern attitude to design.
The use of the term 'utilitarian' seems to give it the simplifying
Victorian interpretation of 'only interested in functionality', which
implies that this chatelaine (despite being a wholly decorative object
– and a long abandoned one at that!) will appeal even to those with
a starker modern aesthetic. However, this is not a strongly articulated point, and it is heavily contradicted by the language representing the object's beauty as produced rather by a decorative than
functional style.

Many comparable commentaries on exhibits could be cited from
the journal, but one further striking example is sufficient, particularly as it represents the Exhibition itself. Page 195 of the catalogue
illustrates:

a vase, intended to represent the triumph of Science and
the Industrial Arts in the Great Exhibition; the style is Elizabethan
enriched. Four statuettes on the body of the vase represent
Newton, Bacon, Shakespeare, and Watt, commemorating Astro-
nomy, Philosophy, Poetry, and Mechanics respectively...between
these figures, the practical operations of Science and Art are
displayed, and their influences typified by the figures on the
base, indicating War, Rebellion, Hatred, and Revenge, overthrown
and chained. The recognition and reward of peaceful industry are
symbolised by the figure of Prince Albert surmounting the composition.

Clearly, no contradiction is felt between the progress of science and the 'enriched Elizabethan style' (that curious 'enriched' may imply that this modern age can further improve past styles by adding even more of that style back into them!). Like Albert's own speech, the theme of this piece is harmony, and the story of progress is one which is both spectacular and yet strangely consistent with gradual development from the past (i.e. is figured as both transforming and smoothly continuous).

The place of 'past styles' in the Great Exhibition can be approached in a number of ways. Asa Briggs suggests that 'both old and new, revival and anticipation, had to be adequately represented if the Exhibition were to fulfil the objectives' of Prince Albert and Henry Cole.[52] Briggs presumably means that this mixture of new and old is needed to show the achievements of human progress up to the present, and the likelihood of their further development. However, this does not quite take account of the fact that the Exhibition did not show actually 'old things', but rather copies of past objects, and modern objects with a decorative style derived from past models. This does not logically represent a smooth history of development in the way Briggs suggests, but rather implies an oddity in attitudes towards the modern. If all the exhibits were new (in fact, they had to be less than three years old), but their styles were often 'old', then this must tell us something about the nature of Victorian modernity. If innovation was to be admired, it was only perfected by being 'dressed' in a tasteful style from the past. Despite the genuine newness of the Crystal Palace itself, there was no generally understood modern style. This could be interpreted as part of Victorian historicism – a tendency to value the past highly and to apply its styles to the new. In this reading, 'past styles' become a way of making the modern acceptable and, possibly, of containing it within or connecting it with older systems of value. However, it could equally be said that the ability to reproduce a range of styles from the past and apply them to any modern artefact is, in fact, a much more positive engagement with the modern than the 'historicism' argument suggests. For if the lack of a modern style and an obsession with the past can be seen as an inability to face the modern, it can also be seen as a situation only possible because of the capacity of modern production to reproduce complex detail on such a scale. It may be that Victorians were more conscious of their historicism than has been allowed, and that approving appraisals of design such as those in *The Art-Journal* were not avoidances of the

modern, but rather celebrations of it. Briggs quotes the architect
Gilbert Scott on history and glosses the comment rather negatively:
'the burdens of history could be as real as its excitements. For...
Gilbert Scott, "the peculiar characteristic of the present day, as
compared with all former periods, is this – that we are acquainted
with the history of art".'[53] It may be that both in this observation
and more generally in Victorian culture it was a question more of
excitement than burden, and that greater access to knowledge, and
productive ability – a result of the kinds of modernity Prince Albert
spoke of – was positively celebrated through a consciousness of the
potential to select at will from the past.

What can this selection of texts about the Great Exhibition tell us
about 'varieties of Victorianism' and 'Victorian modernity'? Above
all, the texts can suggest the importance of notions of progress and
the modern in Victorian culture, and some of the range of complexities that necessary attempts to describe the 'peculiar features of our
present era' led to. Briggs comments on the variousness of Victorian
attitudes to 'old things' and 'new things':

> because so many different, even contradictory answers were
> given, it is as difficult to generalise about the universe of old
> things in Victorian times and how it was related to the universe
> of new things as it is to categorise and to interpret Victorian new
> things. There was parody as well as derivation, escape as well as
> exploration, individual fantasy as well as imitation.[54]

The texts read in this essay are far from homogenous in their
approaches to the modern as represented by the Exhibition (though
only Sibthorpe tries utterly to reject the new), but all do give a sense
of the range of complexity in Victorian attitudes. It may be that
'Victorian modernity' is not only paradoxical for us as a term, but
was also a paradoxical area to Victorians themselves, as they could
both account for it in conventional and traditional languages, and
yet also manifested a (half?)-awareness of the complexities of understanding a genuinely new world.

Notes

1. The title of G.R. Porter's book, first printed in 1837, and reprinted many times; the 1851 edition included a new preface. See Asa Briggs, *Victorian People – a Reassessment of Persons and Themes 1851–67* (Harmondsworth, revised edition, 1965), p. 10.
2. *Principal Speeches and Addresses of H.R.H. the Prince Consort*, 1862, pp. 110–12; reprinted in J.M. Golby (ed.), *Culture and Society in Britain 1850–1890 – A Sourcebook of Contemporary Writings* (Oxford, 1986). Page references are henceforth given in brackets after quotations.
3. Speech to the Society of Arts, quoted by Briggs in *Victorian People*, p. 48.
4. Quoted in Briggs, *Victorian People*, p. 23.
5. *The Times*, 2 May 1851; quoted in Patrick Beaver's *The Crystal Palace*, (London, 1970), pp. 40–2.
6. *Victorian People*, p. 22.
7. W.L. Burn, *The Age of Equipoise* (London, 1964); Geoffrey Best, *Mid-Victorian Britain 1851–75* (London, 1971).
8. G.M. Young, *Portrait of an Age* (London, 1936), p. 87 and note.
9. *Mid-Victorian Britain 1851–75*, p. 20.
10. *Victorian People*, p. 9.
11. Thomas Richards also discusses The Great Exhibition as a transforming event in the invention of a modern commodity culture in *The Commodity Culture of Victorian England – Advertising and Spectacle, 1851–1914* (London, 1991), Chapter 1. However, he does not really discuss Victorian conceptions of modernity so much as a transformation in the theory and practice of consumption.
12. See p. 235 and after, *All That Is Solid*.
13. Ibid., p. 237.
14. Ibid., p. 238.
15. Ibid., p. 239.
16. Ibid., pp. 237–8.
17. Ruskin in his 'The Opening of the Crystal Palace considered in Some of its Relations to the Prospects of Art', 1854, quotes a speech by Mr Laing at the opening of the Exhibition, calling the Palace: 'an entirely new order of architecture, producing, by means of unrivalled mechanical ingenuity, the most marvellous and beautiful effects'. An extract from Ruskin's essay including this portion is reprinted in *Culture and Society in Britain 1850–1890*, pp. 174–7. Laing is quoted on p. 175.
18. *All That is Solid*, p. 238.
19. See Anthony Bird, *Paxton's Palace* (London, 1976), pp. 121–4 and P. Beaver's *The Crystal Palace*, pp. 69 and 79.
20. See *Paxton's Palace*, pp. 124–33.
21. See *Paxton's Palace*, p. 42, and *The Crystal Palace*, pp. 69–103.
22. *The Crystal Palace*, pp. 69–103 includes many excellent Victorian photographs that make clear the solidity of the Sydenham Palace and the extensive landscaping. Transience is not readily suggested.
23. *Paxton's Palace*, p. ix.

24.   See *The Crystal Palace*, pp. 66–8 for examples of cartoons, and pp. 64–5 for texts and illustrations printed on silk handkerchiefs.
25.   All quotations from the speech can be found on pp. 1–2 of *Culture and Society in Britain 1850–1890*.
26.   Yvonne ffrench, *The Great Exhibition: 1851* (London, 1950), pp. 49–50.
27.   *The Communist Party Manifesto*, 1848.
28.   *Victorian People*, pp. 23–30.
29.   *The Crystal Palace*, p. 21.
30.   Ibid.
31.   See *The Great Exhibition: 1851*, pp. 76–9, 99–101 and C.H. Gibbs-Smith's *The Great Exhibition of 1851* (London, 1950), p. 11.
32.   *The Crystal Palace*, p. 21.
33.   Ibid., p. 22.
34.   Ibid., p. 35.
35.   Yvonne ffrench, *The Great Exhibition: 1851*, pp. 153–8.
36.   *The Crystal Palace*, p. 21.
37.   Ibid.
38.   Ibid., p. 35.
39.   Ibid.
40.   *The Times*, 2 May 1851; quoted in *The Crystal Palace*, pp. 40–2.
41.   *The Crystal Palace*, p. 40.
42.   Though this account clearly presents a positive view of the Exhibition, its choice of biblical text may be connected to some of the debates about religion and the Exhibition which were part of early reaction to the proposal. Yvonne ffrench discusses how some saw it as a hubristic celebration of human achievement in *The Great Exhibition: 1851*, pp. 157–8.
43.   Charles Dickens was overwhelmed by a perhaps similar sense of the multiplicity of the Exhibition: 'I find I am "used up" by the Exhibition. I don't say there is nothing in it: there's too much. I have only been twice, so many things bewilder one. I have a natural horror of sights, and the fusion of so many sights in one, has not decreased it.' Quoted in C.H. Gibbs-Smith, *The Great Exhibition of 1851*, pp. 20–1.
44.   Each of the booklet's pages is reproduced in *The Crystal Palace*, p. 60.
45.   Reprinted in facsimile by David and Charles, Newton Abbot, Devon, 1970. References are to this edition.
46.   Original Preface, p. vi.
47.   *Victorian Things*, p. 422.
48.   *The Art-Journal Illustrated Catalogue*, p. V*** (the asterisked Roman numerals are used by the journal to indicate the pagination of the five Essays printed at the end of the catalogue proper. Wornum's essay is printed on pp. I–XXII***).
49.   Ibid., p. V***.
50.   Ibid., p. XXII***.
51.   Ibid., p. 43.
52.   *Victorian People*, p. 48.
53.   *Victorian Things*, p. 423.
54.   Ibid.

4

Black Silk and Red Paisley: the Toxic Woman in Wilkie Collins's *Armadale*

Jessica Maynard

In a much wider degree than people are accustomed to realize, modern civilized life – from the economic system which is constantly becoming more and more a credit-economy, to the pursuit of science, in which the majority of investigators must use countless results obtained by others, and not directly subject to verification – depends upon faith in the honor of others.

Georg Simmel, 'The Sociology of Secrecy'

1

Lydia Gwilt is an affront to common decency, a woman whom it is in the public interest to investigate and expose. Soon after she arrives in the Norfolk village of Thorpe-Ambrose to take up a post as governess, her reputation is thrown into doubt, and a succession of enquiries are instituted. Are her references to be relied upon, is her character really unexceptionable, is she 'genuine'? As a confidence trickster, Gwilt seems inimical to her environment, betraying the trust of those who employ her, and exploiting those unfortunate enough to fall in love with her. She takes advantage of a society of confidence, and in doing so she flouts its codes. To operate under false credentials is the gravest insult to a speculative culture, as legal prohibitions show. Fraud, forgery, impersonation – the criminal staple of Wilkie Collins's novels – attract the highest penalties. Even without recourse to the law, society has other, more diffuse ways of expressing disapproval, through exclusion and rejection. The lie goes against the public good in what Georg Simmel calls the modern 'credit-economy' and the 'enlightenment which aims at elimination of the element of deception from social life is always of a democratic character.'[1]

But, importantly, Simmel goes on to say that this lack of full intelligence – a certain element of mystery, or a kind of lying by omission – is also the principle for the *maintenance* of many relationships, as if exhaustive intimacy spoiled the balance between disclosure and reticence: 'That which we can see through plainly to its last ground shows us therewith the limit of its attraction, and forbids our phantasy to do its utmost in adding to the reality... if the utmost attractiveness of another person is to be preserved for us, it must be presented to us in part in the form of vagueness or impenetrability.'[2] This deficit of knowledge turns out to be an integrating principle, and it is in this hinterland between the *bona fide* and the suspect that the confidence trickster prospers, a kind of counterweight to the official market speculator. Similarly, Lydia Gwilt, criminal seducer and object of so many male fantasies, can, on Simmel's terms, double as ordinary modern lover. Lydia Gwilt, it might be suggested, is simultaneously enemy and exemplum of her culture.

The question of reputation or 'good character' is central to *Armadale*, serialised in the *Cornhill Magazine* between 1864 and 1866, and one of Wilkie Collins's most labyrinthine plots. In broad terms, the novel might be regarded as an exploration of social ambiguity, of a society which, in the absence of all the facts, must acquire the art of discrimination. The novel is, in a sense, an extended enactment of this anxiety of not knowing but being required to believe. This accounts for an unbecoming flurry of detective activity in the novel. As Catherine Peters observes in her introduction, '[i]n *Armadale* the spies are everywhere, and they are not only professional: everyone spies on everyone else.'[3] Character references are held up to scrutiny, read with a practised critical eye: 'The testimonial was very briefly and very coldly expressed, but it was conclusive as far as it went' (*A*, 224). Such vigilance is the product of the credit-economy, as is surveillance, and they are invoked in the public interest. So, in justifying his investigation into Lydia Gwilt, the lawyer Pedgift will argue: 'Read your newspaper... you'll find we live in piping times for the black sheep of the community – if they are only black enough. I insist on asserting, sir, that we have got one of the blackest of the lot to deal with in this case. I insist on asserting that you have had the rare luck, in these unfortunate enquiries, to pitch on a woman who happens to be a fit object for inquiry, in the interests of public protection' (*A*, 358). But *Armadale*, though it must, formally, share this inquisitive enthusiasm, this will to discover, offers not one but two fit objects for inquiry, the first being the criminal woman, the second being what Collins in a prefatory note called 'the Clap-trap morality of the present day' (*A*, xxxix).

Armadale is organised around a quasi-sophoclean proposition: that it is impossible to evade the decrees of fate. It opens with the original sins of the fathers, suggestively played out against a colonial landscape (the West Indies; native poisons; the imminent emancipation of the slaves), and then goes on to test the proposition that these sins are visited on the sons. The original sin is the theft of a (future) wife, and a vengeful murder; the accomplice in these dark events, a servant girl who forges a letter and thus puts in motion a disastrous train of events. Even at the age of the twelve, her capacity to dissemble – 'precocious ability'; 'wicked dexterity' (*A*, 27) – proves lethal. She will be the nemesis that the two sons, Allan Armadale and Ozias Midwinter, seem only narrowly to escape. '"I saw the girl afterwards – and my blood curdled at the sight of her. If she is alive now, woe to the people who trust her! No creature more innately deceitful and more innately pitiless ever walked this earth"' (*A*, 27) is the surviving father's warning, an Old Testament warning to match crimes of biblical proportions: the beguiling of a woman, the deception of an ailing patriarch, the theft of a birthright, and brother killing brother (loosely speaking: they are really cousins).

After this colonial prelude, the woman reappears, now aged thirty-five, presumably (and this the central debate of the text) to fulfil her domesday potential. In the first phase of the novel she seems ubiquitous, improbably present at several different accidents or mishaps, like an avenging angel, or like the crowd perhaps: she reappears to extort some money from her former mistress, and her victim promptly dies from shock. She tries to commit suicide by throwing herself off a boat; a man dies of a chill, after saving her life; he has, we are told, been uncommonly taken with the lady's figure and poise.

These episodes theatricalise the woman; she appears as if within a tableau, and her face is always veiled. Hence it is not the personal detail that arrests her viewers but an abstract generality, a quality located in her body and her 'carriage', a quality that depends on movement, and impersonality – both features of the crowd, both features that can be enlisted to describe fate or force of nature. She is memorable also through what she wears:

Mr Brock was accosted in the village by a neatly-dressed woman, wearing a gown and bonnet of black silk and a red Paisley shawl, and who was a total stranger to him, and who inquired the way to Mrs. Armadale's house. She put the question without raising the thick black veil that hung over her face. Mr. Brock, in giving her the necessary directions, observed that she was a remarkably elegant and graceful woman, and looked after her as she bowed and left him ...   (*A*, 62)

Viewed in isolation, this description may seem unremarkable enough. The woman is decorous and respectable (the black silk dress), and modest (the veil). Yet if we view this as one moment in an incremental description of the woman, then perhaps, with the benefit of hindsight, this ladylike demeanour becomes more questionable. The status of the solitary woman who enjoys such liberty of movement may begin to seem rather more indeterminate. She 'accosts' her man, as perhaps a less reputable woman might, though she is also extremely civil ('she bowed and left him'). As to her clothes, are the red and the black as innocent as they seem, or do they contain counter-signals? Black may mean respectability, but also death; red and black, after all, are also a courtesan's insignia. Could this woman, then, be double-coded, indicative of both domesticity and exoticism? The red Paisley shawl, doubtless British manufactured, mass produced, nevertheless has its origins in the orient.

These contradictory signals are largely what contribute to the 'enigma' of the woman at this moment: boldness and autonomy on the one hand, gentility and constraint on the other. In walking out alone, she raises a problem of classification: she cannot be both a lady, and a free agent. For 'enigma', then, we can read other things beyond the requirements of mere narrative dynamic; we can read the confusion in economies of gender and class that is precipitated by the appearance of this woman in public, a stalling of the process of discrimination.[4] After all, as she walks the streets, she attracts the attention even of the modest country parson, and in her power to do so she erases the very possibility of a line drawn between legitimate and illegitimate, between high and low.

Gwilt is next seen aboard a steamer on the Thames, dressed identically in black silk and red shawl, anonymous behind a veil. Like Mr Brock, Arthur Blanchard is 'struck by the rare grace and elegance of her figure'; and as in the preceding case, Gwilt is, as it were, in contiguous relation to disaster. This scenario provides some important supplementary detail, which perhaps retrospectively informs the earlier account. Now there is more reason to regard her as the woman of questionable virtue, ruined, abandoned and suicidal (though we only know the details later). When she throws herself into the river, Arthur Blanchard rescues her, comes down with fever, and dies. This time, the fatal influence spreads further, to the Alps: father and brother also die while hurrying back to England. 'So,' the text goes, and by this time the coincidence surely does stretch credulity, 'the three lives were mown down by death. So, in a clear sequence of events, a woman's suicide-leap into a river had opened to Allan Armadale the succession to the Thorpe-Ambrose estates' (*A*, 72).

This moment – the woman in black silk with the red Paisley shawl – recurs throughout the first phase of the novel, which leads to the postulation of connection – could this be the same woman? – and from there, to the postulation of culpability – could she be responsible for both incidents? Once this move is made, the language shifts into criminological gear. But where then is the crime? There is no necessary connection between her material presence and these deaths (though she has, admittedly, extorted some money from Mrs Armadale). Rather, the link is forged through superstition, and a superstition easily translatable into the idiom of criminal investigation. Though logic naturally argues against this conclusion, the pursuers of Lydia Gwilt (inside and outside the story) *know* her to be the emissary of that dark colonial past. Now Mr Brock, the clergyman, finds himself in what sounds like the witness box, under examination. What previously seemed to be a casual act of seeing has become crime-watching:

'You saw her yourself in the village. What was she like?
'She kept her veil down. I can't tell you.'
'You can tell me what you *did* see?'
'Certainly. I saw, as she approached me, that she moved very gracefully, that she had a beautiful figure, and that she was a little over the middle height. I noticed, when she asked me the way to Mrs Armadale's house, that her manner was the manner of a lady, and that the tone of her voice was remarkably soft and winning. Lastly, I remembered afterwards, that she wore a thick black veil, a black bonnet, a black silk dress, and a red Paisley shawl. I feel all the importance of your possessing

some better means of identifying her than I can give you. But
unhappily –'   (*A*, 97)

In the retelling of that earlier encounter, black silk dress and red
Paisley shawl become a means of identification, and undergo a
subtle mutation in their cultural application. Where before they
suggested a conflict in meaning, and therefore an enigma, now
they seem to bear the stamp of crime. Where before they were
disruptive in their ambiguity, now the general tenor of this
conversation – that of the witness striving for inclusiveness but
who must always fall short ('But unhappily...') – seems to relocate
their meaning in an explicitly criminal domain. It is now, too, that
Brock articulates the contradiction only implied before: the bearing
of a lady, but the blandishments – 'winning' tone of voice – of a
somewhat different kind of woman. The exchange continues:

> He stopped. Midwinter was leaning eagerly across the table, and
> Midwinter's hand was laid suddenly on his arm.
>   'Is it possible that you know the woman?' asked Mr Brock,
> surprised at the sudden change in his manner.
>   'No.'
>   'What have I said, then, that has startled you so?'
>   'Do you remember the woman who threw herself from the
> river steamer?' asked the other – 'the woman who caused that
> succession of deaths, which opened Allan Armadale's way to the
> Thorpe-Ambrose estate?'
>   'I remember the description of her in the police report.'
>   '*That* woman,' pursued Midwinter, 'moved gracefully, and had
> a beautiful figure. *That* woman wore a black veil, a black bonnet, a
> black silk gown, and a red Paisley shawl –' He stopped, released
> his hold of Mr Brock's arm, and abruptly resumed his chair. 'Can it
> be the same?' he said to himself, in a whisper. '*Is* there a fatality
> that follows men in the dark? And is it following *us* in that
> woman's footsteps?'   (*A*, 97)

Lydia Gwilt is now where she belongs: in the annals of the police.
The 'police report' links her with an entirely different social territ-
ory: that of corruption, sin, despair, officialdom. But she is still only
guilty by association, by contiguity; guilty of the lesser crime of
attempted suicide, of triggering a 'succession of deaths'. These are
displacements of the real criminal history to be revealed later in the

novel. For the time being, though, we are persuaded of Gwilt's as yet unspecified culpability by her mere presence at all these scenes of the 'crime'. Suspicion is endorsed by appeal to intuition, but not through any rational procedure. By now, too, the abstraction of her figure, her way of moving, and her dress, have taken on the character of a criminal profile. It is profile, after all, that has fixed the woman in the memories of these male viewers, and not the specificities of face, a profile being, by definition, incomplete, a 'sketch', which always leaves something in reserve. Brock's description depends on vague impressions of 'figure', 'tone' and 'manner'. Profile, then – the black veil by which the woman withholds the totality of her person – works in opposite directions, as both solicitation and incrimination. It seduces the viewer/reader in the same way as do police reports, and newspaper accounts, and trial transcripts, which are all, as we discover, Gwilt's natural habitat.

There is one further version of this black silk and red Paisley figure which now needs to be considered, and this is the moment when the Reverend Brock identifies Gwilt as the generalised 'feminine' itself. There is no reason, he says, in a moment of male camaraderie, to assume this is one particular woman: 'Need an old man, like me, remind a young man, like you, that there are thousands of women of England, with beautiful figures – thousands of women who are quietly dressed in black silk gowns and red Paisley shawls?' (*A*, 98). Fashion, and mass production, make Lydia Gwilt no more than 'representative', a type endlessly reproducible, endlessly available to the transactions of the exchange economy. Her facelessness seems nothing more than commodified woman herself. Brock follows Baudelaire's painter of modern life in this equation between a woman and her clothes. 'What poet would dare,' asks Baudelaire, 'in depicting the delight caused by a beauteous apparition, to distinguish between the woman and her garb?'[5]

It is this 'making of the woman and her garb an indivisible whole'[6] that enables Gwilt, most crucially for the plot, to elude her pursuers. The identification of woman with what she wears enables Gwilt to escape the Reverend Brock's surveillance by substituting her maid for herself in the same costume. It is indeed her repetitious nature, along with her novelty, that makes her such an unknown quantity. It is her reproducibility that facilitates such a camouflage. 'To wish to see *everything* with this securing eye of the city-dweller ... that is to condemn oneself to see nothing,' says Buci-Glucksmann of the flâneur, whose quest for novelty results only in repetition.[7] Gwilt triumphs at this moment because she has the capacity to make Brock see nothing, though he thinks that he sees everything. His eyes 'are *unlooking eyes*, ever on the look-out for something new which is also always-the-same and therefore a deception,'[8] while Gwilt is that something new which is also always-the-same.

2

The development of big-city prostitution as a widespread phenomenon giving rise to legislation, which involved the conversion of
female bodies into articles of mass consumption, expressed a more
general historical shift that took place in the middle of the nineteenth century. This took the form of a crisis of looking: new
relations between the visible and invisible, representation of the
non-representable, and a series of practices and discourses engen-
dered by it. More than anything else, the female body is the
support of this 'archaeology of the look' to which Foucault
referred. A new stage-setting of bodies now makes them irreducible to their geometric visibility and endows them with a coeffi-
cient of obscurity or mystery.[9]

Perhaps this last manifestation of Lydia Gwilt is the most anxiety-
inducing: the singular woman who could also be any woman, the distinctive which is, at the same time, the standard. She is the type – typical because she, as yet, has no face, because she cannot be known, and she tells us something about Buci-Glucksmann's 'crisis of looking'. This crisis is part of the developing world of novelty and consumption, of voyeurs and window-shoppers, gazing after some-thing they cannot quite reach, cannot hope to own, or love, or know. These viewers will never be in full possession either of the facts, or the goods, or the woman, or authenticity itself: those experiences remain forever round the next corner, they cannot finally be grasped. This culture of seeing and acquisition will always depend on the anticipation of what may come next, but a 'next' that never comes: access will always be barred to the total view, the 'real' experience. There must always remain some areas yet to be charted, a satisfaction perpetually of the future. All this elucidates Lydia Gwilt's spiritual, if not technical, association with the brothel, with the procurer Maria Oldershaw. When her references are

investigated, she is traced to a 'house of ill repute' in Pimlico; in other words, disgraced for metaphorical prostitution (launching herself on to the marriage market, letting cash replace love in the amorous transaction).

Lydia Gwilt fascinates because, as an apparition, she is all about 'what may come next'. This is also why she is a criminal, because she withholds the facts. Her veil in fact obscures a criminal past. She has previously been scandalously revealed, by public prosecution: 'it is the one advantage of the horrible exposure which followed my marriage, that I seldom show myself in public, and never of course in such a populous place as London, without wearing a thick veil and keeping that veil down' (*A*, 208). 'Never of course in such a populous place as London' does not in this case point to laudable feminine modesty, but to the reticence of the social margins, discreet as they are in their absence from respectable view.

But Gwilt as well as being the veiled woman is also the blatant one, not only the stealthy poisoner, but the woman who *is* poison. Her crime goes deeper than mere offences against the person;[10] it is her person itself that is the greatest offence of all, particularly her infernal red hair. Variously referred to as 'terrible' (*A*, 367), 'horrid' (*A*, 279), 'unpardonably remarkable' (*A*, 268), this red hair does not so much testify to the dissimulation and deceit that are an adventuress's stock-in-trade, as to an outrageous availability, a promiscuity even.

When Gwilt embarks upon a plan of marital speculation (the impecunious governess who aims to ensnare the eligible young squire), she does not choose to dissemble as the banally criminal would, but instead seizes the moral initiative. How could she possibly be the same 'Miss Gwilt' as the suspect one already under observation? When challenged, she retorts ' "I don't choose to be mistaken ... for a woman who may be a bad character, because she happens to bear, or to have assumed the same name as mine" ' (*A*, 275). Her weapon is the sanctity of reputation; she bends the society of confidence to her needs. Lydia Gwilt, then, is one step on from Lady Audley, Mary Braddon's governess-adventuress, who still works her diabolical schemes from behind a china-doll exterior, and whose unbecoming conduct is merely underscored and rendered all the more appalling by a profusion of blonde ringlets.[11] Lydia Gwilt is brazen, in colouring and behaviour, and what is interesting is her scorn for cosmetic intervention of any kind, whether in the choice of a name or use of make-up: ' "Keep your odious powders and paints and washes for the spotted shoulders of your customers; not one of them shall touch my skin, I promise you"' (*A*, 154).[12]

How do we account for this hostility to prosthetic enhancements? A brief look at contemporary journalism persuades us of *Armadale*'s textual relation to the world of sales, publicity and scandal. Collins provides the clues himself in the Appendix to the novel, where he describes how he drew on a real gas-poisoning episode reported in the newspapers of the time for the finale of the novel (when Gwilt attempts to administer poison gas to Allan Armadale, so that she may impersonate his widow). *The Times* of November 1865, to which Collins refers, gives us a kind of journalistic matrix of this novel's preoccupations, so that, for example, alongside to the 'Want Places' column, where governesses and ladies' companions advertise their services, we see advertisements for all manner of cosmetic products, from artificial teeth ('Clergymen, lecturers and public speakers will find this system particularly adapted to their wants; it combines complete enunciation and perfect mastication'), to 'Rowland's Kaly-dor – an Oriental Botanical Preparation, for improving and beauti-fying the complexion and skin'. This latter invocation of the mysteries of the harem, the allure of the exotic (the product is apparently 'in high repute from the sultry climes of India to the frozen climes of the Czar') is a common selling point, and it points back to the apothecary's trafficking in arcana.[13] Potency here depends on mystery, just as commercial exclusivity relies on secret ingredients.

But perhaps most immediately relevant to the question of Lydia Gwilt's appearance is the following advertisement: 'Golden tresses and how to get them – By use of the aqua mira, red hair is changed to a charming gold colour. Dark hair, under the same influence, quickly assumes the fashionable tint.' Lydia Gwilt's defiantly red hair, on the other hand, proclaims the natural over the artificial, and it is this unmediated physical power that makes her 'terrible' and 'horrid'. This is why it is necessary to complicate her criminality to include its *natural* content. Gwilt's 'terrible red hair' testifies to an ambivalent construction of the woman in mid-nineteenth-century discourse: she is situated at once within the phantasmagoria of industrial-capitalist culture, and yet, according to the inevitabilities of biology, her body always allies her to the fecundity of nature: 'Woman's productivity, organic in contrast to the mechanical pro-ductivity of nineteenth-century industrialism, appears threatening to capitalist society'; it is the fashion season that replaces the mutabilities of nature, 'the living, human capacity for change and infinite variation'.[14] If fashion now lays claim to what was previously the preserve of nature, then Lydia Gwilt's contradictory status can be explained: she combines the properties of both artifice and nature, capturing the moment when the reproductive and renewing power of the commodity is projected on to the female body. She has reproductive power in either sense.[15]

It is not then inconsistent that she begins her career in the cosmetics trade, the child model who advertises the efficacy of various preparations for an itinerant apothecary and his wife. ' "One day," ' we hear, ' "something like a quarter of a century ago, a travelling quack-doctor, who dealt in perfumery as well as medicines, came to town, with his cart, and exhibited, as a living example of the excellence of his washes and hair-oils and so on, a pretty little girl, with a beautiful complexion and wonderful hair" ' (*A*, 510). This earlier moment of commercial venture is significant in that it shows us how far the nineteenth century has progressed since then. Mother Oldershaw has long since abandoned the pedlar's way of life, preferring to instal herself in 'legitimate' business. She now presides over a beauty emporium or 'Ladies Toilet Repository' in Pimlico, which doubles as a brothel. What does this passage from quackery to enterprise culture tell us? First of all, it is calculated to tell us that Oldershaw's illegitimacy is continuous throughout, regardless of locale, that she is akin to Marx's producer-pander, who 'puts himself at the service of the other's most depraved fancies, plays the pimp between him and his need, excites in him morbid appetites ... all so that he can then demand the cash for this service of love.'[16] What happens is that one form of roguery, that associated with the vagrancy of the open road, is substituted with a settled, urban kind, one that has retreated behind shop windows, one that prefers written slogans to the rhetoric of the street vendor.

But Maria Oldershaw's career is more than old-fashioned villainy rejigged for a modernising society. In its more serious implications it suggests this villainy as endemic to culture rather than situated outside or against it. In *Armadale* the figure of the mountebank – in all his/her guises – can be read not necessarily and not so simply as the enemy of civilised society, but rather as that society's accomplice. Ma Oldershaw, like other speculators, trafficks in confidence – confidence in the power of her beautifying products, confidence too in her discretion – and in this she points to what is a particularly modern transaction. She lives by stealth. Such a transaction is founded on an absence of complete knowledge, it depends 'upon a thousand pre-suppositions which the individual can never trace back to their origins, and verify; but which he must accept upon faith and belief.'[17] The cosmetics industry, perhaps above all others, demands an investment of confidence, and this is an almost tautologous process, since it is only really the illusion of confidence that the product promises in return. 'So essentially confidential a business' – which is Oldershaw's coy description of her trade (in toiletries *and* bodies) – in fact doubles as an account of economic circulation.

Mother Oldershaw has one further business interest. She also deals in drugs, in the 'sleeping drops' or laudanum to which Lydia Gwilt is addicted. This is the final perspective on Lydia Gwilt: her life of dependency, her life of ennui, which can only be combated by narcotics: '"Who was the man who invented laudanum? I thank him from the bottom of my heart, whoever he was... 'Drops', you are a darling! If I love nothing else I love *you*"' (*A*, 414).

3

It is already established that, seemingly, Lydia Gwilt brings destruc-tion in her wake: '"I don't know how she had discovered me, after all the years that have passed – I only know that she *has* discovered me. She will find her way to Allan next, she will poison my son's mind against me. Help me to get away from her! help me to take Allan away before she comes back!"' (*A*, 64). But these appeals come too late and the 'poison' has already begun its deadly work: 'The shock of the previous morning had completed its mischief. Mrs. Armadale's days were numbered' (*A*, 65).

It does seem that Lydia Gwilt's (Jenny Bourne Taylor notes that her name is only one letter away from 'guilt'[18]) appearances display both the grim inexorability of antiquity and the ruthlessness of more contemporary machinery. Her dalliance with poisons has a counter-part of sorts in the catastrophic potential of her personal appear-ance, which repeatedly numbs and incapacitates the male viewer. The overall effect of the novel is to cast her not merely as poisoner (though this is never proved), but as source of poison too. Like other toxins, she works through paralysis, blocking off respiratory func-tions, asphyxiating her victims. She shocks, she immobilises, she robs her admirers of speech: 'As he came within sight of her face, he stopped in ungovernable astonishment. The sudden revelation of her beauty, as she smiled and looked at him, inquiringly, suspended the movement in his limbs and the words on his lips' (*A*, 258). 'He stood looking at me, like a man petrified, without speaking a word. The effect of my horrid red hair perhaps?' (*A*, 279) she says in a letter, and of a further case of petrifaction:

> He turned all manner of colours, and stood trembling and staring at me, as there was something perfectly frightful in my face ... Did you ever see the boa-constrictor fed at the Zoological Gardens? They put a live rabbit in his cage, and there is a moment when the two creatures look at each other. I declare Mr Bashwood reminded me of the rabbit!   (*A*, 280)

There may be romantic echoes here – Lamia, perhaps, the serpentine seductress or Christabel – and reminders of sensation fiction's gothic antecedents, a suggestion even of the gaze of the Medusa.[19]

But what this novel gives us is a modern medusa who advertises through the Situations Wanted column of *The Times*, and who knows how to display herself to best advantage. Gwilt represents a form of enticement that can be best understood if we refer to commodities and markets. Writing in 1896 of the Berlin Trade Exhibition, Georg Simmel would talk of '[t]he way in which the most heterogeneous products are crowded together in close proximity paralyses the senses'. This battery of visual stimuli was 'a veritable hypnosis where only one message gets through to one's consciousness; the idea that one is here to amuse oneself.'[20] Lydia Gwilt exerts a similarly intoxicating effect, and, like the world's fairs Simmel talks about, she too presages an end to traditional sociation, to the bonds of friendship, family, patriarchal community generally (she helps estrange a father from daughter through forgery; she almost breaks up a male friendship; she stands in the way of an old-style match). The only community at Berlin was a community of spectators, united solely in their pursuit of the sensory diversion; for Simmel modern sociation only exists insofar as there is also, contradictorily, dissociation. And these are precisely the kind of social relations which Gwilt, always the circulating, the passing woman, announcing only the impossibility of love, brings to the Norfolk backwater of Thorpe-Ambrose. She brings with her all the distance, the impersonality, the lack of absolute knowledge, the abstract superficiality of capitalist exchange, and the impossibility of love:

'The delight of the city-dweller is not so much love at first sight as love at last sight,' says Benjamin of Baudelaire's poetry. In the modern erotic *'never* marks the high point of the encounter.'[21]

Does she, in this scandalous visibility and intoxicating effect, have something in common with the commodity? It should be recalled that she is marketing herself, as once she marketed elixirs and potions as a child. At every critical moment, she is on display, as in this moment when she frames herself for the viewer she already knows is there: 'Smoothly and gracefully the lady glided nearer and nearer...Noiselessly and smoothly she came on, with a gentle and regular undulation of the print gown...in walk, and look, and manner, in every casual movement that escaped her, expressing that subtle mixture of the voluptuous and the modest...' (*A*, 366–7). Baudelaire noted a similar automatism in the courtesan in 'The Painter of Modern Life': 'She advances, glides, trundles, beneath her load of petticoats which serve her at once as pedestal and a balancing pole. She darts glances from beneath her hat, like a portrait in its frame...To her can be justly applied the words of Bruyère, the inimitable master: Some women have an artificial grandeur which derives from the movement of the eyes, the carriage of the head, a manner of walking and no further significance.' The 'triviality' of such a woman's life,' a life of trickery and combat – shines inexorably through her enveloping apparatus.'[22] This is why Gwilt not only inspires addiction, but is herself the addict, always trying to escape the burden of that triviality.

This lack of significance is the commodity's simple postulation of itself. 'Here I am' is all it says. It is performative:

> The commodity asks for nothing better than to *appear*. And appear it does – visible/readable, in shop windows, and on display racks. Self-exhibition is its forte. Once it is apparent, there is no call to decode it...And yet once it has appeared its mystery only deepens. Who has produced it? Who will buy it? Who will profit from its sale? Who, or what purpose will it serve? Where will the money go? The commodity does not answer these questions; it is simply *there*...[23]

These are questions reformulated in *Armadale* through the figure of the dangerous woman, someone whose origins and intentions are unknown, someone who intoxicates those who look on her, someone who is simply there, 'unpardonably remarkable'. This woman/

commodity is the source of a more significant 'poison' than that to be found in the purple flask of the drug dispensary. What Lydia Gwilt does is much less important than what she *is*. If she is the occasion of paralysis and addiction, if she enchants her viewer, it is because she demonstrates a toxic principle within a culture where, as Baudelaire maintained, a woman *was* the clothes she wore. This poison is to be found in the remedies[24] of capitalist culture – the dependencies of viewing, consuming, acquiring – and, unlike those crimes belonging to the court-room, it cannot be legislated against. The novel appears at a time of increasing government intervention in the pharmaceutical world, and the parliamentary passage of certain reforms testifies to an alarm at the abuse of opiates, the easy availability of lethal poison. The Pharmacy Act of 1868 legislates for clarification and control in the realm of substance abuse: 'Persons selling or compounding Poisons, or assuming the title of Chemist and Druggist' are 'to be qualified' while poisons must be clearly labelled, and their sale recorded in a poison book. But Lydia Gwilt suggests a rather less specific poison, which can neither be labelled nor entered in the chemist's ledger, because it emanates from society itself. *Armadale*, a narrative which elaborates a rhetoric of poison, remedy, consumption and cure, brings to mind Avital Ronell's remark on *Madame Bovary* – 'There is no culture without a drug culture.'[25] Wilkie Collins's novel possesses its own burgeoning society of addicts: the alcoholic (Bashwood), the hobbyist (Colonel Milroy) and, of course, Gwilt herself.

Notes

1. Georg Simmel, 'The Sociology of Secrecy and of Secret Societies', *The American Journal of Sociology* XI, 4 (1906), pp. 441–98; p. 447.
2. Ibid., p. 463.
3. Wilkie Collins, *Armadale* (1866), ed. with intro. by Catherine Peters (Oxford: Oxford University Press, 1989), p. xx. Hereafter referred to as *A* with page references cited parenthetically in the text.
4. In 'The Urban Peripatetic: Spectator, Streetwalker, Woman Writer', Deborah Epstein Nord discusses the stigmatisation of unaccompanied women in public spaces, in *Nineteenth Century Literature* 46, 3 (December 1991).
5. Charles Baudelaire, 'The Painter of Modern Life', in *My Heart Laid Bare and Other Writings*, trans. Norman Cameron, ed. with intro. by Peter Quennell (London: Soho Book Company, 1980), p. 60.

6. Ibid., p. 60.
7. Christine Buci-Glucksmann, _Baroque Allegory: The Aesthetics of Modernity_ (1984), trans. Patrick Camiller (London: Sage Publications Ltd, 1994), p. 75.
8. Ibid., p. 76.
9. Ibid., p. 99.
10. The Offences Against the Person Act 1861 legislated against the abuse of arsenic and other lethal substances.
11. Lady Audley, like Lydia Gwilt, uses her physical charms to combat economic hardship. Apparently abandoned by her husband, she seeks a living as a governess, and marries into wealth and title. When her first husband inconveniently reappears, she pushes him into a well.
12. An interesting point of comparison occurs in Collins's later _The Law and the Lady_ (1875). Here, the heroine Valeria must reluctantly allow herself to be 'made up' before a crucial interview with a man who may be able to help her in her investigation of her husband's past: 'She came back with a box of paints and powders; and I said nothing to check her. I saw, in the glass, my skin take on a false fairness, my cheeks a false colour, my eyes a false brightness – and I never shrank from it. No! I let the odious deceit go on; I even admired the extraordinary delicacy and dexterity with which it was all done' (_The Law and the Lady_, ed. with an intro. by Jenny Bourne Taylor. Oxford and New York: Oxford University Press, 1992, p. 57). Here, the respectable, 'good' woman assumes a mask before she strays outside her sphere. Her 'odious deceit' seems the condition upon which this seizing of the initiative is founded.
13. See Roy Porter, _Health for Sale: Quackery in England 1660–1850_ (Manchester: Manchester University Press, 1989); Kellow Chesney, _The Victorian Underworld_ (London: Temple Smith, 1970). Chesney discusses the woman upon whom Oldershaw is said to have been based, Rachael Leverson.
14. Susan Buck-Morss, _The Dialectics of Seeing: Walter Benjamin and the Arcades Project_ (1989; Cambridge, Massachusetts: MIT Press, 1991), p. 99.
15. It now becomes a woman's lot to attempt to evade the ravages of time, to be eternally 'new'. Fashion becomes a special female burden, as in the case of _Armadale's_ Mrs Milroy: 'The utter wreck of her beauty made a wreck horrible to behold, by her desperate efforts to conceal the sight of it from her own eyes, from the eyes of her husband and child... Her head, from which the greater part of the hair had fallen off, would have been less shocking to see than the hideously youthful wig, by which she tried to hide the loss. No deterioration of her complexion, no wrinkling of her skin, could have been so dreadful to look at as the rouge that lay thick on her cheeks, and the white enamel plastered on her forehead... An illustrated book of the fashions, in which women were represented exhibiting their finery by means of the free use of their limbs, lay on the bed from which she had not moved for years, without being lifted by her nurse.'(_A_, p. 300)

16. Karl Marx, *Economic and Philosophic Manuscripts of 1844*, trans. Martin Milligan, ed. Dirk J Struik (New York: International Publishers, 1964), p. 148.

17. Simmel, p. 445.

18. ' "Gwilt" is emblematically set up as a study of "guilt" in the dual sense of both wickedness and conscience.' Jenny Bourne Taylor, *In the Secret Theatre of Home: Wilkie Collins, sensation narrative, and nineteenth century psychology* (London: Routledge, 1988), p. 168.

19. Freud finds the Medusa's head works dualistically: as threat of castration (the snaky locks as a multiplication of phallic symbols) and reassurance against it (the erectile experience of horror, which reminds the male viewer of his non-castration). See 'Medusa's Head', *Complete Psychological Works of Sigmund Freud*, Vol. XVIII (1920–22), trans. James Strachey, (London: Hogarth Press, 1957), p. 163. Gwilt, correspondingly, shows a propensity for invading traditionally male spaces, recalling Emma Bovary's public exhibitions. She insists on joining Armadale in the smoking carriage of the train: ' "I delight in smoking!," said Miss Gwilt... "It's one of the privileges of the men which I have always envied" ' (*A*, p. 453). Bovary, in turn, 'had the audacity to parade with Monsieur Rodolphe, cigarette in mouth, *just to vex people*', while her sexual misdemeanours are finally confirmed when she is 'seen, one day, stepping down from the *Hirondelle*, squeezed into a tight waistcoat, looking like a man.' Gustave Flaubert, *Madame Bovary* (1857), trans. with an intro. by Geoffrey Wall (Harmondsworth: Penguin, 1992), p. 155.

20. Georg Simmel, 'The Berlin Trade Exhibition' (1896) in *Theory, Culture and Society* 8 (1991), pp. 119–23; p. 119.

21. Walter Benjamin, *Charles Baudelaire: A Lyric Poet in the Era of High Capitalism*, trans. Harry Zohn (London: Verso, 1992), p. 45.

22. Baudelaire, p. 67.

23. Henri Lefebvre, *The Production of Space* (1974), trans. Donald Nicholson-Smith (Oxford: Basil Blackwell Ltd, 1991), p. 340.

24. See Derrida's discussion of the *pharmakon* in 'Plato's Pharmacy' in *Dissemination* (1972), trans. with an intro. by Barbara Johnson (London: Athlone Press, 1993). The Greek word can mean remedy – 'the transparent rationality of science, technique, and therapeutic causality'. On the other hand, it can also mean a poison which 'can worsen the ill instead of remedy it' (p. 97). Derrida here deals with conflicting and co-existent characterisations of writing as remedy (an aid to memory, a useful means of representation) or as poison (dangerous, enchanting, distorting).

25. Avital Ronell, *Crack Wars: Literature, Addiction, Mania* (Lincoln and London: University of Nebraska Press, 1992), p. 96.

5

A Postmodern Victorian?
Lewis Carroll and the
Critique of Totalising
Reason

Simon Malpas

There is a strand of postmodernist literary criticism that constructs itself as something new: it is something that comes after all those other literary and cultural 'isms', such as modernism, Victorianism and Romanticism, whose founding ideas and political dogmas it throws into question with its innovative and advanced critical apparatus. And if the criticism is new, then so is the art. Postmodern art, we are told, makes a profound break from what has gone before: it is variously described as pluralist, fragmentary, intertextual, disruptive, decentering and, perhaps especially, parodic.

There is a double-movement involved in parody: a new text takes the place of the old one but, at the same time, the old text must remain legible beneath the new. Yet parody is neither simply recollection nor merely quotation, as besides incorporating the parodied text it also challenges any meaning that text might have had. If parody mirrors what it recalls then it also distorts it, simultaneously reflecting and refracting what is parodied and re-presenting it in a monstrous form.

According to Linda Hutcheon, parody is the 'perfect postmodern form':

When Eliot recalled Dante or Virgil in *The Waste Land*, one sensed a kind of wishful call to continuity beneath the fragmented echoing. It is precisely this that is contested in postmodern parody where it is often ironic discontinuity that is revealed at the heart of continuity, difference at the heart of similarity. Parody is the perfect postmodern form, in some senses, for it paradoxically incorporates and challenges that which it parodies. It also forces a reconsideration of the idea of origin or originality that is compatible with other postmodern interrogations of liberal humanist assumptions.[1]

For Hutcheon then, parody provides the means by which what Jean-François Lyotard calls the 'postmodern condition' can be discussed in the formal mode of presentation known as postmodernism.[2] Thus, postmodernism, if it is to represent the postmodern 'perfectly', must be parodic. In fact, for Hutcheon parody is what differentiates postmodernism from modernism (and also, by implication, from all of those other 'isms' such as Romanticism or Victorianism that precede modernism): parody permits the replacement of modernism's 'wishful call to continuity' with the attitude of 'ironic discontinuity' that is crucial to her account of postmodernism. It is the attitude of the parodist which forces a 'reconsideration of the idea of origin or originality' that, apparently, has hitherto been taken for granted.

It appears, then, that for Hutcheon parody defines postmodernism. Clearly, however, she is not claiming that parody is an invention of the so-called 'postmodern moment' of the late twentieth century. Such a claim would be patently false unless one was prepared to discount a whole range of parodic literature from Aristophanes to James Joyce as not being 'proper' (i.e. postmodern) parody.[3] Yet it is also clear that these writers cannot be described as postmodernists because of their historical situations. According to Hutcheon's account, postmodernism arises from the 'postmodern condition' which is itself, in Lyotard's words, 'the state of our culture following the transformations which, since the end of the nineteenth century, have altered the game rules for science, literature, and the arts'.[4] This means that the 'crisis of narratives' which constitutes postmodernism is historically grounded: it arises from the social, political, scientific and cultural developments that have occurred during the course of the twentieth century.[5] In other words, because postmodernism is inextricably (but obscurely) related to the events of the twentieth century, the parody that is its 'perfect form' must in some way be different from the parody of those cultural formations which preceded postmodernity.

However, even on its own terms this argument is problematic because, from Hutcheon's own account, the very attempt to identify the origin or originality of what is supposed to be the deconstruction of the idea of origins and originality must, at the very least, be a self-contradictory undertaking. Once the idea of originality has been challenged by parody, any notion that parody is originarily postmodern, or that postmodernism can construct a new or original form of parody, quickly becomes indefensible.

Yet Hutcheon's entire case rests on the idea of parody being the 'perfect postmodern form': the literary and philosophical instantiation of the postmodern condition. The relationship between parody and the postmodern is the relationship that generates postmodernism. But it is this relation which remains underdetermined because postmodern parody 'rejects the resolving urge' of any form of firm definition. This means that, rather than proving a form of continuity between the postmodern condition and its literary formalisation in parody, Hutcheon's description reveals in that relationship its own 'discontinuity... at the heart of continuity, difference at the heart of similarity'. So, even though Hutcheon proceeds to demonstrate quite thoroughly that there is a great deal of parody in many of the texts that she identifies as being postmodernist, the precise relationship between parody as a mode of writing or a literary genre and postmodernism as an aesthetic, theoretical or philosophical discourse remains uncertain. Furthermore, as it is this relationship which is used to construct the historical narrative that differentiates postmodernism from its modernist and Victorian predecessors, the invocation of parody also throws into doubt the validity of the very distinction on which the historical definition of the postmodern condition rests.

How then can one define a relationship between parody and postmodernism? Rather than trying to solve the problem in Hutcheon's terms I want, at least for the moment, to leave the question open in order to examine the position of parody within Victorian thought and literature. From this perspective I hope that it will become clear that, while it is often dismissed (at least by many of those who subscribe to the sort of postmodernism I have just described) as a unitary and totalising system of thought, Victorian culture contains many of the parodic forms of self-reflexive interrogation that are so crucial to postmodernist critique. Thus considered, Victorian parody will also help to shed some light on the problem of the parodic form of postmodernism.

The nineteenth century continued the interest in all forms of parody, from satire and burlesque to lampoon and caricature, that had developed during the preceding century. In 1812 James and Horace Smith published the collection *Rejected Addresses* containing parodies and burlesques of work by Romantic writers such as Wordsworth, Coleridge, Byron and Scott which rapidly became one of the key texts to set the tone of Victorian parody. The satirical paper *Punch* began in 1841 and in its pages many of the major writers of the century parodied, and were parodied by, each other. Perhaps the most notable of the *Punch* parodists was William Make-peace Thackeray, whose 'Novels by Eminent Hands' was published in book form in 1847 as *Punch's Prize Novelists* and can be seen retrospectively to have been part of his ongoing project to prob-lematise literary notions of origin in a series of texts that are so densely allusive that they explicitly generate the type of self-con-scious intertextuality that is so often celebrated in postmodernist fiction. The parodic problematisation of origins and originality in Victorian parody, however, perhaps reached its apotheosis in the epistemological and ontological challenges issued by nonsense lit-erature and, most specifically, by the work of Lewis Carroll.

The narratives of Carroll's two most famous works, *Alice's Adven-tures in Wonderland* (1865) and *Through the Looking-Glass* (1871), are interspersed with nonsense poems recited by Alice to the characters she encounters during her adventures and by those characters to Alice. Practically all of these poems are parodies of verses that were contained in the books read by Victorian schoolchildren and which the contemporary readers of Carroll's work would have known by heart. To cite just one example of the sources of Carroll's parody, the first two stanzas of Robert Southey's 'The Old Man's Comforts and How He Gained Them' run:

> 'You are old, father William,' the young man cried;
>   'The few locks which are left you are grey;
> You are hale, father William, a hearty old man;
>   Now tell me the reason, I pray.'
>
> 'In the days of my youth,' father William replied,
>   'I remember'd that youth would fly fast,
> And abus'd not my health and my vigour at first,
>   That I never might need them at last.'[6]

In Carroll's version the 'improving' message of the poem disappears to be replaced with:

'You are old, father William', the young man said,
    'And your hair has become very white;
And yet you incessantly stand on your head –
    Do you think, at your age, it is right?'

'In my youth,' father William replied to his son,
    'I feared it might injure the brain;
But now I am perfectly sure I have none,
    Why, I do it again and again.'[7]

This is an exemplary instance of parodic writing. Clearly, Carroll's poem is related to Southey's: they share formal qualities of metre and rhythm, the situations described are identical and the speakers retain the same names and relationship. And yet the content of the stanzas has changed completely: the pious and temperate father of Southey's poem has become a deranged, provocative and violent old man who, bored by his son's questions, eventually warns him to 'Be off, or I'll kick you down stairs!'. The bizarre answers of Carroll's Father William replace of the piety of Southey's and yet, at least for an audience familiar with the earlier poem, much of the humour of Carroll's parody is attained from the recollection of Southey's verses and the perception of the violent alterations that have taken place in both the questions asked by the son and the old man's answers. Any moral that the poem may have had in Southey's version disappears under the gleefully twisted logic of Carroll's response.

However, despite its subversion of Southey's moralising, the example of Carroll's 'Father William' does not appear to give parody the radical epistemological thrust that, according to postmodern thinkers, disturbs meaning by problematising the notion of origins through Elizabeth Ermarth's 'ironic mode of intertextuality'.[8] Southey's poem is quite clearly the origin of Carroll's: formally the two poems are identical and the contents of the latter describe a similar situation that has been distorted but not beyond recognition. In this case, Carroll's parody does not appear to challenge the relation between origin and copy in the way Hutcheon argues that postmodern parody should.

Yet this does not immediately indicate a difference between some sort of radical form of postmodern parody and a 'safe' parody in keeping with what Hutcheon calls the 'liberal humanist assumptions' of the Victorians. To cite another example from the *Alice* books, the ideas of origin and originality that postmodernism rejects are expressly addressed by Carroll in the song sung to Alice by the White Knight towards the end of *Through the Looking-Glass*. In announcing the song, the White Knight explicitly raises the problem of origins by interrogating the relationship between a name and the thing it represents:

> '... The name of the song is called *"Haddock's Eyes."* '
> 'Oh, that's the name of the song, is it?' Alice said, trying to feel interested.
> 'No, you don't understand,' the Knight said, looking a little vexed. 'That's what the name is *called*. The name really *is* "The Aged Aged Man".'
> 'Then I ought to have said "That's what the *song* is called"?' Alice corrected herself.
> 'No you oughtn't: that's quite another thing! The *song* is called *"Ways and Means"*: but that's only what it's *called*, you know!'
> 'Well, what *is* the song then?' said Alice, who was by this time completely bewildered.
> 'I was coming to that,' the Knight said. 'The song really *is* "A-sitting On A Gate"*: and the tune's my own invention.'[9]

In his gloss on this passage, Martin Gardner notes that 'to a student of logic and semantics all this is perfectly sensible ... Carroll is distinguishing here among things, the names of things, and the names of names of things. "Haddock's Eyes", the name of a name, belongs to what now logicians call a "metalanguage"'.[10] In logic, a metalanguage is a language that stands outside (or, literally, above) other languages or discourses in order to determine their truth or falsity. The term is taken up again in postmodern theory to identify the final ground of arbitration in any dispute between different discourses or language-systems: a metalanguage provides the origin of the determination of truth as, in Lyotard's words, 'there has to be a metalanguage to determine whether a given language satisfies the formal conditions of an axiomatic'.[11] This means that, just as the name legitimates the thing as a distinct thing, the name of the name legitimates that name as a name. Lyotard defines the postmodern condition as the absence of legitimating metalanguages that are capable of grounding everyday experiences of the world in some sort of universal scheme. The exchange between Alice and the White Knight produces a similar process of delegitimation of the name. This becomes clear when one remembers that in citing 'Haddock's

Eyes' as the metalinguistic origin of the song Gardner omits to observe that there is absolutely no need for Carroll to stop with the name of the name: the name of the name might equally have a name, which name might itself be named by another name, and so on *ad infinitum*. In other words, if a language only gains legitimacy in terms of a metalanguage, then for the metalanguage to gain legitimacy it must in turn have another (meta-)metalanguage, and so on. Gilles Deleuze notes that 'Carroll has voluntarily limited himself...But it goes without saying that that the series, taken in its regressive sense, may be extended to infinity.'[12] Rather than grounding the origin of the song more firmly, the proliferation of names, or of metalanguages, defers the origin indefinitely by subjecting it to a potentially infinite regression.

Not only is the naming of the song problematic, its contents also challenge any straightforward ideas of origins and originality. The White Knight claims that its tune is his own invention but Alice immediately realises that it recalls a poem which she refers to as 'I give thee all, I can no more', and this poem in turn refers to Thomas Moore's song entitled 'My Heart and Lute' of which 'I give thee all, I can no more' is the first line. Once again, it seems that, like 'Father William', the song borrows its formal structure from a contemporary lyric. Unlike 'Father William', however, the content of the White Knight's song is not based upon Moore's but on William Wordsworth's 'Resolution and Independence'. Again, this source poem has been altered, but not beyond recognition: the leech gatherer who teaches the fortitude of resolution and independence in the face of extreme poverty to the narrator of Wordsworth's poem is replaced by an 'aged aged man' whose explanations of the bizarre schemes by which he earns his living are utterly ignored by Carroll's narrator, who has equally outrageous schemes of his own to consider. Immediately, the origin of the White Knight's song becomes problematic: is it based on Moore, Wordsworth, both, or neither of them? The text provides no answer.

Jean-Jacques Lecercle, borrowing a term from Humpty Dumpty, describes the song as a 'portmanteau parody':

> the authorial voice is blurred, not only because there are now two parodied authors instead of one, but because the parodying voice itself becomes uncertain. ... The result of this, of course, is pastiche – a polyphony not of voices, but of discourses, or rather of seemingly individual voices that actually embody social discourses.

Thus, Carroll's poem intermingles his own voice with the voices of Wordsworth, Moore, and 'the people', of Alice as the addressee of the love poem, of the Knight, the aged aged man and the leech gatherer. Not persons of course, hardly individuals, but personae whose points of view are never completely fused.[13]

In fact, the 'points of view' never can be 'completely fused' because there is no original metalinguistic position from which to arbitrate between them and decide which is legitimate and which is not. It seems impossible to claim that Carroll's parody is entirely original and yet, if it is not its own origin, there is no means of discovering any more solid foundation in a specific predecessor: all of the voices that Lecercle identifies are present within the poem but none can take precedence to become its origin.

It appears then that Carroll's parody issues similar structural challenges to the ideas of origins and originality that Hutcheon finds so prevalent in postmodernism. However, despite this formal identity, it cannot be subsumed within this account of postmodernist thought because it is a part of that which is necessarily excluded in the very definition of postmodernism that Hutcheon provides: as it was written over a hundred years ago, it cannot be a text of the 'postmodern age', and also as part of Victorian culture it is inescapably bound up with 'liberal humanism', the assumptions of which Hutcheon sets out to challenge.

The term 'liberal humanism' echoes through a good deal of postmodern literary criticism to refer to some sort of cultural ideology which developed from the discoveries of Enlightenment philosophy and yet seems to cover such a multitude of sins that a precise definition is impossible. As such, postmodernism homogenises that which precedes the 'postmodern moment' by constructing a single dominant cultural ideology based on 'the expression of universal meaning by a transcendental human subject' that ties together the art, philosophy and politics of the eighteenth, nineteenth and early twentieth centuries to form the single, totalising discourse called liberal humanism.[14] At the centre of this tradition stands the Cartesian subject. Hutcheon describes postmodernism's challenge to liberal humanism in terms of its rejection of Descartes's *cogito*:

For the last twenty years, perhaps since the advent of structuralism's rejection of the 'pretensions of the Cartesian...*cogito*', the topic of 'man as a concrete universal', to use Said's term, has hovered over our various intellectual enterprises, descending now and again to become the basis of some attack or other on the humanist tradition...The coincidence of the concerns of criticism and art – their shared focus on the ideological and epistemological nature of the human subject – marks another of those points of intersection that might define a postmodernist poetics.[15]

Thus, to challenge Descartes is to challenge liberal humanism, and this challenge to the Cartesian basis of 'the humanist tradition' is a 'point of intersection' that 'might define a postmodernist poetics'. The other side of this definition remains unstated but the implication is clear: to accept the *cogito* is to partake unquestioningly in the liberal humanist tradition; and to be a liberal humanist is to accept the efficacy of Descartes's formulation of subjectivity. Thus, once again, postmodernism is differentiated from all that has gone before; this time by its scepticism towards the Cartesian subject. But what if *Alice's Adventures in Wonderland* also questions Cartesian rationalism? What would this mean for the postmodernist construction of liberal humanism?

Descartes's *cogito ergo sum*, the argument that 'I think therefore I am', is the first formulation of the status of the human subject to locate subjective certainty of existence within that subject, rather than in some external agency such as God. According to Rodolphe Gasché, Cartesian 'self-reflection marks the human being's rise to the rank of a subject. It makes the human being a subjectivity that has a centre in itself, a self-consciousness certain of itself'.[16] The *cogito* is a logical proof of one's existence based on the proposition that despite the possibility that all of one's sense experiences may, under certain circumstances be false, one cannot doubt the fact that one is doubting these experiences. In doubting one is thinking and, to follow Descartes, in thinking one exists. The certainty of the subject's existence is based upon self-reflection: the subject attains self-certainty through a process of reflecting, or mirroring, its experiences back to itself in order to identify them as its own.

This process of generating identity through reflection is central to *Alice's Adventures in Wonderland*. When Alice follows the White Rabbit down his hole she enters her own world of mirrors, a world in which her 'above ground' beliefs and assumptions are distorted by reversals and inversions of the logical principles that support her sense of selfhood. According to Donald Rackin, Alice is subjected to

Wonderland's pervasive interrogation of stable identity... [manifest in] the destruction of several fundamental above-ground assumptions that give coherence to her old world – the concepts of orderly, progressive growth and development; of 'natural' hierarchical relations between animals and human beings (as well as between various members of a highly stratified, class society); and, consequently, of rationally consistent human identity.[17]

For Alice, the process of doubt begins from the moment she falls down the rabbit hole. In the same way that Descartes, as narrator of the *Meditations*, is stripped of all certainty that is based on his sense experience, the 'destruction' of Alice's 'above-ground assumptions' force her to doubt the validity of her own 'rationally consistent human identity'. The challenges to those fundamental assumptions about the coherence of one's relation to the world which Descartes hypothesises from the comfort and safety of his study are lived out by a child in a strange, disorientating and threatening underground world.

The changes in size that Alice undergoes when she eats or drinks elicit a series of questions that throw into doubt all the certainties that she has hitherto entertained about her identity. Alice remarks

How queer everything is today! And yesterday things went on just as usual. I wonder if I've been changed in the night? Let me think: *was* I the same when I got up this morning? I almost think I can remember feeling a little different. But if I'm not the same the next question is, 'Who in the world am I?' Ah, *that's* the great puzzle![18]

Through a process that ironically recalls Cartesian method, Alice proceeds to test whether she has changed. Does she remember her multiplication tables? Her geography? Can she recite poems that she knows? And when all of these questions have been answered in the negative, she concludes that she is not herself, and decides that when people come to her rescue she will first ask them who they think she is, 'and then, if I like being that person, I'll come up: if not, I'll stay down here till I'm somebody else'.[19] Identity has become fluid: Alice decides that it is simply a matter of time before she will change again; and she is quite correct as, even while she is reasoning with herself, she is shrinking and ends up falling into a pool consisting of her own tears.

It soon becomes clear, however, that she cannot determine the changes that will take place. This indeterminacy is made manifest during her encounter with the Caterpillar:

> 'Who are *You*?' said the Caterpillar.
>
> This was not an encouraging opening for a conversation. Alice replied, rather shyly, 'I – I hardly know, Sir, just at present – at least I know who I *was* when I got up this morning, but I think I must have changed several times since then.'
>
> 'What do you mean by that?' said the Caterpillar, sternly. 'Explain yourself!'
>
> 'I can't explain *myself*, I'm afraid, Sir,' said Alice, 'because I'm not myself, you see.'[20]

Like Descartes's narrator when he is confronted by the 'Evil Genius', all Alice's certainties about her identity have vanished: she can find no ground on which to base an account of herself that will answer the Caterpillar's enquiry because whatever she might count as 'self' has been subjected to violent alterations inflicted on her by the strange new environment. As Rackin states, 'merely to list the reversals Alice encounters underground is to survey at a glance an almost total destruction of our self-styled, logical, orderly, and coherent approach to the world'.[21] Yet, Alice herself is not destroyed as some kernel of her identity persists: her ability to use the word 'I'.

Despite the alterations of size, shape, name and social position, one thing remains constant throughout: even when Alice is not 'Alice' she remains 'I'. This might account for the relative equanimity with which she greets many of the changes that occur. Even the possibility of 'going out like a candle' if she shrinks too far does not appear to evoke any notion of personal annihilation, but rather serves to provoke the question 'I wonder what I should be like then?'[22] *Wonderland* seems, on this reading, to be an almost literal re-enactment of Descartes's argument; an enactment that is so literal that Descartes's position begins to appear absurd. The proposition 'what will I be like when I cease to exist' is clearly self-contradictory and yet, in a sense, Alice's logic is impeccably Cartesian. If her body can change as extremely as it has done without affecting her ability to think, why should she not continue to exist if her body were to 'go out' altogether? For Alice, the changes affecting her body, even its extinction, in being recognised prove her existence.

By taking Descartes at his word, and by taking that word to its logical extreme, the narrative of *Wonderland* drives a wedge between existence and identity. The certainty of one's own existence that is grounded in the *cogito* does not entail any certainty of selfhood. However much one changes, whoever or whatever one becomes, one still exists providing one is thinking, and yet, on the other hand, the mere fact that of one is thinking does not determine what or who one is. The parodic structure of the book is clear: Descartes's formulation of the *cogito* remains, and yet as a basis of identity it is shown to be almost devoid of meaning. Carroll's parody of the Cartesian deduction does not contest the foundational properties of the *cogito*, and yet it shows how abstract and empty that foundation can be.

A similar chain of reasoning leads Jacques Lacan (whose psychoanalytic investigation of the subject pervades postmodernist accounts of subjectivity) to state that 'the status of the *I think* is as reduced, as minimal, as punctual – and might be just as affected by the connotation of the *that is meaningless* – as [the statement] *I am lying*', and to conclude that 'I will now dare to define the Cartesian *I think* as participating, in its striving towards certainty, in a sort of abortion'.[23] The certainty of existence is still-born: it is a certainty and yet it is entirely devoid of any meaning from which an adequate account of the subject can develop.

Thus, both Carroll and Lacan accept Descartes's formulation of the *cogito*, but neither allow it any efficacy. This means that the rejection of the 'pretensions of the Cartesian *cogito*' that Hutcheon identifies as a 'point of intersection that might define a postmodernist poetics' is found not only in Lacan, but also in Carroll. This similarity generates a difficulty that is devastating for Hutcheon's argument. The difference between the 'ironic discontinuity' of postmodern parody and the 'wishful call to continuity beneath the fragmented echoing' of earlier parodic writing, used by Hutcheon to differentiate postmodernism as a literary and philosophical discourse from its modernist and Victorian predecessors, seems to have neither historical nor formal efficacy. Moreover, the similarity between Carroll's and Lacan's positions questions the whole postmodernist construction of a 'liberal humanism' that relies upon the acceptance of Cartesianism. It also illustrates the difficulty of positing some form of epistemological break between the scope and function of parody in Victorian nonsense and its employment in postmodern writing. This means that neither the formal nor the cultural–historical definitions of postmodernism on which Hutcheon's account rests stand up to scrutiny as being capable of clearly differentiating it from what has gone before.

So where does this lead? It is not simply the case that Hutcheon produces an inadequate analysis of the relationship between post-modernism and modernism or Victorianism: in fact, it is the thoroughness and the acuity of her formulations which allows these problems to emerge. Rather, there is a contradiction at the centre of any approach to the idea of postmodernism that sets it up as something that takes the place of what has gone before as the most recent in an endless string of 'world views'.

It is this contradiction that prompts Lyotard to distance his account of postmodernism from the literary-critical movement that Hutcheon exemplifies by supplementing it with the notion of 'rewriting modernity' when he reconsiders the postmodern in *The Inhuman*.[24] Rather than occurring retrospectively, this rewriting is part of a continuing discourse of modernity:

> What I've here called rewriting clearly has nothing to do with what is called postmodernity or postmodernism on the market of contemporary ideologies. This has nothing to do with the use of parodies or quotations of modern or modernist works....Post-modernity is not a new age, but the rewriting of some of the features claimed by modernity, and first of all of modernity's claim to ground its legitimacy on the project of liberating humanity as a whole through science and technology. But as I have said, that rewriting has been at work, for a long time now, in modernity itself... I shall content myself with the following reply: rewriting means resisting the writing of that supposed postmodernity.[25]

According to Lyotard, then, it appears that postmodernity is not simply the latest position that can be occupied in order to produce an 'ism' to subscribe to, but rather is something that emerges from 'the rewriting of some of the features claimed by modernity'.[26] On this account, modernity is a discourse that is unable to provide itself with firm foundations and is constantly open to disturbances of the type that Carroll exemplifies. It is in these disturbances that the postmodern is glimpsed: for Lyotard, a 'work can become modern only if it is first postmodern. Postmodernism thus understood is no modernism at its end but in the nascent state, and this state is constant'.[27] By means of this argument Lyotard disengages a constantly nascent discourse of postmodernity that lies at the margins of the modern from some notion of a 'postmodern condition' that simply comes after modernity. Even so, it is important to note that in the process of rethinking his position, Lyotard has rejected the efficacy of parody as part of the rewriting project. But, as I have tried to show, parody is an important element of deconstructive criticism and his move seems a little precipitous: Lyotard is in danger of throwing out the baby of parodic intertextuality with the bath-water of a postmodern society.

However, besides illustrating a problem with the definition of postmodernism, the structure of Victorian nonsense can also provide the basis for a model of the possibilities open to the form of parodic critique that is frequently carried out under the auspices of postmodernism. This model would develop from the relationship between sense and nonsense. Crucial to this relationship is the fact that nonsense cannot be defined as bad or faulty sense: rather, it is the absence of sense or, as I attempted to show in my analysis of the Carrollian reading of Descartes, the disruption of sense when a logical argument is pushed to, and beyond, its apparent limit. Gilles Deleuze describes this relationship when he argues that:

> sense and nonsense have a specific relation which cannot copy that of the true and false, that is, which cannot be conceived simply on the basis of exclusion. This is indeed the most general problem of the logic of sense: what would be the purpose of rising from the domain of truth to the domain of sense, if it were only to find between sense and nonsense a relation analogous to that of the true and false? . . . The logic of sense is necessarily determined to posit between sense and nonsense an original type of intrinsic relation, a mode of co-presence.[28]

Just as it is inappropriate to describe parody as a 'false' version of that which is parodied, so it is inaccurate to exclude nonsense entirely from thought as 'false sense'. Rather, there is an 'intrinsic relation' between sense and nonsense that implies 'a mode of co-presence': one cannot exist without the other, and every instance of one entails the possibility of the appearance of the other.

An analogous relationship of co-presence obtains between any genre of discourse and its critique, be it Enlightenment modernity,

Victorianism, Romanticism or modernism. Even liberal humanism, if it were to exist in the form that Hutcheon describes, would necessarily have to have its own parodic or deconstructive counter-moment: a counter-moment that one might well find in Victorian nonsense literature. The type of postmodernism that locates itself after or beyond these discourses retrospectively rejects them as totalities that have been surpassed rather than as still capable of affecting the present. Instead of a historically-located notion of postmodernism, what is needed is a recognition of the possibility of parodically rewriting a genre of discourse from within that genre: a mode of analysis that really does reveal the discontinuities that lie at the heart of any continuity.

It is this possibility that Carroll's writing provides. The *Alice* books throw into question a whole range of 'common-sense' beliefs by subverting the logical propositions on which they rely. And instead of presenting an alternative set of beliefs to take their place which can be subscribed to or rejected, they leave a series of unresolvable paradoxes and unanswerable questions. *Through the Looking-Glass* ends with the question 'Which dreamed it?' that, because it is impossible to answer, reflects our reading back to us with the perpetual challenge to choose our own course of action: 'Which do *you* think it was?'[29]

Notes

1. Linda Hutcheon, *A Poetics of Postmodernism: History, Theory, Fiction* (London: Routledge, 1988), p. 11. In a later book Hutcheon makes this argument again when she states that 'Parody – often called ironic quotation, pastiche, appropriation, or intertextuality – is usually considered central to postmodernism, both by its detractors and its defenders' (Hutcheon, *The Politics of Postmodernism*, London: Routledge, 1989, p. 93). Here parody has become an umbrella term that covers a number of other ideas that are frequently associated with postmodern thought. No longer applicable only to literature, parody (considered as 'intertextuality') enters the realms of criticism, theory and philosophy. Moreover, Hutcheon is not the only thinker who extends the notion of parody within postmodernism. Elizabeth Deeds Ermarth provides what might well be the most extended definition when she declares that '*parody is the ironic mode of intertextuality*... Paratactic, parodic, paralogical writing operates simultaneously in more than one mode, and once such multiplication has taken place, we depart from the Euclidean universe of unity, identity, centre, and enter the

non-Euclidean universe of pattern, superimposition, and differential function' (Elizabeth Deeds Ermarth, *Sequel to History: Postmodernism and the Crisis of Representational Time*, Princeton: Princeton University Press, 1992, pp. 165–6). I will take Hutcheon's work as representative of the type of literary critical postmodernism that I am discussing in this essay. This is not because Hutcheon is particularly extreme or excessive in her account but, rather, because the precision and acuity of her discussion serves to highlight problems that less exhaustive descriptions of this approach to postmodernism overlook.

2.   I am taking the term 'postmodern condition' from Jean-François Lyotard, *The Postmodern Condition: A Report on Knowledge*, trans. Geoff Bennington and Brian Massumi (Manchester: Manchester University Press, 1986).

3.   In fact Hutcheon does discriminate between postmodernist parody and the parody of modernism. She points out that 'parody was also the dominant mode of much modernist art, especially the writing of T.S. Eliot, Thomas Mann, and James Joyce... There are significant differences, however, in the final impact of the two uses of parody. It is not that modernism was serious and significant and postmodernism is ironic and parodic, as some have claimed; it is more that postmodernism's irony is one that rejects the resolving urge of modernism toward closure or at least distance' (Hutcheon, *The Politics of Postmodernism*, p. 99). Although Hutcheon is not dismissing modernist parody as 'improper', it is clear that she is drawing a distinction between the uses of parody in the two discourses and implying that postmodern parody is something significantly different, at least in its 'final impact'. This move is necessary if she is to distinguish postmodernity as a distinct and original historical and cultural entity, and yet it is a distinction which is immediately subverted by her own description of postmodern parody...

4.   Lyotard, *The Postmodern Condition*, p. xxiii.

5.   Lyotard, *The Postmodern Condition*, p. xxiii. The underdetermination of this relationship is clear in Hutcheon's account: 'Perhaps, as some have argued, the 1960s themselves (that is, at the time) produced no enduring innovation in aesthetics, but I would argue that they did provide the background, though not the definition, of the postmodern... The political, social, and intellectual experience of the 1960s helped make it possible for postmodernism to be seen as what Kristeva calls "writing-as-experience-of-limits"' (Hutcheon, *A Poetics of Postmodernism*, p. 8). Clearly there is a relation between a certain historical conjunction ('the 1960s') and postmodernism, but it is a relation in which the former does not include or define the latter but, instead, rather obscurely 'provides the background'.

6.   Southey's poem is quoted in Martin Gardner (ed.), *The Annotated Alice: Alice's Adventures in Wonderland and Through the Looking-Glass by Lewis Carroll*, (Harmondsworth: Penguin, 1964), p. 69. Two particularly useful studies that examine the relation between Carroll's parodies and their source poems are Florence Milner's 'The Poems in *Alice in Wonderland*',

and John Ciardi's 'A Burble through the Tulgey Wood', both of which are reprinted in Robert Phillips (ed.), *Aspects of Alice: Lewis Carroll's Dreamchild as seen through the Critics' Looking-Glasses 1865–1971* (Harmondsworth: Penguin, 1974).

7. Gardner (ed.), *The Annotated Alice*, p. 70.
8. Ermarth, *Sequel to History*, p. 165.
9. Gardner (ed.), *The Annotated Alice*, p. 306.
10. Gardner (ed.), *The Annotated Alice*, p. 306.
11. Lyotard, *The Postmodern Condition*, p. 42.
12. Gilles Deleuze, *The Logic of Sense*, ed. Constantin V. Boundas, trans. Mark Lester with Charles Stivale (New York: Columbia University Press, 1990), p. 30.
13. Jean-Jacques Lecercle, *The Philosophy of Nonsense: The Intuitions of Victorian Nonsense Literature* (London: Routledge, 1994), pp. 176–7.
14. Hutcheon, *The Politics of Postmodernism*, p. 143.
15. Hutcheon, *A Poetics of Postmodernism*, p. 158.
16. Rodolphe Gasché, *The Tain of the Mirror: Derrida and the Philosophy of Reflection* (Cambridge, Mass. and London: Harvard University Press, 1986), p. 14.
17. Donald Rackin, *Alice's Adventures in Wonderland and Through the Looking-Glass: Nonsense, Sense, and Meaning* (New York: Twayne, 1991), p. 42.
18. Gardner (ed.), *The Annotated Alice*, p. 37.
19. Gardner (ed.), *The Annotated Alice*, p. 39.
20. Gardner (ed.), *The Annotated Alice*, p. 67.
21. Rackin, *Alice's Adventures*, p. 36.
22. Gardner (ed.), *The Annotated Alice*, p. 32.
23. Jacques Lacan, *The Four Fundamental Concepts of Psychoanalysis*, ed. Jacques-Alain Miller, trans. Alan Sheridan, pp. 140–1. Despite the fact that Lacan has become the postmodernist's theorist of the subject *par excellence*, like a number of the thinkers from which postmodern thought develops he at no point aligned himself with postmodernism, preferring to describe his project as the reinterpretation of Freudian psychoanalysis in the light of modern theories of language and developments in continental philosophy.
24. According to Lyotard, the 'advantage of "rewriting modernity" depends on two displacements: the transformation of the prefix "post-" into "re-" from the lexical point of view, and the syntactical application of this modified prefix to the verb "writing" rather than to the substantive "modernity"' (Lyotard, *The Inhuman: Reflections on Time*, trans. Geoffrey Bennington and Rachel Bowlby, Cambridge: Polity Press, 1991, p. 24).
25. Lyotard, *The Inhuman*, pp. 34–5.
26. In fact, Lyotard has already posited a similar definition of postmodernism in *The Postmodern Condition* when he argues that the postmodern is something that is never present but constantly about to be born: subject to 'the paradox of the future (*post*) anterior (*modo*)' (Lyotard, *The Postmodern Condition*, p. 81).
27. Lyotard, *The Postmodern Condition*, p. 79.

28. Deleuze, *The Logic of Sense*, p. 68.
29. Gardner (ed.), *The Annotated Alice*, p. 344.

6

Politics as Antagonism and Diversity: Mill and Lyotard

Peter R. Sedgwick

At first glance, John Stuart Mill's *On Liberty*[1] would seem an obvious target for postmodernist criticism. Yet, I will argue, Mill's analysis of the problem of individual liberty in this text, although flawed, can serve to reveal something relevant to our understanding of the political implications of the conventionalist account of language offered by the philosopher Jean-François Lyotard in his book *The Differend: Phrases in Dispute*.[2] Lyotard's position in this text differs in some measure from the views advocated earlier in *The Postmodern Condition*,[3] in so far as the postmodern project is regarded as being more problematic and partial.[4] However, an emphasis upon the elucidation of an economy of meaning which resists strategies of totalisation is common to both *The Postmodern Condition* and *The Differend*. It is in this sense that *The Differend* situates itself within a postmodern context. Before discussing Lyotard's views, however, I will turn to the text of *On Liberty*.

First published in 1859 by Victorian Britain's most famous philosopher, *On Liberty* may be justifiably regarded as one of the most eloquent expressions of the principles which underlie the individualistic philosophy of political liberalism. Mill's avowed aim in the text is to explore 'the nature and limits of the power which can be legitimately exercised by society over the individual' in the context of the social 'struggle between liberty and authority' (*On Liberty*, 59). The inherent political tension which exists between liberty and authority, Mill notes, is not a new one; it was also a central feature of the political organisations of Ancient Greece and Ancient Rome (not to mention early English civil society). However, modern society bears the fruit of a process of historical development which has served to redefine the nature and terms of this struggle. In earlier civil societies the struggle over authority took the form of a contest between subjects and rulers, and was thus concerned solely with establishing the limits of the power of monarchies or aristocracies. However, the modern social provisions required to meet the 'new demand for elective and temporary rulers' (60) led to the formation of institutions of representative democracy. This raises a different problem:

> What was now wanted was that the rulers should be identified with the people, that their interest and will should be the interest and will of the nation. The nation did not need to be protected against its own will. There was no fear of its tyrannizing over itself [...].

> But [...] when society itself is the tyrant – society collectively over the separate individuals who compose it – its means of tyranniz-ing are not restricted to the acts which it may do by the hands of its political functionaries. Society can and does execute its own mandates; and if it issues wrong mandates instead of right, or any mandates at all in things with which it ought not to meddle, it practises a tyranny more formidable than many kinds of political oppression [...].   (61, 63)

In short, a society in which the ideal of popular democracy is realised will necessarily also be open to the establishment of a new form of collectively grounded, authoritarian tyranny. This tyranny, of course, is Mill's famous 'tyranny of the majority', the political condition in which 'society itself is the tyrant' (62, 63).

The problem, as Mill presents it, is to be understood in terms of a conflict between two distinctive types of interest: those of the indi-vidual and those of society – 'collective opinion' versus 'individual independence' (63). For Mill, the individual is always already an independent entity: 'his independence is, of right, absolute' (69). To elaborate upon Mill's point: an individual exhibits abilities (such as those of reflection and choice) as well as passions, desires and purposes. Taken together, these features allow for the identification of the individual as that which possess interests. Given a situation in which a diversity of individuals are present in a society, it follows that such a society will also contain a diversity of interests. It is just such a form of society, one which both contains and is an expression of the diversity of human possibility manifested in the form of the individual, that Mill favours as being the most progressive: 'A people, it appears, may be progressive for a certain length of time, and then stop: when does it stop? When it ceases to possess individuality' (136). The individual is, moreover, that which is capable of possessing interests which are 'anti-social', in so far as they may come into conflict with the practices and norms which regulate collective behaviour. The individual subject's relative autonomy with regard to collective norms means that this is an ever-present possibility. In short, there is a necessary disjunction between collective modes of social organisation and the individuated, and hence particular, interests which can be present within such social formations. This, in turn, is a necessary outcome of the fact that individuals can and do make choices, given their own particular circumstances and the existence of a range of possible choices open to them within that context. Opposed to this ability to choose are the normative regulations of custom: 'He who does anything because it is the custom makes no choice' (122). The 'tyranny of the majority' is thereby identified by Mill with the force of the collective will of society, which is realised in the form of the normative regulations which serve to contextualise and thereby govern the behaviour of individual political subjects.

Of course, Mill's account of the individual is problematic. In the first instance, one might object that the text of *On Liberty* places too much emphasis on the issue of autonomy, and in so doing draws a distinction between self- and other-regarding actions which is unworkable. 'In the part which merely concerns himself [...] over his own body and mind, the individual is sovereign' (69). In what way, one might object, is it possible to secure a criterion which enables us to separate an individual's actions from their public consequences? Even the most private and self-regarding actions are susceptible to producing consequences which affect others. This, and a number of other possible objections, however, I leave to one side. Rather, I shall now address an aspect of Mill's argument which relates to the political implications inherent in the conventionalist account of language presented in Lyotard's *The Differend*. By way of doing so, some discussion of Lyotard's text is required.

In *The Differend* Lyotard poses a question about the nature, scope and limits of politics. The question can be put thus: how are we to understand the meaning of the term 'politics'? This is asked within the context of Lyotard's linguistic conventionalism. According to Lyotard, languages operate in terms of what he calls 'phrases' and 'genres'. A 'phrase' can be any form of utterance and is composed of four 'instances' (an addressor, an addressee, a sense, and a referent)

(*The Differend*, 25). It is not necessary that there be a named addressor or addressee, a determined sense, or a designated referent in order for a phrase to function. Every phrase presents a 'phrase universe', and determines the nature of each universe according to the way in which each of the four 'instances' which constitute it function in relation to one another (28). There are many different kinds of phrases, for example, cognitive, aesthetic, ethical, political. Lyotard characterises each of these phrases as belonging to different 'phrase regimens'. Phrases belonging to different regimens are heterogeneous and cannot therefore be translated from one into another (178). Genres of discourse are different from regimens: they supply rules for linking phrases together in particular ways according to particular purposes (179ff). It thus is impossible, Lyotard holds, to validate any genre of discourse from outside itself by way of resorting to a meta-language.

Thus, to illustrate the above point, just as the cognitive phrase regimen is one regimen amongst many, the cognitive genre is likewise merely one amongst many genres. The legitimation of genres is therefore a matter of internal consistency. Hence, any legitimate linking of phrases cannot be deduced from a position external to the particular genre in which a phrase is at that moment situated. Regimens, in contrast to genres, do not provide rules for linking phrases. They are non-teleological and contain the 'rules of formation' whereby a phrase can be characterised as being cognitive (that is, concerned with matters of fact), aesthetic, metaphysical, etc. But these rules cannot prescribe which phrase from which regimen ought next to be linked onto a preceding phrase. Linking, it follows, is necessary but how to link is a contingent matter (136). It is hence impossible to assert with any degree of legitimacy from a position outside of, for example, the cognitive genre that one ought to link on to a cognitive phrase with another compatible with the rules of that genre. In a manner akin to the view presented in *The Postmodern Condition*, this argument precludes any establishment of meta-narratives external to the cultural conditions under which genres are formulated and put into practice.

What Lyotard does attempt to make room for, however, are those instances of phrases which cannot be voiced within a particular genre. Such phrases would be the phrases of victims who, because of the way in which genres operate, are silenced by them. These phrases Lyotard terms 'differends'. A differend is thus characterised as 'a damage accompanied by the loss of means to prove the damage' (7). Lyotard here gives the example of a French citizen who is a Martinican: such a person cannot complain about the possible wrongs they may suffer as a result of being a French citizen because the genre of French law, as the only genre in which such a complaint could be lodged, prevents the possibility of making it. A differend is thus 'the unstable state and instant of language wherein something which must be put into phrases cannot yet be' (22). In arguing that such phrases must be phrased (as a matter of principle), *The Differend* announces its ethico-political concern with the proper goal of culture. 'Culture', Lyotard argues in a manner once again reminiscent of *The Postmodern Condition*, has come to mean 'the putting into circulation of information rather than the work that needs to be done in order to arrive at presenting what is not presentable under the circumstances' (260). With this statement one may conclude that Lyotard's later work, in so far as it establishes its own stakes in terms of arguing for the need to voice differends, conceives of politics as involving the expression of a view of culture voiced as far back as 1962, in the essay 'Dead Letter': 'Culture is lending an ear to what strives to be said, culture is giving a voice to those who do not have a voice and who seek one'.[5] Thus, for Lyotard, genuine cultural activity is both an ethical and a political pursuit. This view has parallels with some aspects of Mill's position.[6]

Turning to the question of politics, Lyotard argues that we are mistaken if we assume politics to be a mode of human interaction which has a definable purpose. Rather, according to him, the political realm is to be understood as a space in which competing discourses meet. Put another way, politics is not a genre of discourse:

> Were politics a genre and were that genre to pretend to that supreme status, its vanity would be quickly revealed. Politics, however, is the threat of the differend. It is not a genre, it is the multiplicity of genres, the diversity of ends, and par excellence the question of linkage [...] It is, if you will, the state of language, but it is not *a* language. Politics consists in the fact that language is not a language, but phrases [...].   (190)

The problem with politics is that, although it is not a genre, it 'always gives rise to misunderstandings because it takes place as a genre' (199). Thus, Lyotard is committed to an account of the political sphere which is obliged to maintain a distinction between (i) the general state of language, understood as a range of phrases which cannot be exhausted by any single generic account of them, and (ii) the fact that, substantively speaking, politics must actually 'take place' in the form of a particular genre. Politics, therefore, always raises its head whenever the question of how to link phrases occurs.

However, the question of linking cannot be subsumed under an answer offered, as necessarily it must be, from within the perspective of any single genre. This latter point is generated by Lyotard from his acceptance of 'Russell's aporia', that is, the fact that any attempt within one genre to supply a universal solution to the questions posed by all other genres of discourse founders. This is because either 'this genre is part of the set of genres, and what is at stake in it is but one among others, and therefore its answer is not supreme [...] Or else, it is not part of the set of genres, and therefore does not encompass all that is at stake [...]' (189).

Hence, with regard to politics, which is the sphere in which the linkage of phrases by different and thus competing genres is played out in terms of the pursuit of a diversity of potentially incompatible ends, no genre is capable of supplying an all-inclusive and therefore universally applicable means of choosing one genre or set of genres over and above any others. In consequence, there is no means of providing universal legitimacy for the advocacy of any one mode of social organisation above another. This is because the stakes of that genre will necessarily conflict both with the stakes of other genres and the diversity of phrases which constitute the existence of languages. In turn, the advocacy of any universal solution to particular social ills (for example, revolution), even if it were to right old wrongs, would create new ones: 'supposing the change took place, it is impossible that the judgments of the new tribunal would not create new wrongs, since they would regulate (or think they were regulating) differends as though they were litigations [i.e. according to a rule which is universally applied]' (197). Consequently, for Lyotard, politicians cannot with any justification be said to 'have the good at stake, but they ought to have the lesser evil'. In short, politics cannot be pursued as if it were a genre with a defined set of stakes or goals. To treat the political realm as if it were a genre would necessarily be to engage in an activity which would create new wrongs, and therefore new victims (differends) who lack the means even to assert their status as victims. But if this is the case, then one is entitled to ask: what notion of the political realm is being foregrounded in Lyotard's account?

Lyotard's position entails a commitment to the view that no single generically derived view of politics, which necessarily will treat political questions as if they may be understood in terms of a particular goal, is valid. It follows that for him politics is not a matter of the establishment of tribunals which have the power to settle disputes between competing modes of life, expressed through the diversity of actual and possible phrases. 'Society' is this diversity of phrases, and this very variety brings with it 'politics', understood as the issue of how to link phrases together in appropriate ways: 'The social is implicated in the universe of a phrase and the political in its mode of linking' (198). Thus, we are always already implicated within the social world by virtue of being linguistic subjects, and in consequence also in politics; for politics is the issue of how one ought to link phrases together. If this is the case, then the political realm, properly regarded, is a space of possibility which offers an unlimited potentiality for linking phrases together in possible ways, and hence cannot be used to supply a rule which dictates *how* phrases *ought* to be linked. Therefore, Lyotard is committed to the view that one cannot legislate about the goal of politics. In short, his case is that it is impossible to provide a universal rule concerning the purpose of politics which can then be applied as a means for solving disputes between differing and necessarily competing viewpoints (genres of discourse). This is because the activity of solving disputes is, practically speaking, endless. For if language is defined in terms of phrases rather than genres, then it follows that the act of linking any particular phrase with another phrase according to a rule supplied from one genre cannot exclude the possibility of other modes of linkage, of other genres. This is an extension of the principle, noted above; namely, that 'To link is necessary, but a particular linkage is not' (136).

The outcome of such a view, however, entails a commitment to a view which has more than a merely passing resemblance to Mill's with regard to its commitment to the notion of diversity. Where for Lyotard politics must concern maximising the range of possible ends that may be pursued within any particular social context (and it is a condition of phrases that they are inherently social (193)), so for Mill the diversity and inherent antagonism of 'political life' is what defines it in its truest sense:

Unless opinions favourable to democracy and to aristocracy, to property and to equality, to coperation and to competition, to

luxury and to abstinence, to sociality and individuality, to liberty
and discipline, and all the other standing antagonisms of practical
life, are expressed with equal freedom and enforced and defended
with equal talent and energy, there is no chance of both elements
obtaining their due. Truth, in the great practical concerns of life, is
so much a question of the reconciling and combining of opposites
that [...] it has to be made by the rough process of struggle
between combatants fighting under hostile banners.

(On Liberty, 110–11)

In other words, there is no final means of reconciling disputes
between competing modes of life. This is because such disputes
are a condition of social existence.

Putting it another way, one can extrapolate from Mill the view
that politics *is* the engaging in disputes over what rules are appropriate in particular contexts consisting of individual agents pursuing
particular goals. Lyotard would, of course, object that, on his
account, individual agency (subjectivity) is inseparable from the
fact that there are phrases: 'A "subject" is situated in a universe
presented by a phrase' (*The Differend*, 119). Thus, one cannot hold
the view that subjects are distinct from the conditions they inhabit.
Rather, subjects are constructed within the context of these conditions (that is, within phrase universes) and such conditions are
intrinsic to the notion of subjectivity. In short, there is no notion of
self which is not bound up with the fact that there are phrases and
genres. A cursory analysis of Mill's view of the self, as exemplified in
(i) the presentation of the problem of liberty in terms of a dichotomy
between individuality and authority, and (ii) a rigidly held distinction between the public and private spheres (*On Liberty*, 59, 71),
might conclude that he falls foul of this view. But it is worth noting
that Mill does not suggest that individuality is an a-historical ontological category. Societies can exist in which there is no individuality,
but individuality is the precondition of a healthy culture, that is, one
in which the diversity of human potential is best recognised. And
such potential is realised through endorsing the view 'that free
scope should be given to varieties of character' (120).

However, even if the above criticism were granted, Lyotard is still
committed to a position which has much in common with Mill's. For
when Mill argues that 'different persons also require different conditions for their spiritual development' (133), he is in effect asserting
the heterogeneity of differing and competing modes of social

existence. This principle finds analogous expression in Lyotard's conception of the incommensurability of different genres and his argument that a phrase which is subjected to an inappropriate mode of linkage by a genre is inevitably wronged. Likewise, Mill's contention that 'the liberty of the individual must be thus far limited; he must not make himself a nuisance to other people' (119) leads to two conclusions, which can in turn be re-phrased in Lyotard's terms: (i) that no single goal (genre) should dominate over all others, (ii) that individuation presupposes a diversity of subject positions (individual cases of phrases), each of which needs to be given its due. Hence, whatever conception of the subject one might be tempted to favour, it is the case that the 'lesser evil' that Lyotard advocates as a guiding political principle is one which implicitly rejects the majoritarian approach to political life which is also the target of Mill's critique. This, in turn, leads to similar conclusions concerning the nature of politics.

Above all, it is this last point which must be of concern. For, whatever the approach to the question of the nature of politics – whether it is taken to be an issue concerning the practical limits of normative power exercised over the individual (Mill) or the metaphysically necessary conditions of language use and their political implications (Lyotard) – both thinkers derive their conclusions from a common set of presuppositions concerning it. Lyotard's postmodernism (even as it is expressed through the ambivalent metaphor of an old man picking through the various political and aesthetic relics of a failed modernism[7]), and likewise his attempt at an immanent transcendence of the limits of the postmodernism put forward in *The Postmodern Condition* through the development and application of a philosophy of phrases and genres, still situates itself within the presuppositions of Mill's liberalism. This is not to deny, as Lyotard says elsewhere, that liberalism can serve the ends of capitalism.[8] But from this fact one cannot necessarily conclude that liberalism is itself identical with that genre for, as a reading of Mill's text can show us, the key political problem for him concerns the irreconcilable conflict between differing modes of life which are realised through the activity of pursuing particular ends. Such a concern cannot be reduced to a matter of mere capital.

In Lyotard's case, too, the political implications of how phrases are linked, even though situated within the context of an anti-humanist project[9] which would have been anathema to Mill, must still revolve around the question of diversity. One can develop this point by noting that even Lyotard's anti-humanism does not offer a ready means of escape from Mill's key contention. For the issue of political diversity and the question of whether or not there are subjects who 'use' a language (rather than subjects of a language) are matters of a different order. What a subject is must always remain a metaphysical question, since the subject presented with one phrase cannot be used to secure a definition of other modes of subjectivity as they will be presented within other kinds of phrases. One might seek to derive a particular politics from a given notion of the subject, and thus a specific set of political concerns may well centre on debates about the nature of subjectivity. But this must remain a metaphysical matter rather than a specifically 'political' one unless it can be shown that there is a necessary connection between the genre of metaphysical inquiry and the state of heterogeneity and antagonism Lyotard asserts to exist between phrases and genres of discourse. This, latter claim, however, is itself a metaphysical one made with the aim of proving a point about what politics is. Hence, the con- nection can only be shown by presupposing the authority of meta- physical investigation (which is a genre of discourse).

The political question, for both Mill and Lyotard, is not 'What is the purpose of politics?' Rather, both thinkers assert it to be the case that politics is the engagement between conflicting purposes. In consequence, the position Lyotard takes with regard to politics cannot escape from the key concern underlying Mill's advocacy of individual liberty, that is, the principle that particular cases (be it of 'subjects' or 'phrases') when they are subsumed under a general rule will be in danger of being rendered the victims of a wrong. Lyotard, therefore, cannot avoid the charge of providing a justifica- tion for a liberalism re-articulated in postmodern form. Moreover, it is not sufficient to object that these principles, although identifiable in the work of a tradition of 'liberal' thinkers (from Locke to Rawls), denote the existence of a 'liberal' genre of discourse. For, if the key aspect of Mill's liberalism is his concern with diversity, it may be that 'liberalism' in this sense is not itself a genre. Rather, it is an expres- sion (presented in the form of a proper name) of the irreconcilable antagonisms which necessarily and always exist between differing subject positions as a condition of their possibility. Additionally, if the principles noted above are identifiable as being situated within a genre, then Lyotard's own conception of the realm of politics must also fall prey to the objection that he, too, treats politics as if it were a genre of discourse. This is because Lyotard, like Mill, is committed to the position that in politics diversity ought to be pursued *as a matter of principle*. But what is this if it is not treating the arena of politics as if it were a genre?[10]

Mill's text situates itself within the boundaries of a specific set of social conditions which are characterised by a crisis over the nature of political authority. From an historical vantage point, one might say that this is a specifically 'Victorian' crisis, in that this period of British history saw the rise of representative democracy and an accompanying intellectual anxiety about its implications. But the actual problem of political authority as Mill identified it in this context is the same problem as that identified by Lyotard. To this extent, Lyotard's politics might well be said to embody a kind of 'Victorianism' with regard to its attitude to delineating the realm of politics.

Notes

1. J.S. Mill, *On Liberty* (Harmondsworth: Penguin, 1984). All further references are given in the text with page number.
2. Jean-François Lyotard, *The Differend: Phrases in Dispute*, trans. Georges Van Den Abeele (Manchester: Manchester University Press, 1988). All further references are given in the text with section number.
3. Lyotard, *The Postmodern Condition: A Report on Knowledge*, trans. Geoff Bennington & Brian Massumi (Manchester; Manchester University Press, 1989).
4. See *The Differend*, p. 182, where Lyotard characterises postmodernism as 'the pastime of an old man who scrounges in the garbage-heap of finality looking for leftovers', as a genre fitting for 'a certain [type of] humanity'.
5. Lyotard, *Political Writings*, trans. Bill Readings & Kevin Paul Geiman (Minneapolis: University of Minnesota Press, 1993), p.33.
6. See *On Liberty*, pp. 127ff. Although Mill's argument is often couched in terms of the threat of mediocrity, it is nevertheless the case that he endorses the view that the development of new practices and competences (in Lyotard's terminology, new genres) is culturally beneficial: 'There is always a need of persons not only to discover new truths and point out what were once truths are true no longer, but also to commence new practices and set the example of more enlightened conduct and better taste and sense in human life' (129).
7. *The Differend*, p. 182 (see footnote 3, above).
8. See Lyotard, *Political Writings*, p. 11.
9. Lyotard, *Political Writings*: '[T]he first task is that of overcoming this humanist obstacle [i.e. the anthropocentric view that humans are *users* of language] to the analysis of phrase regimes, to make philosophy

inhuman. Humanity is not the user of language, nor even its guardian; there is no more one subject than one language' (p.21).

10. One might call this conception of politics a genre, in so far as it has as its aim the pursuit of a plurality of aims.

7

'Victorian Values' and *Silas Marner*

K. M. Newton

In the good (or bad, depending on one's point of view) old days when it was taken as a matter of course that classic literary texts were central to any English syllabus, *Silas Marner* was one of the most widely studied of Victorian novels in schools. Part of the reason for this, no doubt, was that it was short by nineteenth-century standards, as well as being perceived as a simple story written in an accessible style. But perhaps even more important was its identification with Victorian moral idealism since it would appear to present a world in which moral order is intrinsic and triumphs over moral disorder, with the good being rewarded and the bad being punished. In an edition of the novel for schools first published in 1912 and often reprinted, the editor discusses the appropriateness of *Silas Marner* as a school text and states:

> above all, the ethical interest must be paramount; and no treat-
> ment of *Silas Marner* can be really educative which does not make
> its appeal to the moral consciousness. It is in the belief justified by
> a long experience that in this lies the true value of the teaching of
> literature, that this edition of *Silas Marner* is included in the series
> of English Literature for Schools.[1]

What now tend to be referred to as 'Victorian values' remained powerful well into the twentieth century, and the prescribing of literary texts in schools must have played some part in sustaining them. *Silas Marner* is a particularly significant text in cultural terms because the ethical certainties associated with 'Victorian values' appeared to be more straightforwardly asserted in this novel than in almost any other literary text of the period. A recent critic, Sandra Gilbert, has stated that its 'status as a schoolroom classic makes it almost as much a textbook as a novel'.[2] Indeed it might be claimed

that it exemplifies the theory of fiction proclaimed by Miss Prism in
The Importance of Being Earnest when she describes her lost novel in
the following terms: 'The good ended happily, and the bad unhappily. That is what Fiction means.' Wilde was clearly satirising what
he believed to be the simple-minded moralism and optimism of
Victorian fiction which *Silas Marner* can be perceived as exemplify-
ing and which almost certainly accounts for its former prominence
as a school text.

In certain political circles there have recently been demands both
for a 'return to Victorian values' and for the restoration of classic
literary texts to English syllabuses in schools, demands that are
clearly not unconnected. It may be that *Silas Marner* will again be
thought of as an ideal school text. In this essay I shall suggest that it
is not as amenable a text as modern proponents of 'Victorian values'
may think and that only critical impercipience allowed it to be seen
in such terms in the past. Even though there has recently been
critically sophisticated discussion of *Silas Marner*, as in Sandra Gilbert's feminist reading, such criticism has not, I think, directly called
into question the novel's apparent commitment to promulgating
Victorian moral certainties.

Silas Marner is difficult to categorise within George Eliot's fiction.
It can either be seen as the end of her early phase or the beginning of
her mature style. It has links with her first novel *Adam Bede* in that it
deals with English rural life, yet in structure it is similar to her later
work since all of her novels from *Silas Marner* onwards employ a
double plot. George Eliot is of course noted for her commitment to
realism in fiction yet *Silas Marner* has often been seen as more akin
to myth or fairy tale: '*Silas Marner* is simply an allegorical fairy-tale';[3]
it is 'essentially a myth of spiritual rebirth'.[4] Also divine providence
appears to be at work in the novel, rewarding the good and punishing the bad, which would suggest that it embodies a religious or
metaphysical meaning, yet how is this to be reconciled with the fact
that George Eliot's other writings indicate that she had rejected
religious and metaphysical beliefs? Readings of the novel which
assume that it is a simple and straightforward moral fable are
weakened by ignoring these considerations, which complicate the
question of interpretation.

One significant fact that needs to be taken into account is that
George Eliot acknowledged the influence of Wordsworth on the
novel and its connections with certain of the poems in *Lyrical Ballads*
is obvious.[5] Both *Lyrical Ballads* and *Silas Marner* are simple in style

when compared with other texts by their authors and both writers are clearly drawing on traditional ballads and fairy tales, but one should not forget that they are sophisticated writers adopting an apparently simple style for their own purposes. Their texts cannot be credibly interpreted as if they were genuine ballads or fairy tales.

To look at the question of realism in *Silas Marner* first of all: though critics have seen the novel as resembling a fairy tale or myth and therefore as a departure from the realistic representation associated with her other fiction – as Leavis puts it: 'the atmosphere precludes too direct a reference... to our everyday sense of how things happen'[6] – there is no evidence that George Eliot regarded the novel as a break from realism. Though the 'atmosphere' may often resemble a fairy tale nothing that happens in the novel is irreconcilable with a rational perspective on the world, as one critic admits: '[It] is constructed completely within the limits of conventional realism, with careful attention to probability and verisimilitude of detail'.[7] Of course, the novel contains what appear to be some striking departures from the conventions of realism, but these, I believe, should not be seen as belonging to the 'world' of the novel but as the outcome of an aesthetic strategy. In other words what I am suggesting is that the events and situations in themselves are not fundamentally different from those depicted in her other novels but that at the level of style and narrative structure the novel draws upon fairy tale and myth. To put the matter in terms of narrative theory, there is a discontinuity between 'story' – the basic material of the novel – and 'discourse' – how that material is rendered in artistic terms;[8] a story that creates a 'world' in accordance with a rational or scientific perspective – unlike fairy tales, myths and legends – nevertheless uses some of the devices of fairy tales, myths and legends in representing that world.

An example of such discontinuity is the association of weavers at the beginning of the novel with 'the remnants of a disinherited race',[9] 'alien-looking men' (51) who 'rarely stirred abroad without that mysterious burden' (51). They are 'wandering men' (51) who are viewed with suspicion by their rural neighbours. Yet these weavers are not in reality Wandering Jew figures belonging to a Romantic world remote from historical specificity. They are clearly products of the Industrial Revolution and the burden they carry is not the consequence of some mysterious sin committed in the past but contains the thread and other materials they require to practise their trade. The dehumanising effect of the Industrial Revolution is conveyed by using language and symbols associated with early Romanticism to turn the weavers into alienated, rootless wanderers, but the historical reality retains its integrity. This illustrates in miniature the aesthetic strategy employed in the novel.

Another example of this discontinuity is Silas's strange fits in which he goes into a death-like trance. These are crucial to the plot yet they seem too bizarre to be appropriate normally to fiction in a realist tradition. People in Lantern Yard or Raveloe have no idea what causes them and they contribute to the Romantic or fairy-tale atmosphere of the novel. Yet the narrator makes it clear that there is a medical explanation for Silas's condition, namely catalepsy. Silas's association with Romantic figures such as Wordsworth's leech gatherer or Michael and of course Coleridge's Ancient Mariner is obvious from the way he is presented but realism is, I would suggest, not compromised at the level of 'story'.

As I mentioned above, this is the first of George Eliot's novels to use a double plot and it is clear that Silas's and Godfrey Cass's stories are inextricably connected. The Romantic atmosphere of the novel allows George Eliot to create a more fable-like structure than would be possible in conventionally realist fiction where such structuring would have to be understated so as not to undermine the realistic illusion. Silas and Godfrey represent two differing perspectives on life which are brought into confrontation with experience. It is not insignificant that *Silas Marner* was written shortly after Darwin's *Origin of Species* was published in 1859, for the world that Silas and Godfrey have to face – far from being fairy tale-like – is Darwinian in basis; that is, a world in which there is no evidence of a divine or providential order, a world in which events are the product of chance, circumstance and accident. It is striking how often the word 'chance' occurs in the *Origin*:

as there is a frequently recurring struggle for existence, it follows that any being, if it vary however slightly in any manner profitable to itself, under the complex and sometimes varying conditions of life, will have a better chance of surviving, and thus be *naturally selected*.

every slight modification, which in the course of ages chanced to arise ...

under such circumstances ... the swiftest and the slimmest wolves
would have the best chance of surviving ...

the more diversified these descendants become, the better will be
their chance of succeeding in the battle of life.[10]

It is such a world that Silas and Godfrey have to confront.

Chance is a significant factor in *Silas Marner*. The narrator informs
us that 'Favourable Chance is the god of all men who follow their
own devices instead of obeying a law they believe in' (126). Silas has
been brought up to accept the view that the world is governed by a
divine order and when accused of robbery he puts his faith in the
drawing of lots to prove his innocence, believing that 'God will clear
me' (59). Godfrey, on the other hand, relies on chance to rescue him
from a set of circumstances that threatens to ruin his life: a degrad-
ing marriage that would result in his losing his inheritance and
being denied the possibility of marrying Nancy Lammeter. When
chance in the form of drawing lots goes against Silas, it destroys his
faith in a beneficent God and he retreats into despair: ' "there is no
just God that governs the earth righteously, but a God of lies, that
bears witness against the innocent" ' (61). Godfrey, however, profits
from chance. By waiting on events and being prepared to adapt to
them, he avoids ruin: 'The longer the interval, the more chance
there was of deliverance from some, at least, of the hateful consequences to which he had sold himself' (81). His wife dies without
their marriage or the fact that he has fathered a child being disclosed, and his brother Dunstan, the only other person who knows
about the marriage, disappears. Godfrey has gambled with events
and won. He is now free to marry his 'paradise' (81), Nancy Lammeter, and inherits his father's property on his death. No relation is
revealed between human desert or justice and what happens in the
world. Silas had put his faith in a moral order in the world con-
trolled by a beneficent God but that faith is shattered. In contrast,
Godfrey has gambled with events and won.

Though the world of *Silas Marner* may be Darwinian in its basis in
that chance, accident and circumstance are intrinsic to it, the novel
nevertheless suggests that this need not undermine human notions
of a moral order since the absence of an immanent moral order in
the world should have no bearing on how human beings ought to
live. Those characters in George Eliot's novels, such as Godfrey, who
try to exploit chance and circumstance to serve their own immoral

or amoral purposes are clearly treated with little sympathy, for she believes that Darwinian natural selection has no tenable application to human society.

This attitude to Darwinism was untypical of the period. Those who grasped what the theory meant in scientific terms but who believed that morality was dependent on the existence of a moral order in the world tended to take the view that Darwinian theory could have negative social consequences; human individuals would no longer have any incentive to behave morally since Darwin implied that the survival of species had no relation to morality but was dependent on adaptation to a constantly changing world. Others who interpreted Darwin less scientifically and who were influenced by Herbert Spencer's translation of natural selection into the 'survival of the fittest' believed that Darwinism demonstrated the existence of an order in the world founded upon struggle and conflict and that this had human and social implications. Whereas Darwin's concept of 'natural selection' was neutral in evaluative terms, the term 'fittest' could be taken to mean those most fit to survive. This interpretation led eventually to Social Darwinism. *Silas Marner* suggests that George Eliot rejected both these readings of Darwinism.[11]

The novel recognises, however, that the undermining of the idea of an immanent moral order could have disastrous effects. Silas's response to the shattering of his faith when the drawing of lots reveals him to be guilty when he knows he is innocent is to construct a mechanical way of life for himself: 'Strangely Marner's face and figure shrank and bent themselves into a constant mechanical relation to the objects of his life' (69). The main elements of this mechanical life are work and money; nothing else matters to him until his encounter with Eppie. Of course, work and money were all too prominent features of Victorian life and it seems certain the George Eliot is implying a relation between the Victorian preoccupation with them and loss of faith. Marner's mechanistic life functions allegorically as a commentary on the alienation which George Eliot suggests underlies Victorian culture. Likewise Godfrey's hope that he will be rescued by a fortunate turn of events has wider implications. The reader is told that Godfrey 'can hardly be called old-fashioned' (126) in conducting his life in this way. He is seen as typical of people in George Eliot's own time, even though the novel is set some sixty years in the past: 'Let even a polished man of these days get into a position he is ashamed to avow, and his mind will be

bent on all the possible issues that may deliver him from the calcul-
able results of his position' (126). Silas with his Ancient Mariner
associations and Godfrey (God-free) represent different forms of
Victorian alienation.

Yet, apparently, good finally triumphs: the man who had believed
there was an immanent moral order in the world wins out eventually over the calculating gambler on chance. It is this triumph of
good that has persuaded some critics that the novel fundamentally
supports a providentialist view of the world. Thus U.C. Knoepflmacher writes: 'The "mystery" previously denied to Dinah, Latimer, or
Maggie, is allowed to survive in this legendary tale.... In a story
where obstacles come in threes... such beliefs [Nancy Lammeter's]
cannot be laughed away.'[12] This is to mistake style and artistic
expression for philosophical content. The triumph of 'good' in the
novel is not a matter of arbitrary rewards and punishments being
administered to Silas and Godfrey. Indeed, I shall suggest that the
moral position the novel takes would be unchanged if Silas had lost
Eppie and Godfrey had succeeded in taking her from Silas.

Silas had believed that moral equilibrium is structured into the
world and is thus shattered when he is unjustly pronounced guilty
of theft. Godfrey in gambling with events in effect rejects such moral
equilibrium. The novel suggests, however, that people have a psychological need for such equilibrium even if it does not exist. As
George Eliot writes in *Romola*: 'Justice is like the Kingdom of God – it
is not without us as a fact, it is within us as a great yearning' (Chap.
67). Because Godfrey's rewards are not in equilibrium with his sense
of his deserts, he is vulnerable to guilt. He also has to adopt a role
which is at odds with his inner self since he cannot acknowledge his
past actions to others, not even to Nancy, the person closest to him.
Because of the fear that the past may come to light he is accompanied by 'his importunate companion, Anxiety' (142). Godfrey's
eventual acknowledgement of providence – ' "Everything comes to
light, Nancy, sooner or later. When God Almighty wills it, our secrets
are found out" ' (223) – has to be seen in this psychological context.

David Cecil argues, however, that George Eliot imposes an
arbitrary moral order on the text by punishing Godfrey through
making him childless:

> George Eliot vindicates the moral order by making him [Godfrey]
> childless. This is not in the least an inevitable consequence of his
> act. There is no inherent reason in the nature of things why a

morally-feeble man should not beget twenty children. In consequence we feel Godfrey's discontent to be no inevitable expression of the moral law, but a gratuitous piece of poetic justice imposed on him by the arbitrary will of his creator.[13]

Cecil ignores the fact that Godfrey's success in avoiding the consequences of his past actions and marrying Nancy resulted from his gambling with events and winning. But gamblers always lose sooner or later. Godfrey's predicament is not so much 'a gratuitious piece of poetic justice' as a piece of bad luck. Since he has had so much good luck previously, it is not difficult for the reader to accept that his luck should run out. Although he interprets it as God's retribution – understandable in the light of his continuous sense of guilt and anxiety – there is no reason why the reader should agree with him.

Silas, however, would seem to provide support for Godfrey's view as he has his belief in providence restored. He says to Dolly Winthrop: '"There's good i' this world – I've a feeling o' that now... That drawing o' the lots is dark; but the child was sent to me: there's dealings with us – there's dealings"' (205). Yet even though his money is returned he says that if he lost Eppie '"I might come to think I was forsaken again, and lose the feeling that God was good to me"' (226). He has no sooner said that than Godfrey and Nancy come knocking at his door to ask for Eppie. Just as in Lantern Yard his belief in providence will be tested.

But whereas in Lantern Yard Silas's identity had been shattered with the collapse of his faith in benevolent providence, the significance of this second crisis is that it indicates that a belief in providence is no longer central to Silas's identity. Though he had regarded Eppie as having been sent to him as a substitute for the loss of his gold, he is able to rise above such views and ceases to regard her as his possession. He allows her to choose: '"Eppie, my child, speak. I won't stand in your way. Thank Mr and Mrs Cass"' (229). But when Eppie rejects Godfrey's offer and he then asserts his claim to her as her natural father, Silas suffers his greatest test. Though he had been prepared to let Eppie choose, confident perhaps that she would choose him, Godfrey's claim that she is his by right again creates the spectre that there is no beneficent God and that the world is devoid of justice – '"God gave her to me because you turned your back upon her, and He looks upon her as mine: you've no right to her!"' (231) – a view that Godfrey regards as 'very selfish' (231). Yet instead of reacting in the same way as he had done in Lantern Yard when the drawing of lots goes against him, Silas transcends questions of theology through experiencing the primary Wordsworthian feeling of sympathy. Fearing that 'he should be raising his own will as an obstacle to Eppie's good' (232), the question as to who has the greater right to Eppie – a mechanical view of the issue – ceases to matter: the right is what is good for Eppie: ' "I'll say no more. Let it be as you will. Speak to the child. I'll hinder nothing" ' (232).

The significance of this is that Silas is able to set aside absolute notions of what is right or what is good and instead sees the right and the good in humanist terms. The right is what is good for Eppie; it is not an absolute which exists external to humanity. Whether God has decreed that he is entitled to Eppie becomes a matter of no importance; it is the human considerations that are paramount. Even if Eppie had chosen to go with her natural father, it is clear that Silas would not have retreated into his previous sense of alienation. He would have borne her loss through renunciation since the relation to the world he has established in Raveloe is one which is no longer dependent on the sense that the world is providentially ordered. If one interprets the novel as a fairy tale about a man who is rewarded by the workings of a benevolent providence, the novel's humanist message is lost.

What makes Silas able to allow Eppie to choose the good rather than to see the good in absolute terms is that he is now an integrated member of the community of Raveloe and Eppie is a living person to him, not a mere possession like his gold. The theft of his gold and then the coming of Eppie had resulted in Silas's becoming more and more a part of this community, and significantly in Raveloe rigid theological ideas such as divine providence have no place. The religious life of Raveloe is one which emphasises human relationship, not theological concepts. Even without Eppie, Silas would have had the community to fall back on.

Notoriously Margaret Thatcher – who urged a return to Victorian values – asserted that 'There is no such thing as society. There are individual men and women, there are families.'[14] This view is certainly not borne out in *Silas Marner*. Indeed, for George Eliot human identity is social in a constitutive sense and those of her characters who attempt to live purely individualistic human lives virtually cease to have human identities. Thus Tito in *Romola* is said by Bernardo to be ' "one of the *demoni*, who are of no particular country" ' (Chap. 19), and the calculating individualism of Christian in

Felix Holt reduces him to the status of an animal in a Darwinian environment: 'Mr Christian ... had been remarkable through life for that power of adapting himself to circumstances which enables a man to fall safely on all-fours in the most hurried expulsions and escapes' (Chap. 12).

Silas Marner attacks on a number of fronts ideas and beliefs that have been seen as characteristically Victorian. Morality and justice are shown not as immanent in the world, as most Victorians would have believed, but as social in origin and thus purely human constructions. The devotion to work and money, strongly associated with the Victorian ethos and a feature of Victorianism much admired by those who support a 'return to Victorian values', is represented as symptomatic of an alienation from the human. Silas becomes humanised not merely by having to care for another human being but by taking part in the community life of Raveloe. It would not be wrong to describe Raveloe as an organic community and to see *Silas Marner* as a novel that uses organicist ideas derived from the Romantics and from such writers as Carlyle as part of an implicit attack on the dominance of mechanistic structures in mid-Victorian British society.

However, organicist ideas have been vulnerable to attack on the grounds that they idealise the past. Yet Raveloe is not idealised despite the fairy-tale and mythic atmosphere of the novel. Raveloe is certainly not perfect. The upper class represented by the Casses is largely cut off from the community. The people of the town are in many respects unenlightened; they make little effort at first to help Silas and treat him with suspicion. It is years before he is accepted by them. Dolly Winthrop may be a warm and generous person but her ignorance is apparent and her advice to Silas at times unreliable, notably when she urges the necessity to discipline Eppie: ' " ... I put it upo' your conscience, Master Marner, as there's one of 'em you must choose – ayther smacking or the coal-hole – else she'll get so masterful, there'll be no holding her" ' (186).

Yet the value of Raveloe is clear: it does possess a spirit of community, and though people in the village are reluctant to reach out to what they perceive as other, Silas is finally accepted by them. This spirit of community is reinforced by various ceremonies, such as going to church and the New Year dance, that are fundamental to Raveloe life and which, together with a story such as the Lammeters' wedding that has become something of a community myth, create a sense of shared consciousness. At Eppie's christening,

Silas 'shared in the observances held sacred by his neighbours' (183). Religion in Raveloe is not associated with a rigid theology; rather, it is inseparable from the social fabric. Silas has become integrated into a society that can absorb good and bad fortune and which is thus is not vulnerable to the amoral development of events.

Though superficially it might seem that Silas is rewarded and Godfrey punished when Eppie chooses to stay with Silas rather than go with her natural father, Eppie's choice of Silas is not an arbitrary one. It is in keeping with the novel's attack on the 'mechanical'. Godfrey may be Eppie's natural father but her relationship to him has no human substance; Silas is her father in human terms. It is also more than Silas that she chooses. To take her place in the class-conscious world of the Casses would be to reject the community in which she has been brought up and would cut her off from her past: ' "I wasn't brought up to be a lady, and I can't turn my mind to it. I like the working-folks, and their victuals, and their ways" ' (234). Modern advocates of 'Victorian values' often point to the importance of the nuclear family in creating stability and security in both social and individual terms during the Victorian period and contrast this with the instability and insecurity created in the late twentieth century by the emergence of large numbers of one-parent families. It is worth pointing out, therefore, that in *Silas Marner*, a one-parent family – admittedly with community support – is seen in very positive terms, with one parent successfully combining paternal and maternal roles and bringing up a child who shows every sign of developing into a well-adjusted and socially responsible adult.

It is possible to undermine further the view that the 'good' are rewarded and the 'bad' punished by arguing that even if Godfrey had been successful in gaining Eppie, the moral scheme of the novel would have been unchanged. David Cecil suggests that in depriving Godfrey of children, George Eliot is arbitrarily punishing him. But what the novel suggests is that even if Godfrey's luck had persisted, his life would have continued to be a failure in human terms. For Godfrey's life is founded upon the search for gratification. Exploiting chance and the desire for gratification are connected: 'The longer the interval, the more chance there was of deliverance from some, at least, of the hateful consequences to which he had sold himself; the more opportunities remained for him to snatch the strange gratification of seeing Nancy, and gathering some faint indications of her lingering regard' (81). Even Nancy is associated with gratification though he thinks of her in religious terms: he had 'wooed her with tacit patient worship, as the woman who made him think of the future with joy' (80). Yet we are told that 'the hope of this paradise had not been enough to save him from a course which shut him out of it for ever' (81).

In paradise one is beyond desire and the quest for gratification, because paradise by definition implies that one's desires are completely fulfilled and therefore no lack persists leading to further desire for gratification. Yet Nancy as 'paradise' had been unable prevent him succumbing to the kind of life that led to marriage with Molly Farren, and even after he has achieved paradise by marrying Nancy, having exploited chance to escape from his past actions, desire as lack does not cease as his failure to father a child by Nancy prevents gratification being complete. The language used to describe his feelings when he fails to gain Eppie imply that it is gratification that motivates him: 'Godfrey felt an irritation inevitable to almost all of us when we encounter an unexpected obstacle' (230), and at the end of the chapter his feelings on failure consist in 'frustration' (235).

One can conclude from this that even if Eppie had chosen to go with him and Nancy, gratification would have been only temporarily satisfied for Godfrey because there would always be something lacking to make happiness complete. Nancy as 'paradise' had proved insufficient; her childlessness was a lack which generated a new desire. Godfrey cannot accept renunciation, like Silas, or Nancy with her more rigid identification of the development of events with providence, as ways of controlling desire:

> Meanwhile, why could he not make up his mind to the absence of children from a hearth brightened by such a wife? Why did his mind fly uneasily to that void, as if it were the sole reason why life was not thoroughly joyous to him? I suppose it is the way with all men and women who reach middle age without the clear perception that life never *can* be thoroughly joyous: under the vague dulness of the grey hours, dissatisfaction seeks a definite object, and finds it in the privation of an untried good.   (219–20)

One can see a Schoperhauerian type of philosophy underlying this aspect of the novel, and Schopenhauer was a writer whom George Eliot had read.[15] Desire is seen as an intrinsic force within human beings that cannot be quenched since no gratification of desire can be complete. Again this suggests that those characters who commit themselves to desire or the will and experience frustration are not defeated arbitrarily; for George Eliot, as for Schopenhauer, people such as Godfrey who live a life based upon the gratification of desire will always end up frustrated.

At the level of the individual, then, the underlying philosophy of the novel is one of pessimism: there is no God, at least no just God who takes account of human hopes or deserts, and even if one obtains everything that one desires, it will never be enough to satisfy. Nancy articulates the latter philosophy when she remarks to Godfrey after he has disclosed the fact that he is Eppie's father: '" . . . I wasn't worth doing wrong for – nothing is in this world. Nothing is so good as it seems beforehand – not even our marrying wasn't, you see"' (224). One has, of course, to balance against this the loving relationship between Silas and Eppie that is at the centre of the novel. However, even here Silas is never free from the anxiety that Eppie will be taken away from him, leaving him bereft in a similar manner to his experience in Lantern Yard. He tells Eppie 'how his soul was utterly desolate till she was sent to him' (226) and the fear that he could return to this state if he lost her, in addition to the fear that God having abandoned him once could do so again, means that his happiness is constantly compromised by a sense of anxiety. She has mysteriously come into his life and she could just as easily be taken away from him, as he finds out. Silas's anxiety about losing Eppie is only a heightened form of that which all people – consciously or subconsciously – experience, as eventually a symbolic 'knocking at the door' (226) will come to threaten all relationships as human beings exist in a world of change which, the novel suggests, is indifferent to human feeling.

It could be argued that even if the novel takes a pessimistic view of human life at the level of the individual, it is more optimistic at the social level. Marner is eventually integrated into Raveloe, a society with shared implicit values and assumptions which provides some protection from the amoral world of chance that is a continual threat to human beings at an individual level. In an earlier discussion of the novel I suggested that one of the functions of Raveloe was as a kind of model of an organic society for George Eliot's contemporary Victorian society, performing a role similar to that of feudal society in Carlyle's *Past and Present*.[16] Though the latter sort of societies belonged to the past and could not be imitated in the present, they could serve as examples of a shared corporate consciousness that industrialised societies needed to recreate in the contemporary world. However, another perspective is also implied. Even if Raveloe acts as a model for the present, it also testifies to the disappearance in Victorian Britain of the kind of community spirit achieved in such a society. Carlyle's writings are full of despair about the inability of Victorian industrialised society to change course and make itself 'organic'. He refers in *Past and Present* to 'the immense Industrial Ages, as yet all inorganic, and in a quite pulpy condition, requiring desperately to harden themselves into some organism!'[17] but the impression one forms from most of his writing is of profound pessimism that such a change can happen. The emphasis is very much on the spiritual disaster that will result if contemporary society remains mechanistic.

Likewise George Eliot expresses a Carlylean despair at the consequences for any society that remains inorganic, as in this passage from her poem, 'In a London Drawing Room':

> All hurry on & look upon the ground,
> Or glance unmarking at the passers by
> The wheels are hurrying too, cabs, carriages
> All closed, in multiple identity.
> The world seems one huge prison-house & court
> Where men are punished at the slightest cost
> With lowest rate of colour, warmth & joy.[18]

Though her writing continually emphasises the importance of ideals in shaping action, there seems little optimism that Victorian society can be changed. As with Carlyle, though of course less melodramatically expressed, pessimism about the mechanistic tendencies of contemporary British society is the dominating tone. This culminates in *Daniel Deronda*, where the hero rejects England in favour of a proto-Zionist ideal. There seems little possibility of organicist values having any impact in Britain. In relation to *Silas Marner*, this suggests that the positive social forces of the pre-industrialised Raveloe which reclaim Marner from his mechanistic devotion to work and money no longer exist in the present and seem unlikely to exist in the future.

What I have tried to suggest in this essay is that *Silas Marner* is a work which in important respects presents a radical critique of the dominant Victorian ideology. Its fairy-tale-like surface masks a world which, far from exhibiting the presence of an immanent moral order, is Darwinian in its nature and thus takes no account of human needs or hopes. Silas Marner's religious world-view cannot survive confrontation with such a world and the work ethic he constructs as a response to his alienation is depicted as a desperate, mechanistic attempt to impose some kind of order on a life devoid of meaning, while the money he accumulates by work only accentuates his estrangement. Optimism and a belief in progress are ideas very much associated with the Victorian ethos but they are little in evidence in this novel. The only reason that the 'bad' end unhappily is that, since desire can never be fully satisfied, they are bound to be frustrated. Instead of the future promising improvement, the novel suggests in its implicit contrast between Raveloe and contemporary Victorian society that organic social structures belong to the past and that their existence in post-industrial society is problematic. All of this of course was clearly not evident to earlier generations who prescribed the novel as a set text in schools. I would suggest that modern enthusiasts for Victorian values looking for texts to promote them would be well advised to steer clear of *Silas Marner*.

Notes

1. George Eliot, *Silas Marner*, ed. F.E. Bevan (Cambridge: Cambridge University Press, 1923), p. vi.
2. See Sandra M. Gilbert, 'Life's Empty Pack: Notes toward a Literary Daughteronomy', in *George Eliot*, ed. K.M. Newton (London and New York: Longman, 1991), p. 102.
3. Mario Praz, *The Hero in Eclipse in Victorian Fiction*, trans. Angus Davidson (Oxford: Oxford University Press, 1956), p. 352.
4. Walter Allen, *George Eliot* (London: Weidenfeld and Nicolson, 1965), p. 120.
5. See *The George Eliot Letters*, ed. Gordon S. Haight (9 vols, New Haven: Yale University Press, 1954–78), III, 382.
6. F.R. Leavis, *The Great Tradition* (Harmondsworth: Penguin Books, 1966), p. 59.
7. Jerome Thale, *The Novels of George Eliot* (New York: Columbia University Press, 1959), p. 59.
8. For a detailed discussion of this distinction, see Seymour Chatman, *Story and Discourse: Narrative Structure in Fiction and Film* (Ithaca and London: Cornell University Press, 1978).
9. George Eliot, *Silas Marner*, ed. Q.D. Leavis (Harmondsworth: Penguin Books, 1967), p. 52. Page numbers from this edition will subsequently be incorporated in the text.

10.   Charles Darwin, *The Origin of Species*, ed. J.W. Burrow (Harmonds-worth: Penguin Books, 1968), pp. 68, 131, 138, 170. This edition is a reprint of the first edition of 1859.

11.   For a fuller discussion of Darwinism in relation to George Eliot, see K. M. Newton, 'George Eliot, George Henry Lewes and Darwinism', *Durham University Journal* 66 (1973–4), pp. 278–93.

12.   U.C. Knoepflmacher, *George Eliot's Early Novels: The Limits of Realism* (Berkeley: University of California Press, 1968), p. 247.

13.   David Cecil, *Early Victorian Novelists: Essays in Revaluation* (Harmonds-worth: Penguin Books, 1948), p. 244.

14.   See interview with Margaret Thatcher in *Woman's Own*, 31 October 1987.

15.   See James Sully's memoir of her in *My Life and Friends: A Psychologist's Memoirs* (London, 1918), p. 264. Similar ideas, however, can be found in Carlyle, for example in *Sartor Resartus*.

16.   See K.M. Newton, *George Eliot: Romantic Humanist* (London: Macmillan Press, 1981), pp. 82–3.

17.   Thomas Carlyle, *Past and Present* (London: Chapman and Hall, 1894), p. 214.

18.   Bernard J. Paris, 'George Eliot's Unpublished Poetry', *Studies in Philology* 56 (1959), pp. 541–2.

8

Racism in the Mid-Victorian Novel: Thackeray's *Philip*

John Peck

I

The final chapter of Thackeray's last completed novel, *Philip*, is extraordinarily distasteful. By this stage, the problems the hero, Philip Firmin, has had to contend with have been resolved: he will not have to honour the debt his father has incurred, and his reconciliation with his employer has restored his financial security. But then, in the closing pages, Philip visits his family seat, inherits a fortune when a lost will is discovered, and gets the better of a character called Woolcomb who is standing for parliament. What makes the chapter so unpleasant is that Woolcomb is of mixed race and ridicule of him on the grounds of colour seems to be Thackeray's overriding intention. Philip arranges for 'a cart drawn by two donkeys, and driven by a negro, beasts and men all wearing Woolcomb's colours'[1] to be driven into the market-place:

> In the cart was fixed a placard on which a most undeniable likeness of Mr Woolcomb was designed: who was made to say, 'VOTE FOR ME! AM I NOT A MAN AND A BRUDDER?' (p. 642)

Pendennis, the narrator of the novel, refers to 'our fine joke' (p. 643); one searches in vain for a trace of irony. Indeed, Thackeray seems to share Philip's delight in getting the better of Woolcomb in this way. Such a scene creates a problem for the reader: it is easy to take a superior critical line with a novel like *Philip* (using it, for example, to illustrate the mentality that shaped and was shaped by Victorian colonialism[2]), but is there any other way of coming to terms with a text that is so overtly offensive?

Philip is not the only Thackeray novel marked by racism, but it is the only one where the hatred is so extreme as to unbalance the

126

work. For the most part, Thackeray's racism is incidental, something that remains the case in his references to Jews in *Philip*.[3] When Philip's father flees the country, his good are sold at auction: 'and as for the doctor's own state portrait, I am afraid it went for a few shillings only, and in the midst of a roar of Hebrew laughter' (p. 206). This kind of casual jibe is common in Thackeray; everywhere we turn, there are unpleasant asides and caricatures of Irish, Jewish and black characters. The tone is offensive, but seems merely unthinking. Usually his caricatures, particularly of Irish characters, fall into that dubious category where the victim is meant to feel flattered at the insult; a failure to see the patronising affection of the insult would mark the recipient as lacking an English sense of humour. Consequently, Thackeray's novels are full of drunken Irish rogues, such as Costigan in *Pendennis*, playing the part the English expect of them. Essentially, Thackeray offers racial stereotypes in the same way that stand-up comedians have over the years.

Sometimes, however, the issue of race is irrelevant. In *Vanity Fair*, a black servant appears on the first page of the novel, but the text displays an uncomplicated attitude towards him: he is simply a servant. And, as was the case with black people in the eighteenth and early nineteenth centuries, he is absorbed into English society: 'Black Sambo, with the infatuation of his profession, determined on setting up a public-house.'[4] Despite the name, Sambo is grouped with servants as a whole rather than being seen as in any way an exceptional case. But Sambo does not represent a threat. The issue of race only becomes complicated in the Victorian period when two additional factors are introduced: class and America. A class dimension becomes apparent with Miss Swartz, 'the rich woolly-haired mulatto from St Kitts',[5] in *Vanity Fair*, who, because of her colour, has to pay double to attend Miss Pinkerton's school. Much could be made of Thackeray's particular animus towards characters of mixed race,[6] but what is most significant is that Miss Swartz is a black character with money. Douglas Lorimer, in the context of discussing how the English became more racist in the 1850s and 1860s, suggests that it 'was not so much the black poor, but . . . black gentlemen who most directly encountered the growth of racial antipathy'.[7] A servant can be treated benevolently, but a black character with money unsettles the status quo; a predictable picture therefore appears of Miss Swartz festooned with the material good of Europe: 'Swartz in her favourite amber-coloured satin, with turquoise bracelets, countless rings, flowers, feathers, and all sorts of tags and gimcracks . . .'[8]

The economic and cultural threat Miss Swartz represents is countered through mockery.

Such an attitude might seem difficult to reconcile with British opposition to slavery, but the slavery debate was far from straightforward. Essentially, emancipation was enthusiastically embraced as an abstract concept, but actual contact with slaves provoked a different response. Thackeray, on a visit to America in 1853, wrote:

> They are not my men and brethren, these strange people with retreating foreheads, and with great obtruding lips and jaws: with capacities for thought, pleasure, endurance quite different to mine...[9]

The paternalistic fiction of a bond between master and servant has been displaced by a sense of an unruly mass. Thackeray's comment indicates the extent to which, by the 1850s, the view from America was determining British thinking about race. It was no longer a case of the individual black servant, but the thought of large numbers, and this more than anything else created the mid-Victorian sense of a savage threat.[10] An aspect of this is the way in which a culture needs a symbol to crystallise a fear: the English obviously had nothing to fear from black Americans, but fears about the working class in England could be brought into focus through this oblique parallel. *The Virginians* is the novel that most fully reflects these anxieties. Gumbo, a slave, is seen as a child who thrives under a good master. When he attains his freedom, however, he becomes a disruptive nuisance: 'He was free, and they were not: he was, as it were, a centre of insurrection...bragging of his friends in Europe...like the monkey who had seen the world.'[11] Thackeray resorts to the crudest animal imagery for the beast who threatens the social order.

In reading *The Virginians*, however, the reader could easily miss such slurs; they are a minor element. And generally, before *Philip*, Thackeray's racism is never central enough to unsettle the tone of a novel. In *Philip*, though, all sense of proportion disappears; in addition, we encounter aspects of Victorian racism that are not present in Thackeray's earlier novels. The tone is set from Woolcomb's first appearance:

> the fact is, that young Woolcomb of the Life Guards Green, who had inherited immense West India property, and, we will say, just

a teaspoonful of that dark blood which makes a man preternat-
urally partial to blonde beauties, has cast his opal eyes very
warmly upon the golden-haired Agnes of late.   (p. 105)

This is a rich black man in London society, a social equal but also a
sexual rival to the white male. The sexual slur here is new in Thackeray, as is another myth, that the savagery of the black character will
display itself in cruel behaviour: Woolcomb beats his wife, and we
are left in no doubt that he is a 'jealous, stingy, ostentatious, cruel
little brute' (pp. 332–3).[12] Critics have, of course, attempted to deal
with the nastiness of *Philip*. Most recently, Deborah Thomas, working within Lorimer's framework of ideas, explains *Philip's* racism in
terms of attitudes that had taken root in English society by 1862:

> this regrettable calcification of Thackeray's racial attitudes should
> be seen primarily not as his individual humanitarian failure but
> rather as a manifestation of a general hardening of attitudes on
> the subject of race in British thinking in the 1850s and 1860s.[13]

The flaw in this approach, however, is that, although attitudes may
have hardened, *Philip* is the only novel of the period that sinks to the
level of the racist taunt. Others might have shared Thackeray's
prejudices, but they do not betray them in print in the same kind
of way.[14] Indeed, *Philip* is such an intemperate performance, from a
novelist commonly noted for both his intelligence and liberalism,
that it is tempting to dismiss it as an aberration, a tired, and best-
ignored, work from a writer who has lost his sense of proportion
and tact, not to mention his sense of humour.

II

If we invoke an idea of Thackeray's tiredness, however, we risk
losing sight of something complex in *Philip*, particularly in the area
of its deep-rooted anxieties. These begin to become evident in the
jaundiced view that infects the whole novel. The overwhelming
impression is of a world where sickness reigns, and the only movement is towards death. The novel starts with Philip ill as a child. His
father is a doctor, but Dr Firmin's whole life is a betrayal of his trust.
There is a good doctor, Goodenough, who plays his part as a Good
Samaritan, but he is a minor character in a novel where recovery

seems unlikely. Barbara Hardy has made a case for the redemptive power of love in Thackeray's fiction,[15] and Caroline Gann – as nurse and substitute-mother to Philip – occupies a relevant role in the text, but generally the sense of infection is greater than any sense of a power to heal. It is an impression that is reinforced by the frequency of the references to death, even in inconsequential asides such as 'the corpses of our dead lovers' (p. 22). It is a world bounded by, and often described in terms of, death. Family life offers no consolation: Philip's mother fails to visit him when he is ill; within a few pages, Philip and his father are at odds; all of Philip's extended family are loathsome; and Philip's father-in-law, Baynes, is trapped in a terrible marriage. It is an exceptionally sour vision of family life, often extending into the idea of physical cruelty, even murder.[16]

What the negativity of Thackeray's vision suggests is that he is at a remove from, and unable to share in, ways of thinking that had become established by the middle of the century. The Victorians as a whole, for example, found a source of strength in the family, seeing a reinscription in family life of what had collapsed elsewhere.[17] Thackeray, however, does not share this view. He is even more ill-at-ease with Victorian ideas about the self. Mary Poovey, writing about *David Copperfield*, provides a widely-accepted view of the central role of Victorian fiction in constructing

> a psychological narrative of individual development, which both provided individual readers with an imaginative image of what identity was and created a subject position that reproduced this kind of identity in the individual reader... one effect of the 'literary' in this period was the textual construction of an individualist psychology...[18]

It would, we can start by saying, be a very odd reader who chose Philip as a role model. He is a disturbingly anti-social hero, quite different from the maturing hero or heroine we encounter in many Victorian novels. But what the text also suggests is that everything is on the surface with Philip, and, as such, the novel seems to take issue with the whole notion of an individualist psychology. The issue is encapsulated in a short comment by Major Pendennis:

> 'Stuff! nonsense – no patience with these personalities begad! Firmin is a doctor, certainly – so are you so are others. But

Firmin is a university man, and a gentleman. Firmin has
travelled.'   (p. 3)

The major rejects the idea of a unique personality; everything is
explicable in terms of background, rank, education and profession.
There are general truths about human nature rather than everyone
being a special case. The Major turns out to be wrong, to have
misread his man, but, none the less, Thackeray seems to agree
with the Major's approach to character.

At a fundamental level, *Philip* consistently rejects a notion of the
complex self, preferring to read experience in terms of class and
gender; not surprisingly, race needs to be added as a third term.
Philip, it is true, might come across to the reader as a psychological
peculiarity, but he is certainly not conceived of as a complex character. He is, just literally, a misfit: tall, clumsy, blundering. We are
made to feel that he is a man from the past who cannot adapt to the
present. Where he differs most radically from the new kind of hero is
that he is incapable of self-fashioning; unlike David Copperfield, for
example, he has no ability to construct a self in response to the
demands of middle-class society. This can, of course, be read as
autobiographical, that Thackeray is registering his own sense of
being out of step with the times, but if we take the biographical
line we miss the larger point that the Victorians developed new
assumptions about society and the self in order to control their
world, and Thackeray is outside this new consensus. Again and
again, therefore, we encounter passages such as this: 'as for Philip –
he is a man; he is a gentleman; he has brains in his head, and a
great honest heart of which he has offered to give the best feelings to
his cousin...' (p. 183). The same key words – man, gentleman,
honest, heart, generous – are repeated throughout the novel as
touchstones by which a man is to be judged. It is a commonplace
that Thackeray's characters never change, that they do not go
through the process of individual development that is at the heart
of so much Victorian fiction, but by the time of *Philip* this has become
more than just a defining feature of his fiction. It has become a
provocative challenge to new ideas about the self, Thackeray maintaining that there is no need to move beyond what can be defined at
the outset.

Of course, we could say that Thackeray is simply old-fashioned,
but that would be to concede that by the 1860s a new kind
of truthfulness about character had made Thackeray's view

redundant. What critics such as Mary Poovey demonstrate, however, is that new ideas about the self were an invention of the nineteenth century, designed to cope with fundamental changes in daily living (essentially the fact of living in a town-centred industrial society). Rather than dismissing Thackeray as old-fashioned, we can regard him as provocatively standing apart from the middle-classness of Victorian fiction; indeed, what is so telling about his more ponderous (and unfunny) later novels – specifically, *The Newcomes*, *The Virginians* and *Philip* – is that they not only engage with but also take issue with the new middle-class orthodoxy. At the same time, Thackeray is realistic enough to accept that it is the new middle class who will come out on top; it is, after all, Woolcomb who, despite Philip's attempt to humiliate him, is returned as the successful candidate at the election. More troublesomely, however, we have to deal with the fact that a novel that deliberately sets itself against the mainstream in a society will encounter problems; specifically, the misjudged tone of all the scenes involving Woolcomb suggests a writer who has lost touch with an appropriate mode of expression for his age. England may have become more racist in the 1850s and 1860s, but the simultaneous development of a middle-class mentality ensured that at least the expression of racist views was circumspect and cautious. We can point, for example, to Charles Kingsley's notorious description of the Irish as 'human chimpanzees', but this remark was made in a private letter; Kingsley would not have used such a phrase in a published context, knowing, as he did, that many of his closest friends would have been amongst the most offended at any such expression of racist sentiments.[19] Thackeray, in contrast, blunders in, as if picking up the new racism but refusing to accommodate himself within the new delicacy of the mid-Victorian period.

Perhaps more fundamentally, however, there is the point that his refusal of the idea of the complex self drives him back into a social analysis that has to be conducted along the lines of class, gender and race; for, in a secular age, if the new sense of self is removed, there is nothing else available as a way of codifying experience other than group identity, male and female identity, and national identity. In *Philip* this old matrix of analysis is found conspiring, somewhat oddly, with the newer impulses of mid-Victorian racism. The direction in which this leads is to a recognition of how Thackeray's racism is rather different from the most common manifestations of racism in the 1860s: rather than being a knee-jerk response to a perceived threat, *Philip's* racism reflects a more fundamental lack of identification with the spirit of the period. To some extent the novel even turns its back on realism. Lacking any conviction about the self, *Philip* offers an impression of archetypal fears. As is the case with the Dracula myth later in the century, there is a sense of Woolcomb as the dark primitive revenger. He confronts Philip who, unusually for a character in Victorian fiction, has a father; indeed, Philip, despite the fact that he loses his inheritance, is carrying the burden of the sins of his father. There is, therefore, both a sense of guilt and a sense of a dark figure of retribution and judgement. At some level, clean-ness is confronting a stain, with the complication that Philip knows he carries forward his father's stain. The point is that Thackeray is heading so much in an opposite direction from his age that to a certain extent he comes close to a symbolic narrative of sin, guilt and punishment. But the novel cannot simply be removed from the world of realistic narrative in this kind of way. Woolcomb is *not* a dark primitive revenge figure; on the contrary, he is a precisely imagined black character in a specific society. For, although Thack-eray might not identify with the spirit of the period, as a competent novelist he cannot avoid engaging with the period.

III

We might understand Thackeray's position rather more fully if we set *Philip* against two other overtly racist texts from the Victorian period. The Victorian writer who is even more offensive than Thackeray on the subject of race is Carlyle. It is a fact that Caryle's admirers by and large choose to ignore. In 'The Nigger Question', Carlyle writes:

Do I, then, hate the Negro? No ... I decidedly like poor Qua-shee ... A swift, supple fellow; a merry-hearted grinning, dancing, singing affectionate kind of creature, with a great deal of melody and amenability in his composition.[20]

This appeared in 1849; in 'Shooting Niagara: and After?', published in 1867, his views are much the same:

One always rather likes the Nigger: evidently a poor blockhead with good dispositions, with affections, attachments – with a turn for Nigger Melodies and the like.[21]

Superficially, Carlyle's position resembles Thackeray's. Both argue for a hierarchy in society, with the black man in the role of servant, but the difference is that in Carlyle there is not a trace of self-questioning. His contempt fuels the mentality of colonialism, preparing the ground for late-century 'Jingoism'. But his position is even more unsavoury than this, for, as Harold Bloom maintains, 'It is Carlyle, and not his critic Nietszche, who is the true forerunner of twentieth-century fascism, with its mystical exaltation of the state and its obliteration of compassion and the rights of the individual'.[22] Thackeray is always too much of a sceptic to be lured in this direction; in *Philip*, the sense of a threat from an other always co-exists with self-doubt.

It is on a similar basis that we can draw a distinction between Thackeray and the 'Muscular' novelists of the period. There is an obvious area of overlap between Philip Firmin and Charles Kingsley's 'manly' heroes, and, as might be expected, novelists such as Kingsley, Thomas Hughes and G.A. Lawrence share Thackeray's impatience with psychological interiority. But their heroes are not – or, at least, not meant to be – as off-putting as Philip. The issue of violence might clarify the difference. The Muscular novelists have few reservations about violence: in G.A. Lawrence, for example, as John Sutherland puts it, the hero 'degenerates into the condition of a thug in evening dress'.[23] But such a hero is presented as the hope for his race rather than as a misfit out of his time. What is also noticeably absent in Thackeray is the idea found in works such as *Hereward the Wake* and *Brakespeare* of a mystical celebration of the English national struggle. Along with Carlyle, the Muscular novelists represent the cruder edge of a national debate, revealing a desire for conviction in a period of change; fear is transformed into political dogma, with characteristics that will eventually lead towards fascism. Thackeray's fiction might be provoked by a similar sense of insecurity, but his fears about the present do not lead him to believe that anything can be salvaged from the past or that any hope can be held out for the future. It is a deeper pessimism, in which nothing really counts for very much except death.

It is, of course, no defence of Thackeray to suggest that, although he is a racist writer, some of his contemporaries are even more unpalatable. But it is interesting to explore the nature of his reactionary stance and the curious way that this expresses itself in *Philip*: in what seems like an involuntary nervous gesture, Woolcomb suddenly appears or is referred to when there is a tense scene for Philip.

For example, at a party Philip's relative Ringwood Twysden deliberately barges into him; Philip staggers and his coat rips, revealing 'a great, heartrending scar' (p. 358). Philip retreats into the garden where he again encounters his cousin Ringwood, but also 'Mr Woolcomb, whose countenance the lamps lit up in a fine lurid manner, and whose eyeballs gleamed in the twilight' (p. 358). Woolcomb does not appear all that often in the novel, yet by the end he does seem to have been one of the principal characters. The main reason for this is that his appearances are always associated with moments such as this, when Philip is not only humiliated but his pride in his social class is challenged. At a later point in the novel, for example, Philip is angry at the way that his relative Philip Ringwood treats him. Pendennis comments: 'I cannot tell why this man's patronage chafed and goaded our worthy friend so as to drive him beyond the bounds of all politeness and reason' (p. 595). Ringwood's familiarity with Philip's wife is part of the problem, but in addition Philip feels he is not being accorded the respect that he merits. Woolcomb does not actually appear, but the novel makes an immediate shift from discussing Philip's marriage to discussing the state of Woolcomb's marriage. It is a repeated pattern in *Philip*: when questions are asked about Philip's status in society, Woolcomb is reintroduced. He pops up at these flashpoints as the person who might usurp the position that Philip believes to be his by right.

Philip is involved in a great many clashes in the novel, and, indeed, one of the things that most characterises *Philip* is the abrasiveness of the encounters between people. It is something that is encountered again and again; there is a constant note of anger and confrontation. At the very start of the novel, for example, we are told about Philip's grandfather: 'Firebrand Firmin, they used to call him – a red-headed fellow – a tremendous duellist' (p. 3). The essential thing about a duel is that it institutionalises, and so controls, the violent instincts in man, but a duel belongs to the past; in the present-day world of the novel the old checks on behaviour have disappeared. Pendennis, as narrator, represents a tolerant code, but most of the characters are at each others' throats. There might be a level at which the novel distinguishes Philip from the rest because of his bluff honesty (and certainly Pendennis insists, indeed overinsists, on Philip's kindness and gentleness), but the impression that actually comes across is that he is as violent as anyone else. One of the oddest moments in this respect is a comment Philip makes about Mrs Woolcomb:

'I wonder he has not Othello'd her,' remarks Philip, with his
hands in his pockets. 'I should, if she had been mine, and gone
on as they say she is going on.'   (p. 597)

There are various dimensions to this short speech, not least what we
might make of the phrase 'Othello'd her', but the central point of
interest is that there is a level of savagery in Philip himself that
matches the savagery detected in Woolcomb. What we might suggest is that what is most fearful in a stranger is the quality we do not
want to recognise in ourselves; the presence of Woolcomb helps
Thackeray come to a recognition of the violent instinct that is always
present in men. This is another way in which Thackeray stands
aside from the new assumptions of the Victorian period: rather
than accept the fiction of a sensitive, thoughtful, individualised
hero, there is an immovable idea of a capacity for violence in
human nature that cannot be tamed or assimilated.

It is at this point that many of Thackeray's critics would introduce
the idea of the gentleman, that there is a civilised stance that can be
adopted.[24] In *Philip*, however, there is a deeper failing of manliness
that undermines this social answer. Just as Woolcomb surfaces at
moments when Philip is engaged in a class challenge, he also reappears at key stages in Philip's emotional life. He is first introduced
as the 'besides' (p. 105), that explains why Agnes' parents will not let
her marry Philip. When Philip marries Charlotte, no sooner has the
reader been told that they are wed than they encounter Woolcomb
and his wife on the Champs Elysées (p. 332). And then, just after a
discussion of the poverty of Philip and his wife, there is a discussion
of Mrs Woolcomb's wealth, with the reservation that her wealth is
accompanied by her husband's cruelty (p. 450). In such scenes,
Woolcomb is seen both as a sexual rival to Philip and the opposite
of Philip in terms of conduct towards a partner. What also comes
across, however, is a kind of limpness in Philip. Dr Firmin had been
a sexual predator in his day and Woolcomb is seen as a sexual
predator, but there is something lacking about Philip. He throws
himself into confrontations with people, but the fact is that, except
for his hollow victory over Woolcomb at the end of the novel, he is
usually humiliated. He marries and has children, it is true, but there
is no real conviction in the courtship scenes; interestingly, the novel
mentions that Philip's father, for all his faults, married for love – 'a
match of the affections' (p. 11) – whereas it is hard to see any more to
Philip's choice of Charlotte beyond the fact that she is available.

Philip's lack of a certain kind of manliness is also seen in his working life, where he is forever dependent upon the help of others, including the benevolence of the vulgar Mugford. Most humiliating of all, however, is the fact that he has to rely upon his substitute-mother, Caroline Gann, to fight his battles for him, for it is Caroline who by her guile saves Philip from the financial clutches of Tufton Hunt. It is, more specifically, through her use of chloroform, still something of a medical novelty in 1862.[25] Philip has to rely, therefore, upon both a woman and a new invention to maintain his traditional role. Every detail adds to a sense of an impotent and inadequate hero; for all his bluster and readiness to fight, he is curiously unmanned.

If Woolcomb was white rather than black, *Philip* as a novel might have received rather more attention and praise, for, as against the over-sized and redundant hero, Woolcomb could be seen to represent a new, if cruel, energy that manifests itself in the Victorian age. A close parallel would be the upwardly mobile, wife-beating banker Barnes Newcome, in *The Newcomes*. *Philip* deals with a fundamental redistribution of power within nineteenth-century society, and part of this is a recognition that it is not just a money-making energy that has passed to people like Woolcomb but also sexual energy; the sources of productivity and creativity have been relocated. There is, therefore, potentially, a link between Philip and Woolcomb that could be as interesting as the link between David Copperfield and Steerforth. But when it comes to the crunch, *Philip* is too distorted by venom to stand as an analytic exploration of such issues. It is, however, a wrong-headed criticism that maintains *Philip* would be a better novel if it simply steered clear of racism; this is what Deborah Thomas suggests, who argues that racism obscures the true subject of the work.[26] It seems much more sensible to suggest that the peculiar power *Philip* does have as a novel is in no small measure generated by its hatred; rather than being a detached analysis of a process of social realignment, it emerges from the heart of the battle, snapping and spitting with resentment. It sympathises with its eponymous hero, who cannot adjust to the modern world, and who, in a curious way, through being so isolated and alienated, becomes the kind of psychological hero the novel does not want him to be. *Philip* is not a balanced performance, but, to the extent that it lets us explore Philip's antipathies, it does offer us a revelation of what lies behind one version of racism rather than being just an expression of racism.

IV

Thackeray liked to think of himself as a historian. The majority of his novels are set in the past, but *The Four Georges*, published in 1860, is his only real contribution to historical writing. Very much the work of an amateur, it serves, none the less, to remind us how popular history became in the Victorian period. It is easy to understand why: with the disintegration of traditional certainties, the Victorians endlessly sought new frames of interpretation and self-understanding. History was one of the most appealing. As Robin Gilmour writes:

> The various pasts which a period chooses to investigate, and the contemporary uses to which these pasts are put, tell us much about the anxieties of the present and the identity – or identities – which a society chooses to affirm.[27]

The past Thackeray most often chose to explore was the eighteenth century; indeed, although he is merely an amateur historian, he is often credited with creating the idea of a peaceful Augustan Age.[28] We, of course, are likely to stand aside from his view of the eighteenth century, to look with more than a little scepticism at the constructions he imposed upon the past. In so far as we read *The Four Georges* at all, we are going to read it as symptomatic of Thackeray's nineteenth-century anxieties rather than for what it might tell us about the eighteenth century. It is as well to bear this in mind if we are at all tempted to read the nineteenth-century *Philip* as a clue to, or anticipation of, twentieth-century racism. It is, on the face of it, a novel that is very much concerned with issues that engage us today; not just the issues of race and empire, but also the rejection in criticism today of a liberal humanist emphasis on the individual in favour of an analysis that focuses on class, race and gender. Thackeray is as uneasy with the notion of the individual as many modern critics are; indeed, Thackeray could even be argued to be fashionable in his views simply by virtue of being so old-fashioned.

But the drawing of parallels between the Victorian period and our own is inherently suspect; for the moment we begin to use history in this way we simplify and falsify both the past and the present. What is interesting about Thackeray's racism is that it is different from racism today and different from other manifestations of racism in the Victorian period (and, if we looked more closely at Carlyle and the Muscular novelists, we would see that they all have far less in common than might initially appear to be the case). Thackeray's racism might be crude in expression, but it is complex in its origins; similarly, racism at all times might have shared characteristics, but, as is the case with Thackeray's racism, it is also always the unique product of a particular culture and a specific historical situation. It is, of course, a twentieth-century awareness of racism and Britain's colonial past that prompts our current critical interest in these issues, but we soon arrive at a point where it is less than productive to conduct our own debates about national identity in the light of the state of affairs that prevailed over a hundred years ago; if the argument is conducted along these lines we are simply using an old pattern to try and make sense of a new pattern. A work like *Philip* might, therefore, provide us with a starting point for a discussion that moves beyond the text itself, but what *Philip* really illustrates, despite its crudeness of tone as a novel, is the complexity and mid-nineteenth century specificity of the issues it raises.

Notes

1.   William Makepeace Thackeray, *The Adventures of Philip*, vol. XVI of *The Oxford Thackeray* (London: Oxford University Press, 1908), p. 206. All references are to this edition.
2.   Patrick Brantlinger offers the best commentary on Thackeray and colonialism. In relation to the character of Rummum Loll in *The Newcomes*, for example, he makes the sort of astute remark that characterises his whole discussion: 'Thackeray's treatment of the Bengali businessman offers an especially clear instance of blaming the victim, a racist pattern that underwrites all imperialist ideology' – *Rule of Darkness: British Literature and Imperialism, 1830–1914* (Ithaca: Cornell University Press, 1988), p. 102. In the course of his chapter, 'Thackeray's India' (pp. 73–107), Brantlinger suggests that 'Thackeray's novels offer a clear expression of average, bourgeois, mid-Victorian values and ideas about many social issues' (p. 105). The gist of this present essay, however, is that Thackeray's position is, in the final estimate, far from representative.
3.   Little has been written on the subject of Thackeray's racism. One critic who does deal with the issue is John Sutherland in 'Thackeray as Victorian Racialist', *Essays in Criticism* XX (1970), 441–5. Sutherland focuses on Thackeray's use of Josiah Wedgwood's phrase 'Am I not a man and a brother too?' More recently, S.S. Prawer has published *Israel at Vanity Fair: Jews and Judaism in the Writings of W.M. Thackeray* (Leiden: Brill, 1992). Joseph E. Baker in 'Thackeray's Recantation', *PMLA* LXXVII (1962), 586–94, touches briefly on the issue of race in the course

of a discussion of the general unpleasantness of Thackeray's stance and attitudes in *Philip*. There is also Deborah A. Thomas's *Thackeray and Slavery* (1993), which is referred to in the course of this essay.

4. *Vanity Fair*, vol. XI of *The Oxford Thackeray* (London: Oxford University Press, 1908), p. 214.

5. Ibid., p. 7.

6. 'Commentators have noted Thackeray's animus against wealthy mulattoes...George P. Davies ascribes the hostility to Thackeray's resentment at his half-sister, Sarah Bleckynden, the illegitimate offspring of his father's Eurasian mistress.' John Sutherland (ed.), *Vanity Fair* (Oxford: Oxford University Press, 1983), p. 884.

7. Douglas A. Lorimer, *Colour, Class and the Victorians* (Leicester: Leicester University Press, 1978), p. 45. The best account of the growth of racialism in the mid-nineteenth century remains Lorimer's. Other books dealing with the subject include Kenneth Little, *Negroes in Britain: A Study of Race Relations in English Society* (London, Kegan Paul, Trench, Trubner, 1947) and James Walvin, *Black and White: The Negro and English Society, 1555–1945* (London, Allen Lane, 1973).

8. Op. cit., p. 252.

9. *The Letters of William Makepeace Thackeray*, ed. Gordon Ray (New York, Octagon, 1980), vol. 2, p. 199.

10. See Lorimer's chapter, 'English Opinion on the Negro in the American Civil War', op.cit., pp. 162–77.

11. *The Virginians*, vol. XV of *The Oxford Thackeray* (London: Oxford University Press, 1908), p. 934.

12. See Folarin Shyllon, *Black People in Britain, 1555–1833* (London: Oxford University Press, 1977), pp. 106–7, and Lorimer, op.cit., pp. 147, 151, 160.

13. Deborah A. Thomas, *Thackeray and Slavery* (Athens: Ohio University Press, 1993), p. 167.

14. The General Eyre case of 1865 brought out into the open the attitudes of many leading Victorians. Charles Kingsley, however, who we might expect to see noisily airing his views, was extremely hesitant about openly committing himself in support of Eyre. And with good reason, for even though Kingsley deliberated over his words and actions, there was a rift with his former friends Thomas Hughes (author of *Tom Brown's Schooldays*) and John Ludlow on the issue of race. See Susan Chitty, *The Beast and the Monk: A Life of Charles Kingsley* (London: Hodder and Stoughton, 1974), pp. 241–2.

15. *The Exposure of Luxury: Radical Themes in Thackeray* (London: Peter Owen, 1972), pp. 161–88.

16. See Juliet McMaster, 'Funeral Baked Meats: Thackeray's Last Novel', *Studies in the Novel* XIII (1981), p. 141. McMaster recognises 'an intense though intermittent energy' (p. 133) in *Philip*, and sees it as 'deeply disturbing' (p. 133), particularly 'the panic and hatred within, the irrational fantasies and suppressed desperation...' (p. 136) It is a brilliant essay, McMaster being one of the few critics who recognises that *Philip* is not just a tired novel in which Thackeray defends the

gentleman, but her essay does weaken a little towards the end as she makes too many connections between Philip and Thackeray himself.

17.   On Victorian notions of the family, see, for example, David Mussel-white, *Partings Welded Together* (London: Methuen, 1987), pp. 140–1.
18.   Mary Poovey, *Uneven Developments: The Ideological Work of Gender in Mid-Victorian England* (London: Virago, 1989), p. 89.
19.   'I am haunted by the human chimpanzees I saw along that 100 miles of horrible country. To see white chimpanzees is dreadful; if they were black, one would not feel it so much. But their skins are as white as ours'. Quoted in Chitty, op. cit., p. 209. Kingsley's book about a trip to the West Indies – *At Last: A Christmas in the West Indies* (London: Macmillan, 1871) – is surprisingly benign in tone. With Kingsley, there is always a sense of a gap between his public statements and his private sentiments.
20.   Thomas Carlyle, 'Occasional Discourse on the Nigger Question', in *The Works of Thomas Carlyle* (London: The Chesterfield Society, n.d.), vol. XVI, p. 302.
21.   Ibid., p. 424.
22.   *Thomas Carlyle: Modern Critical Views* (New York: Chelsea House, 1986), p. 14.
23.   *The Longman Companion to Victorian Fiction* (Harlow: Longman, 1988), p. 453. David Rosen discusses G.A. Lawrence's 'muscular Blackguard-ism' in 'The Volcano and the Cathedral: Muscular Christianity and the Origins of Primal Manliness', in Donald E. Hall (ed.), *Muscular Christianity: Embodying the Victorian Age* (Cambridge: Cambridge University Press, 1994), pp. 17–34.
24.   'And as he grew older he did tend to retreat into the seeming safety of gentlemanly prejudice, in novels like *The Virginians* and *Philip*' – Robin Gilmour, *The Idea of the Gentleman in the Victorian Novel* (London: George Allen and Unwin, 1981), p. 38.
25.   See A.J. Youngson, *The Scientific Revolution in Victorian Medicine* (New York: Holmes and Meier, 1979), p. 122.
26.   Op.cit., p. 187.
27.   *The Victorian Period: The Intellectual and Cultural Context of English Literature 1830–1890* (Harlow: Longman, 1993), p. 31.
28.   See A. Dwight Culler, *The Victorian Mirror of History* (New Haven and London: Yale University Press, 1985), p. 14.

9

The Reason for Drinking in Hardy's *The Mayor of Casterbridge*

Steven Earnshaw

'I don't drink,' he said in a low, halting, apologetic voice. 'You hear, Susan? – I don't drink now – I haven't since that night.' Those were his first words. – *The Mayor of Casterbridge*

'I am as willing as any man to have a free trade in beer, but let us have some control over it' – Sir Thomas Gooch (1830)[1]

In 1830 'The Beerhouse Act' came into force. For the price of two guineas paid to the Excise anyone could sell beer. This was not simply a freeing-up of trade for the sake of *laissez-faire* economic philosophy, it was in part a measure to control the consumption of alcohol through encouraging people to switch from spirits to weaker alcoholic beverages. If beer were sold separately, people wouldn't get so drunk, or so the thinking went. It would also, according to the free-traders, 'advance morality' and 'national prosperity',[2] and would even help promote democracy.[3] Another factor behind the Beerhouse Act may have been an attempt to win popularity for a faltering government.[4] It was also seen as a gesture towards the ending of hierarchical privilege – the tax on beer then seen as an indirect tax on the poor, as Thomas Paine had once complained.[5] Before the Act came into force the licensing system gave magistrates sole control over the renewal of licences each year, a power that was seen as an outdated preserve of the upper classes which some thought should be overturned.[6]

For the rest of the century the drink question vexed Victorian society, embodying the age's struggle to come to terms with itself, the desire to control free trade not the least of the paradoxes generated (see Gooch's gaffe above). If there was an argument that

142

tax on alcohol hit the poor in the same way that expensive bread did, the Chartists could later argue that the government reduced taxes on alcohol to keep the working classes drinking rather than thinking;[7] if it could be argued that drinking was good for the economy 'and would save English agriculture',[8] it could also be argued by temperance reformers that the trade in drink led to 'trade depression'.[9] For the medical profession, intemperance might be the cause of 90 per cent of all insanity, or, conversely, 'there was a direct correlation between the amount of beer and wine insane patients consumed and the speed of their recovery'.[10] Temperance reformers blamed moral failing when someone turned to drink, whereas the socialists blamed the poverty-stricken environment, and thus absolved individual responsibility. In turn the socialists had to answer the argument that drinking was at its most virulent when times were most prosperous.[11] The temperance movement itself became riven with opposing aims and philosophies, especially that between the 'moral suasionists', who had given the main impetus to the movement in the 1830s, and 'the legal suppressionists' ('prohibitionists'), whose United Kingdom Alliance for the Suppression of the Traffic in all Intoxicating Liquours (UKA) was formed in 1853. For the UKA it was the government's duty to stop the trade in drink, in other words, it was primarily a legal issue, although it is also true that they could argue that the government shirked its moral responsibility by not prohibiting drink traffic. For the moral suasionists, on the other hand, it was a question of individual agency. As Joseph Livesey, founder of the English Total Abstinence Movement put it, 'the evil is in the drink, not in the trade'.[12] Although the effect upon legislation by the activities of the temperance movement was not great, its power filtered through in other ways, (adversely) powerful enough by the end of the century to (allegedly) contribute to the defeat of the Liberal Party in 1895, after the Liberals had formally aligned themselves with the temperance campaigners in 1890.[13] Before then the argument had not been drawn up along party lines, although even in 1874 Gladstone was blaming drink for his defeat at the general election.[14]

Although there had been problems with drink in the eighteenth century, notably gin, 'drunkenness carried no social stigma'.[15] We have only to think of the attitude adopted towards drink in *Tom Jones* (1749), particularly Mr Western, or *The Adventures of Joseph Andrews* (1742) to see that no one thought especially ill of heavy drinkers or drinking in general, notwithstanding the evil of gin.[16] According to Lillian Lewis Shiman the change in attitude arose in the nineteenth century, where 'The "work discipline" concept brought into being by industrialisation transformed drunkenness from a personal state of excess socialibility into an anti-social vice'.[17] The change in attitude is identifiable in novels. Indeed, Mairi McCormick turns to fiction for a record of first depictions of alcoholics because they are not available in medical records. 'First representations of the gamma alcoholic in the English novel' can be found in fiction from 1830 onwards, whereas gamma alcoholism was still not recognised 'in 1850 by the learned professions'.[18] Elsewhere, John Peck notes the change in attitude towards drink and drunkenness occurring within the space of a few years. Thackeray's 1848 novel *Vanity Fair*, 'an astonishing drinks manual of the early nineteenth century', 'seems entirely free of any air of moral condemnation' amongst all of the drinking, whereas *The Newcomes*, published only seven years later, is on the defensive, thanks to the general change in social attitudes.[19]

As well as the role of the state in trade and morality, drink was also a distinctly class issue, as has already been suggested. The temperance movement is (and was) often seen as a body which foisted middle-class interests upon the lower classes. More accurately, there was an alliance between certain sections of the middle classes and the respectable working classes as regards temperance, with a kind of closing of the circle whereby the debauched leisure classes were on a par with the lower orders when it came to loutish drinking habits.[20] But with the Drink Question what was also at stake, in retrospect, was the limit of reason: 'as rationalistic movements growing out of the enlightenment, abstainers and free licensers had fears in common: of traditionalist class privilege (consolidated through the licensing system), and of urban populations maddened by gin'.[21] The use of reason meant that anything connected with the old, medieval hierarchy had to go, and that the masses should be kept within reason at all times – hence the ban on alcohol at the Great Exhibition in 1851, 'following pressure from temperance campaigners'.[22] Drunkenness and insanity were also quite commonly linked, most likely because the symptoms were regarded as similar.[23] Why would a rational person drink, when all it could lead to was 'crime, pauperism, disease, insanity'?[24]

The issue of drink takes us to the heart of our comprehension of the Victorians: we see their desire for social engineering, that is, the

application of reason to society; we observe their appeal to individual agency in a world which, as it became more anonymous for
any one individual, was now tending to grant psychological uniqueness to those very same individuals; and there is their belief that
moral and financial well being were compatible and achievable
through self-discipline. The issue of drink sets us firmly and
squarely into the middle of discussions concerning industrialisation,
class perception and the rise of mass entertainment. For Brian Harrison in *Drink and the Victorians*, 'the history of the temperance
movement... [is] of the greatest historical interest if one wishes to
understand how we differ from the Victorians'.[25] He also points out
that 'Whereas the twentieth century idolizes "heroes of consumption", the nineteenth idolized "heroes of abstinence" '.[26] It is here
that the broader cultural outlook is apparent: our approach to life in
its postmodern mode tends to be 'both/and', in effect there is no
pressing need to choose between alternatives, we can have it all
ways, or, obversely, can find no reason to select one thing over
another. This compares to the Victorian 'either/or' *Weltanschaaung*,
exemplified by their attitude to drink – drink and you will suffer
disease, poverty, violence, insanity, waste and death; give up drink
and you will live in domestic bliss and affluence.

Classifying the Victorian attitude towards drink as one of abhor-
rence is obviously to re-iterate a particular view that passes for
Victorian, the view of the metropolitan middle classes and respectable working classes. The twentieth-century official attitude to
'drugs', drawing its arguments from discourses in medicine, law,
education and popular (usually conservative) conceptions, is often
indistinguishable from the nineteenth-century public outcry against
drink: 'just say no'. The idea that certain drugs are recreational and
under control, in the manner that drinking is a social activity when
not debilitatingly addictive, is found difficult to accept. This is
further complicated by our own fascination when people *are* addicts
(Irvine Welsh's *Trainspotting* is the most recent example), in much
the same way that the best advertisements for the temperance
advocates were reformed characters who could detail the depths
of depravity they had suffered. Where we differ, perhaps, is that for
the Victorians it was relatively easy to demonise alcohol, whereas an
absolute concept such as that of evil lacks common acceptance in the
late twentieth century. Nevertheless, there must be a certain *frisson*
attached to our looking into the extremes of consumption similar to
that of the Victorians, the idea that there is no way back from

addiction. We might state that our medical understanding of the physiological, psychological and nutritional value of drink is much greater than that of the Victorians, so that we are able come to terms with drink in a more effective manner. For example, the law, supposedly backed by medical evidence, states precisely how many units of alcohol we can consume before it is unsafe to drive. We are also able to acknowledge, unlike the Victorians, that there is a difference between drunkenness and alcoholism.[27] Undoubtedly we believe that our attitude to drink is a sensible one, or that at least we know what a sensible attitude to adopt is, since we have all the facts to hand. Yet no matter how far we think we may have come since the Victorians, we still flounder when it comes to drink. English licensing law has only recently changed from what was essentially legislation emerging from debates during the First World War, in itself a carry-over from Victorian beliefs about the evils of drink and the demoralising effect it had on the working classes. Every few months information regarding the beneficial or deleterious nature of drink issues forth from health bodies and the government,[28] and the physiological and psychological effects of alcohol remain unclear and surrounded by myths.[29] Given all this current confusion, in conjunction with the variety of responses to drink in the Victorian period as they came to terms with new pressures caused by industrialisation and the inroads of enlightenment progress, what does drink tell us about the Victorians and our relationship to them?

Annette Federico in her discussion of the Victorian novel and addiction[30] goes out of her way to show that our interest in characters in Victorian fiction is most likely to be in those consuming alcohol or opium, since they are the ones who face existential despair. The implication is that we are farthest from those characters who exhibit what we have come to see as representative Victorian values, 'hard work, energy, self-help, individualism, earnestness, domesticity',[31] and, conversely, hypocrisy and dogmatism. Federico discusses alcoholics in Gaskell's *Mary Barton*, Ann Brontë's *The Tenant of Wildfell Hall*, and George Eliot's 'Janet's Repentance' in *Scenes of Clerical Life*. In conclusion she wishes to 'stress especially the idea that alcoholism is a spiritual illness, a crisis in understanding, even an existential dilemma, since in its self-destructiveness drug addiction is not far from suicide'.[32] It is tempting to follow this route, to show that the most distance we have put between ourselves and the public Victorian world (that of the middle class and the respectable working class) is in our refusal to accept their work ethics and moral codifications, and that we are closest to them when we descend into our subjective depths, into our singular consciousnesses to face a world without meaning. Alcoholism is then seen as an exercise in existential freedom akin to self-annihilation. We could further refine our charting of epistemic change by adding the postmodern twist, that rather than despairing at a world without value we celebrate our freedom to create whatever worlds we want, free to do it chemically either to enhance our mood or to alter our perception, to dip into whichever consciousness takes our fancy. The alcoholics of the Victorian era would then be the forebears of the collapse of a cohesive society and the champions of postmodern consumption. But this depends upon too narrow an understanding of drink in its Victorian context. The idea that the alcoholics in the fiction discussed by Federico represent some attempt on each author's part to look into the abyss is overplayed. Compare any of these vignettes with Lowry's *Under the Volcano* to understand what such a work would really look like, or with Patrick Hamilton's *Hangover Square*. To be sure, the addicts Federico cites have lost faith in religion and the values of society, but they are there precisely to underscore the necessity for an ethical framework by showing the antisocial nature of addiction, drink and drugs (I am using the cultural and social distinction which differentiates drink from drugs). They are not there to undermine the Victorian moral universe through antiheroic rebellion. Given the economic, social and symbolic significance of drink to the Victorians, I would like to look at Hardy's *The Mayor of Casterbridge*, since it too is permeated by drink in a number of ways, and see how we might understand this novel in its relation to the Victorians, as well as using it as an opportunity to understand our own relationship to the Victorians, drink, and related issues.

The narrator of Hardy's novel informs us towards the end that Casterbridge has for many years been an assize town.[33] In the course of the novel's events it is the nature of man that is measured in Casterbridge, as one might do with bread and ale – the two are linked in the minds of the Casterbridge inhabitants, as when someone tells Susan Henchard 'There's less good bread than good beer in Casterbridge now' (p. 33) – and Hardy's measure of man is his measure of Henchard. In its own way, then, *The Mayor of Casterbridge* is a measure of Victorian society, and Hardy has used the framework of what appears to be a straightforward temperance narrative with which to do it.[34] Henchard's drunkenness leads to the break-up of the family unit, literally, when he sells his wife at a fair after too much to drink. He repents, swears to abstain from strong liquor, and subsequently becomes a successful business man with attendant social status in the local community. His later decline is exacerbated by his return to drink. Nothing could be clearer. Drink is the ruin of domesticity and prosperity, whereas temperance enables a man to devote his energies to the pursuit of wealth, respectability and high moral standing. How accurate is this?

We can provisionally discount the temperance gloss that would see the initial scenario as a case where the husband's drinking is to blame for the family's poverty since Henchard has in fact come looking for work.[35] That Henchard does drink is made clear, but it is also stated later that Henchard 'had been given to bouts only, and was not a habitual drunkard' (p. 29). The fact that Henchard is not an alcoholic places him firmly within the social fabric rather than making him a more extreme case, that of the addict. This is especially so since, as Barr notes, '[agricultural] work was sporadic and seasonal, and [the workers] had tended to fill in the gaps with drink. They did not take regular holidays, but indulged in random drinking sprees'.[36] It is also worth noting that Susan takes a milder version of the rum-laced furmity when Henchard drinks at the fair without the same consequent desire to drink until drunk, in other words, the liquor is not seen as inherently addictive.[37] Nor is this the result of the trade in drink itself. The first tent is licensed whereas the second provides smuggled spirit, a state of affairs suggesting that no matter what, people will want to drink and that there will be ways and means to drink regardless of the law of the land. It also scotches the idea that by making alternative refreshments available the desire for drink can be displaced. There is neither a defence of drink nor a castigation of drink, yet drink lies at the heart of the story.

The morning after selling his wife Henchard regrets his actions, but before searching for her he wishes to register an oath, 'a greater oath than he had ever sworn before: and to do it properly he required a fit place and imagery; for there was something fetichistic in this man's beliefs' (pp. 17–18). The fit place is the church where he declares ' "I, Michael Henchard ... do take an oath before God here in this solemn place that I will avoid all strong liquors for the space of twenty-one years to come, being a year for every year that I have lived. And this I swear upon the book before me" ' (p. 18). The oath is rough and ready but does suggest an acquaintance with temperance oaths.[38] The inclusion of a time period looks like Hardy's own dramatic invention, but there is a suggestion that, by abstaining for exactly the same time period he has already lived, he is in some way redeeming time, making himself morally useful. By making himself morally useful he is thus symbolically placed at the centre of Victorian society, since, as Harrison argues, the Victorians placed stress on 'individual moral effort', something lacking in the twentieth century thanks to the inroads made by Marx and Freud.[39] Henchard's act is symbolically central in another way. It has been argued that the rise of capitalism shifted the state's understanding of time into a conceptualisation which was (is) antagonistic to personal time (or the older, task-oriented agricultural time). In redeeming time there is a sense in which Henchard is allying himself with Victorian capitalism.[40] Further to this, the refusal to drink takes him out of the pattern of behaviour where drinking patterns had been essential to social bonding in 'pre-industrial artisan society' and into the 'purely market economy' of industrialisation.[41] The swearing of the oath in a church gives the religious spin to the story, and follows the temperance narrative paradigm of offering paradise on earth after the repentance of the sinner.[42] Initially what is at issue, it seems, is the question of character, and since we are at this point in the essay dealing with the measure of man, let us look more closely at Henchard's character.

What are the possible ways of viewing character in the Victorian period? There is the residual idea of universal man, with his universal faults, essentially, the 'classic ideal', with states of affairs to a large extent preordained. Arguably the dominant notion is that of man as an autonomous agent, with his life in his own hands (Protestantism). And then there is the emerging notion of man as a product of his environment (the socialist view). We might see a mixture of all three in the novel. The world the characters inhabit is fatalistic in tone, the drama of human affairs played out in an indifferent universe. Hardy even places some of the action in a Roman amphitheatre as if to underscore the point. But against this there also appears to be a sense in which people have their futures in their own hands, as in the success of Donald Farfrae, Henchard's friend turned rival, even if the narrator puts part of this success down to Farfrae's background, northern energy against a more easy-going south. It is 'with the instinct of a perverse character' that Henchard espies the furmity woman's trick of lacing the drinks with something stronger (p. 6). Why should this be perverse?

It is as if Henchard deliberately seeks out what is not natural or, possibly, what the order of things hides, as if he wants to go against what is natural. Is 'character' natural? At one point in the novel the narrator states: 'Character is Fate, said Novalis, and Farfrae's character was just the reverse of Henchard's, who might not inaptly be described as Faust has been described – as a vehement gloomy being who had quitted the ways of vulgar men without light to guide him on a better way' (p. 131). So according to the narrative's logic Henchard's character is his destiny, and it is thus his perversity which will determine his life.

The drinking leads him to sell his wife; although he has talked about doing this before, he has not gone through with it. Here it would seem that drink is very much to blame since it is the spur for an action that has only been a 'harmless' jest in the past. But as a drinking man he is also very much a part of his culture. It is the consequent renunciation of drink which sets him apart from the rest of Casterbridge. In other words, his refusal to drink is what makes him so unusual, a genuine sign of his perversity. Drinking is the norm, as the amount of time spent in the public houses in Casterbridge attests to. But what does this signify? There is a grim irony at work. Henchard swears his pledge in a church, before God. He is making his pact with God to abstain, which contrasts with the Faustian reference attached to him and the implication of a pact with the devil. The logic of this would be that, indeed, as temperance reformers consistently argued, drink is evil.

Hardy then skips the next nineteen years when Henchard becomes prosperous and mayor and magistrate. The good times, under God's aegis, are of no interest. What does interest the author (and us) is watching Henchard slide back to destitution. During these nineteen years Henchard has mastered his own perversity. He has been the Victorian ideal man of action, raising himself up from nothing, the autonomous agent. It is as if the novel is saying yes, this Victorian dream of the hero as self-made man is possible, and to reiterate the point Farfrae does the same. Nor does the latter have to go to America to make his fortune, as was his original plan. More importantly, he has not had to renounce drink. On the one hand Hardy gives us a picture of men who can take their lives in their own hands and prosper, rise to the top, that is, the Victorian's ideal masculine self-image, but on the other hand he can show that for no good reason at all prosperity is in the lap of the Gods. Now of course this might simply be chalked up to Hardy's pessimism, fatalism or scepticism, depending on which shade we prefer, and I would not argue against this. But in addition I think we might also pick out something else. By renouncing drink Henchard also renounces his society. It appears from our current perspective that the kind of personality which had the strength to carry out such an oath also had the kind of will-power to succeed in business.[43] But such will-power is not natural to Henchard in the sense that he must hold down his natural character in order to persevere.[44]

In some ways, the universe's indifference to human striving is mirrored in the narrative's attitude to drink and the nature of drink. Henchard's lot is not much different from others when we first meet him, and it is noteworthy that we do not find out his name until he swears the oath (the morning after the night before he wonders whether he gave his name out to the crowd in the tent and is relieved to remember he hasn't, p. 17). He is thus not named as an individual self until he goes against his natural self, that is, he is not a unique individual until he has transformed his being into a kind of self-consciousness, or consciousness of the self of Michael Henchard. By naming himself as an abstainer he separates himself from his immediate society. His first words to Susan on their reunion are 'I don't drink', the one guarantee he can give to his wife that he has changed character. Drink is throughout symbolic of his volcanic nature, since its own effects are unstable, and to renounce this is to renounce his nature. In contemplating what might have happened to Henchard before she finds out he is still alive, Susan thinks: 'He had possibly drunk himself into his tomb. But he might, on the other hand, have had too much sense to do so' because he wasn't 'a habitual drunkard' (p. 29). It is in his nature to be inconsistent since consistency would mean being habitually drunk or a teetotaller. Stirling Haig believes that rather than the characters being fixed, as 'character is fate' would suggest, 'the characters are portrayed in a constant state of suspension marked by fluidity and rootlessness' (p. 56) and traces this in the motif of 'water' used throughout the novel. He makes the interesting observation that 'Henchard is either up or down, which is to say *dry* or *wet*' (p. 56). For our own purposes we can see that this is in accord with the idea of trying to fix life in some way (through the Victorian archetype rather than giving in to the vagaries of self). To be dry (sober) is to be fixed, to be wet is to be prey to contingency. But I also think it points to the distinction between character and self. The former is 'assumed' by Henchard as he rises to the top, the latter is what he emerges from and slips back into. Character is fate only in the sense that if Henchard adopts a Victorian character his fate is sealed (he becomes the successful business man), but without character he is back with his existential, contingent self – fluid, 'wet'. It is perhaps the novel's own confusion between 'character' and 'self' that has led to the many discussions on the significance of the narrator's comment that 'character is fate'.

With respect to self rather than character, late on in the narrative we are given a small insight into the novel's view of the psychology of the mind, and this also helps explain why drink may or may not be regarded as 'evil' in the novel and the society it describes. When Henchard discovers that Elizabeth-Jane is to marry the one man he would wish her not to, Farfrae, he thinks of wrecking the whole plan by telling Farfrae that Elizabeth is 'legally, nobody's child'. Such information in a society built upon respectability would be devastating. This is how the narrator understands human psychology: 'There is an outer chamber of the brain in which thoughts unowned, unsolicited, and of noxious kind, are sometimes allowed to wander for a moment prior to being sent off whence they came. One of these thoughts sailed into Henchard's ken now'. Henchard dismisses it with, ' "God forbid such a thing! Why should I still be subject to these visitations of the devil, when I try so hard to keep him away?" ' (p. 354). It is evident that Henchard's struggle with moral self-worth is a struggle with what he chooses to see as the work of the devil, the temptation to do evil, as he himself sees it. The temperance oath has thus been part of this longer struggle. Looking back at his life from this particular psychological viewpoint it can be seen that drink was the catalyst to allow 'these visitations of the devil' to come to the fore, but also the 'twenty-one years' is to be seen as a self-imposed sentence, since once it is over he feels he can drink 'with a good conscience' (p. 270). On the day the pledge is over Henchard also says that he means 'to enjoy myself', making clear the distinction that business is not pleasure. The twenty-one years thus represent the novel's version of Victorian earnestness.

Hardy has taken what might be seen as the biggest threat and/or temptation to individual will-power in Victorian society and shown that that society will neither be dragged down by drink nor dragged up by teetotalism. The intersection of drink and a particular personality might have dire consequences, but even here the argument against drink is not allowed much leeway. The novel refuses to allow drink to be the scapegoat for all society's troubles, as many avowed. What of the society that Henchard takes himself out of?

The town is quite clearly differentiated along class lines, or, to be more precise, along a hierarchical line of social respectability, through symbolic use of the three public houses, the King's Arms, the Three Mariners, and Peter's Finger. At the top of the heap is the King's Arms. It is here that Susan first sees Henchard when she arrives in Casterbridge, where he is presiding over the Great Public Dinner as mayor. Not only is the hotel at the top of the social ladder, it is representative of what we might call 'official England', associated through its name to the monarchy, through its function to the official business in Casterbridge, and through an 'incidental' descriptive touch, to Englishness: the band is playing 'The Roast Beef of Olde England' directly in front of it (p. 35). Having risen therefore to the top of middle-class society, Henchard takes his place at the head of Casterbridge's version of the state and monarchy. By redeeming his time into moral time, that is, capitalist time, he gets his just rewards (see above). By turning himself into Victorian man he places himself at the head of Victorian society, at the expense of sociability and pleasure (unofficial Victorian society) – as Susan notices, his wine glasses are empty (p. 37). The narrator makes a point of detailing the ritual of social drinking in which Henchard takes no part (p. 38). It is at this function someone points up that Henchard is responsible for the recent bad wheat/bread in the town and asks what he is to do about it.

> 'But what are you going to do to repay us for the past?' inquired the man who had before spoken, and who seemed to be a baker or miller. 'Will you replace the grown flour we've still got by sound grain?'
> Henchard's face had become still more stern at these interruptions, and he drank from his tumbler of water as if to calm himself or gain time. Instead of vouchsafing a direct reply, he stiffly observed –
> 'If anybody will tell me how to turn grown wheat into wholesome wheat I'll take it back with pleasure. But it can't be done.'
> (p. 41)

Hardy is piling on the ironies in this section. The lightest hint of irony is the narrator's uncertainty as to whether Henchard takes water to calm himself, in implicit contradistinction to (the missing) alcohol which would inflame him and exacerbate his irascibility, or whether it is used to gain time, and is thus a twist on Henchard's oath to redeem time.

Repaying the past is of course what Henchard's temperance oath represents, the attempt to redeem the past through making himself into a wholesome character. Yet this is in the face of his observation that in nature such a thing is not possible. It is Farfrae who shows him how to restore the overgrown wheat. Henchard declares: ' "It's complete! – quite restored, or – well – nearly." ' Farfrae returns with ' "Quite enough restored to make good seconds out of it.... To fetch it back entirely is impossible; Nature won't stand so much as that, but here you go a great way towards it" ' (p. 53). There is an implicit warning, that by tampering with nature (Henchard's oath goes against his own nature) there is a limit on how much it is possible to achieve. With Henchard's later reversion to bad ways the novel appears to bear out the observation that Nature will only stand so much, that the restoration of a good (Edenic?) nature is only a temporary measure (the significance of Henchard's 'redemptive' oath fittingly in the church suggestive in the light of this of atonement for the Fall). Man's nature is thus more akin to Henchard's pre-oath days, and, by implication, Victorian society's moral worth is, and can only be, 'temporary'.

As the narrative shows Henchard spiritually separate from his social environment through his teetotalism, it also shows how drink bonds that society, showing that the teetotaller's lot is a lonely one. He briefly leaves the dinner at the hotel to look for Farfrae. When he returns 'The Corporation, private residents, and major and minor tradesmen had, in fact, gone in for comforting beverages to such an extent that they had quite forgotten, not only the Mayor, but all those vast political, religious, and social differences which they felt necessary to maintain in the daytime, and which separated them like iron grills' (p. 45). So, far from drink being represented as the evil in society, it is the bringer in this instance of a conviviality that crosses all social divides. Henchard at this time is not a part of it.

After Farfrae has passed a message to Henchard to the effect that he knows of a process to restore the taste of grown wheat, Henchard automatically assumes Farfrae has put up at the most respectable place, the King's Arms. However, Henchard is informed that Farfrae has gone to the Three Mariners. The name of the pub itself suggests a more down-to-earth crowd, defined by its homage to an occupation rather than the monarchy, although like the King's Arms it can still claim to be part of English tradition since it dates back to Elizabethan times. It is also the case that the narrator, in a rare value judgement,[45] approves of the place: 'This ancient house of accommodation for man and beast, now, unfortunately, pulled down' (pp. 45–6), and further, 'The good stabling and the good ale of the Mariners... (were) perseveringly sought out by the sagacious old heads who knew what was what in Casterbridge' (p. 47). 'Inside these illuminated holes [windows], at a distance of about three inches, were ranged at this hour, as every passer knew, the ruddy polls of Billy Wills the glazier, Smart the shoe-maker, Buzzford the general dealer, and others of a secondary set of worthies, of a grade somewhat below that of the diners at the King's Arms, each with his yard of clay' (p. 46). What this description does is give a good sense of the social make-up of Casterbridge, in addition to that of those attending the public dinner (and later rounded off with a description of the public house at the lowest end of the social scale, Peter's Finger). What differentiates these from those at the King's Arms, apart from the obvious 'secondary' social standing, is that this is not a special occasion, that these are regulars, frittering away their time without regard for the demands of state or governance. There is no sense of progression, of Enlightenment reason channelled into the success of capitalism, there is only sameness. That the Three Mariners has disappeared by the time the narrative is related perhaps vouchsafes for the disappearance of the older way of life and rhythm that the thrusting Victorian dynamos and their investment in 'time' have usurped, men like the sober Henchard and Farfrae, along with the new machinery. Not only then is drink the great social leveller, as described in the King's Arms, it is the representative, in its middle social setting, of the link with the traditional, unofficial past.[46]

The issue of respectability as crucial to Victorian society is further enhanced in a couple of ways. When Henchard seeks Farfrae in the Three Mariners, he deliberately tones down his appearance before entering. When Elizabeth-Jane and Susan arrive in Casterbridge, on looking for a respectable place they decide to follow Farfrae who himself looks respectable. They must choose somewhere respectable even if they can't afford it, although there is also the worry that the Three Mariners is not respectable enough and would be an embarrassment to Henchard if he discovered they had stayed there. Once here Elizabeth-Jane has to work to pay off some of the cost of their lodging, a fact that returns to haunt her when her own maid later on brings up the incident to humble her in front of Henchard.

In completing the panoramic view of the social strata of Caster-bridge the story finally takes us to the region inhabited by the lower classes, where vice runs freely 'in and out of certain doors of the neighbourhood' (p. 293). At the heart of it is Mixen Lane, 'the inn called Peter's Finger was the church' – again the connection between religion and alcohol not too metaphorically distant. 'It was centrally situate, as such places should be, and bore about the same social relation to the Three Mariners as the latter bore to the King's Arms' (p. 295). (There is the suggestion of a joke on Hardy's part, with the main body of people 'the three mariners' and either end of society represented by the body's extremities, arms and fingers.) It is in Peter's Finger that we find that the furmity woman mixes with poachers and others. The narrator makes the point that nothing has changed in the time that both Henchard and Farfrae have been mayors. It's as if the story has given us the drama of public Victorian society by showing us the only area where it is actually capable of dramatic movement, in the new middling classes, with the upper and lower classes static. (Farfrae has the chance to be a 'gentleman', that is, the opportunity to live off residual wealth thanks to Lucetta's money, but refuses it, as if there were no life there, the only action available being that of monetary mobility and respectability, the cut and thrust of the marketplace.) At the other end, the life of the inhabitants of the Three Mariners appears change-less, as does the kind of life enjoyed by the frequenters of Peter's Finger. Like those who enjoy hereditary wealth, their lives are untouched by the Victorian great and good. Symbolically, the func-tion of those linked to Peter's Finger is to disrupt this Victorian edifice. The mere existence of Mixen Lane and Peter's Finger shows a distinct lack of civic progress and the unreachable nature of certain sections of society. We are taken there to show the hatch-ing of the skimmity-ride, an old tradition whereby a couple of worthies are mocked by a ride through town of their effigies. The discovery of love letters between Lucetta and Henchard is the occa-sion for this year's mockery. It leads to Lucetta's death and Hench-ard's confrontation with his own image and death. Hardy also juxtaposes the preparations for the skimmity-ride with the prepara-tions for the royal visit to emphasise the undermining of the received image of what is worthy and what is not. By doing so he closes that circle that was often drawn by comparing the habits o the upper classes to those of the lower (as mentioned above). It is perhaps noticeable that Jopp is distracted from going about his errands by the temptation of the public house, drawn into the idle time that Peter's Finger offers. In all three public houses, drink is simply there, and, for better or for worse, it brings their societies together. In a Victorian novel where the overwhelming tone is one of equanimity in the face of human striving, it is perhaps unsurprising that both at the level of character and social observation, drink is everywhere, yet unfathomable.

Any Victorian looking for a definitive answer to the Drink Question would be stimied by *The Mayor of Casterbridge*. The one man who ostensibly uses his reason, maintains his 'senses' by not drinking and thus attains character rather than wallowing in an unreconstructed self, fails according to those very criteria which would judge whether he were successful or not. There is no sustained reason in the novel not to drink, although there may be reason enough not to drink to excess, whilst there are plenty of good reasons to take to drink, not least for sociability, serenity, pleasure and social status. Susan drinks, Farfrae drinks, all the worthies drink, and all the lower orders drink. To be seen in a public house can be the sign of greatest achievement – Henchard at the King's Arms – or of social sliding – Henchard's visit to the Three Mariners to find Farfrae; Susan's and Elizabeth's stay there. Or it can designate mutual membership of the margins of society. In the face of drink, it is clear that the Victorians could not understand it through the use of the particular kind of reason they would wish to apply to it.

Notes

1. Quoted in Brian Harrison, *Drink and the Victorians: The Temperance Question in England 1815–1872*, 2nd edition (Keele, Staffordshire: Keele University Press, 1994), p. 75.
2. Ibid., p. 63.
3. Henry Carter, *The English Temperance Movement* (London: Epworth, 1933), p. 25.
4. Harrison, op.cit., pp. 72–4.
5. Ibid., p. 69.
6. Carter calls 'The Beer House Act' a 'Parliamentary Blunder' (op. cit., p. 16) and 'a disastrous experiment' (ibid., p. 18) in that it led to a massive increase in the consumption of drink. Harrison is much more

circumspect, and argues that what figures we do have suggest only a moderate increase in consumption after the Act came into force (op. cit., pp. 79–80). He argues that the notion of the 'Beer Act' as an unmitigated disaster lies with the *History of Liquor Licensing* (1903) by the Webbs, who, for personal reasons, were attracted to the 'debauchery theory' (ibid., p. 84).

7. Andrew Barr, *Drink: An Informal Social History* (London: Bantam Press, 1995), pp. 10–11.

8. Carter, op. cit., p. 25.

9. Lilian Lewis Shiman, *Crusade Against Drink in Victorian England* (Basingstoke: Macmillan, 1988), p. 209.

10. Peter McCandless, ' "Curses of Civilization": Insanity and Drunkenness in Victorian Britain', *British Journal of Addiction* 79 (1984), 49–58; p. 51.

11. Shiman, op. cit., pp. 209–10.

12. Livesey was one of the more respected campaigners, and Carter dedicates his book to him. However, the father of temperance had his own extreme moments: 'Joseph Livesey even believed *all* the troubles in nineteenth-century Ireland were caused by drink. "Drain Ireland of whiskey, and persuade the Irish in America from drinking it, and you will not be much troubled about Fenians" ' (ibid., p. 291).

13. For discussion of the temperance movements see Brian Harrison, op. cit., and Lilian Lewis Shiman *Crusade Against Drink*. Henry Carter's *The English Temperance Movement* is an interesting account biased in favour of the 'moral suasionists' headed by Livesey. Shiman covers ground previous to Carter by looking at the temperance movement in the 1820s which did not call for teetotalism but only regarded excessive use of distilled spirits as open to condemnation. Harrison nominally stops his study at 1872, partly because the issues change to ones of legal technicalities and because drink is no longer seen as a moral failing but as a disease. Shiman, though, sees in the 1870s a revival in 'the moral suasionist' argument thanks to 'gospel temperance', and traces the increased political influence of the temperance movement in the 1880s and 1890s.

14. Barr, op. cit., p. 139.

15. Shiman, op. cit., p. 1.

16. However, this needs to be tempered with the fact that Fielding wrote elsewhere *against* the kind of drunkenness produced by spirits, particularly gin, in his *Enquiries into the Causes of the Late Increase of Robbers* in 1751 (see Barr, op. cit., pp. 9–10), and it should be borne in mind that the public perception of gin and its accompanying social environment was different from that of beer and ale. Barr himself appears to perpetuate the dismissal of spirits as somehow inferior: 'Whereas wine, beer and cider are the natural produce of fermented fruit, spirits are the artificial concentration of that natural produce. Instead of evolving naturally as fermented drinks had done, they had to be invented' (p. 8). Yet, as Barr himself makes clear, spirits were not 'invented' as an alcoholic beverage but changed from being for medicinal purposes only.

17.   Shiman, op. cit., p. 2.
18.   Mairi, McCormick, 'First Representations of the Gamma Alcoholic in the English Novel', *Quarterly Journal of Studies on Alcoholism* 30 (1969), 957–80; p. 959. 'Gamma alcoholism means that species of alcoholism in which (1) acquired increased tissue tolerance to alcohol, (2) adaptive cell metabolism, (3) withdrawal symptoms and "craving," i.e., physical dependence, and (4) loss of control are involved'. E. M. Jellinek, quoted in McCormick, p. 960. The first 'real use of the word' alcoholic is by W. Marcet in 1860 (from John Peck, 'Thackeray and Drink: *Vanity Fair* and *The Newcomes*', *Dionysos: The Literature and Addiction TriQuarterly*, 4: 1 (1992), 14–18; p. 18, n. 4).
19.   Ibid., p. 14 and p. 16.
20.   Harrison, op. cit., p. 141.
21.   Ibid., p. 63.
22.   Barr, op. cit., pp. 37–8.
23.   McCandless, op. cit., esp. pp. 49–50.
24.   Joseph Livesey, quoted in Carter, op.cit., p. 15.
25.   Harrison, op. cit., p. 11.
26.   Ibid., p. 28.
27.   Ibid., p. 23.
28.   See, for example, an article in response to the Health Minister, Stephen Dorrell, who claimed that drinking is good for your health, Richard Boston, 'Surely shome mishtake...', *Guardian*, 13 December 1995 (tabloid section), pp. 2–3.
29.   See Barr, op. cit., pp. 314–26.
30.   Annette Federico, '"I must have drink": Addiction, Angst, and Victorian Realism', *Dionysos: The Literature and Addiction TriQuarterly*, 2.2 (Fall 1990), 11–25.
31.   Robin Gilmour, *The Victorian Period: The Intellectual and Cultural Context of English Literature 1830–1890* (London: Longman, 1993), p. 14.
32.   Federico, op. cit., p. 24.
33.   Thomas Hardy, *The Mayor of Casterbridge* (Harmondsworth: Penguin, 1994), p. 378. All future references will be included in the main body of the text.
34.   'The story of the teetotaller who started life at the very bottom of the ladder as an itinerant handloom weaver, usually unemployed, and rose to be mayor of Chester and its first teetotal sheriff, was one duplicated by other temperance colleagues' (Shiman, op. cit., p. 30. The weaver in question was William Farish).
35.   A middle-class complaint was that fairs were moving away from commercial benefit towards becoming places of pleasure, that is, sites for drinking (Nicholas Dorn, *Alcohol, Youth and the State*, London: Croom Helm, 1983). This is evident in the novel. When Henchard arrives at the fair, someone points out to him that the main business is already done with (p. 4), and the narrator comments that the crowd is bigger now in the afternoon than when business was being done before. Peter Clark has the actual transition starting a century earlier: 'By the mid eighteenth century... many fairs were starting to lose

their old commercial importance' (Peter A. Clark, *The English Alehouse: A Social History 1200–1830*, London: Longman, 1983, p. 200).

36.   Barr, op. cit., p. 138.

37.   This was a belief of the temperance reformers, Harrison, op. cit., p. 23.

38.   Carter, op. cit., reprints some temperance pledges in his book, Appendix One.

39.   Harrison, op. cit., p. 25.

40.   Although at other points in the narrative Henchard is representative of the traditional way of life in comparison to Farfrae's efficient new methods, illustrated amongst other things by Farfrae's introduction of the 'seed drill' and Henchard's dismissal of it.

41.   Barr, op. cit., pp. 174–5. John Dunlop's *The Philosophy of Artificial and Compulsory Drinking Usage in Great Britain and Northern Ireland* (London: Houlston and Stoneman, 1839) shows how pervasive drinking is as a mechanism for social bonding, listing its ritualistic usage in hundreds of trades and the penalties involved for those who attempt to opt out.

42.   Harrison, op. cit., p. 33.

43.   Shiman, op. cit., p. 30.

44.   I am not arguing that there is such a thing as a 'natural character' given to us from birth, but this is the way it operates in the novel.

45.   Most judgements are reserved for nostalgic comments. This also applies to the changing fortunes of the brewing industry in the face of monopolisation.

46.   Similarly, George Eliot in *Felix Holt* (London: Penguin, 1995), uses inns to suggest an England some time before the 1830s but now (1860s) lost: 'the great roadside inns were still brilliant with well-polished tankards, the smiling glances of pretty barmaids, and the repartees of jocose ostlers' (p. 3). This is contrasted with the now current 'gin-breathing tramps' (p. 5), again emphasising the divide between desirable brews and the unwelcome introduction and adoption of distilled liquors.

See also, Stirling Haig, ' "By the Rivers of Babylon": Water and Exile in *The Mayor of Casterbridge*', *The Thomas Hardy Yearbook*, 11 (1984), 55–62.

10

'To Whom Does He Address Himself?': Reading Wordsworth in Browning's *Pauline*[1]

Carl Plasa

Twentieth-century criticism approaches questions of influence and intertextuality in Browning's *Pauline: A Fragment of a Confession* (1833) by focusing exclusively upon Browning's relation to Shelley.[2] Such an emphasis is hardly surprising, given the fact that Browning's first published poem invokes and alludes to Shelley as poetic ideal and tutelary spirit in a manner which is as pervasive as it is overt. Yet it is precisely the conspicuousness with which Shelley figures in Browning's text that allows an alternative reading of its intertextual relations to emerge. As Harold Bloom has shown, what poems consciously *say* about their intertextual provenance is often discrepant from what they *do*, the ways in which they behave or perform, as it were.[3] An adoption of the kind of 'hermeneutics of suspicion' undergirding Bloom's work enables us, in the first instance, to read *Pauline* against the grain of its own reading of itself. Even as the 'I' of Browning's text enters into poetic dialogue with Shelley, his poem's language is simultaneously drawn, for reasons to be discussed, toward Wordsworth and, in particular, 'Tintern Abbey'. Yet while the persona's blindness toward Wordsworth's complicating presence in *Pauline* is invariably shared by the poem's critics, it is significantly not reproduced by the text itself, which recurrently signals and acknowledges its engagement with Wordsworth by means of a specific (inter)textual effect. The language of the earlier poet is not only incorporated into the later text but also translated into a medium through which that text variously figures and comments upon its own revisionary operations. In this way what becomes evident is that the relation between Browning's poem and its twentieth-century critical readers is in the end a reciprocal one: the critics illuminate the poem but the poem at the same time highlights the limits of the criticism, problematising – in its self-reflexiveness – one of the major critical orthodoxies with which *Pauline* is circumscribed.

SHELLEYAN ORIGINS AND WORDSWORTHIAN DEPARTURES

As if to confirm Shelley in the role of exclusive poetic interlocutor, *Pauline*'s peroration (ll. 1020–31) circles back to the sustained invocation of the redoubtable 'Sun-treader' with which it begins (ll. 151–229), structurally enacting his centring effect. Between these moments occurs a passage in which the persona recalls the period just prior to his encounter with the earlier poet:

> schemes and systems went and came,
> And I was proud (being vainest of the weak),
> In wandering o'er them, to seek out some one
> To be my own; as one should wander o'er
> The white way for a star.

> (ll. 399–403)[4]

The figuration of that 'one' as 'star' makes it implicitly clear that the persona's quest is directed toward the discovery of another poet as an influence to be exerted over him: in its literal meaning, as the *OED* informs us, 'influence' is an astrological term for the 'supposed flowing from the stars of an ethereal fluid acting upon the character and destiny of men'. In the final version of *Pauline*, the active nature of the persona's role in the shaping of his own poetic origins is underscored by the formulation added immediately after the (revised) lines cited above: 'And my *choice* fell / Not so much on a system as on a man – ' (1888, ll. 403–5, emphasis added). The later insertion of this statement clarifies the underlying assumption in *Pauline* that a poet can be fully conversant with the forces which determine his identity. One need not, however, be a Bloomian critic versed in the links between poetry and repression to recognise how the paradoxical rhetoric of influence-as-choice cannot quite exhaust or account for the intertextual operations of the persona's language. We can consider instead, by way of initial examples, two sequences in the text, situated before and after the passage previously cited, in which, despite *Pauline's* concern for the knowability of poetic origins and identities, the poem's speaker emerges as a stranger to his own beginnings, doomed to misconstrue the intertextual 'schemes and systems' in which he is located. The first of these passages occurs at lines 230–5:

> Autumn has come – like Spring returned to us,
> Won from her girlishness – like one returned
> A friend that was a lover – nor forgets
> The first warm love, but full of sober thoughts
> Of fading years; whose soft mouth quivers yet
> With the old smile – but yet so changed and still!

Figuring 'Autumn' as 'Spring', substituting earliness for lateness, Browning's text specifically reverses the pattern of mournful temporal transformation outlined in Shelley's 'Adonais':

> Grief made the young Spring wild, and she threw down
> Her kindling buds, as if she Autumn were,
> Or they dead leaves.

> (ll. 136–8)[5]

Yet while they seem to operate purely within the terms of a relation to Shelley, Browning's lines are complicated by the inadvertent revival of the language of both 'Tintern Abbey' and, that other great poem of Wordsworthian loss, the 'Intimations' ode. Browning's persona turns toward his Shelleyan 'Sun-treader', even as, in a subversive counter-tropism, his text veers toward Wordsworth. Revisionary intent is eclipsed by unconscious allusion in a way which questions the rhetoric of mastery that seems to dominate *Pauline* – 'Yet I can take a secret pride in calling / The dark past up – to quell it regally' (ll. 289–90).

'Autumn''s revision into 'Spring', the friendly form of an ex-lover, is thus significant because it obliquely recalls and parallels the terms in which Wordsworth struggles to understand the nature of his return to the Wye in 'Tintern Abbey'. In the latter context, the difference between present and past selves is both couched erotically and also figured as a sobering modulation from sight to sound:

> For I have learned
> To look on nature, not as in the hour
> Of thoughtless youth; but hearing oftentimes
> The still, sad music of humanity
> Nor harsh nor grating, though of ample power
> To chasten and subdue.

(ll. 88–93)

The inward change has its outward corollary in a transposition of desire from nature's 'beauteous forms', hauntingly half-eroticised as 'An appetite; a feeling and a love, / That had no need of a remoter charm, / By thought supplied' (ll. 22, 80–2) to Wordsworth's 'dearest Friend', Dorothy, as 'warmer love' is oxymoronically cooled into a 'deeper zeal / Of holier love' (ll. 115, 154–5).

In tracing out a path to sublimation, 'Tintern Abbey' is typically Wordsworthian. In the 'Intimations' ode this path leads to the 'sober colouring' of the 'philosophic mind' (ll. 200, 189) as in 'Elegiac Stanzas' to a 'Soul' that has been 'humanised' (l. 36). Equally, however, the text strives to resist its own trajectory. The assertion of an 'Abundant recompense' (l. 88) is ultimately a hollow one, undercut by a consciousness of the temporal losses it claims to transcend.[6] In an affirmation whose quasi-interrogative impetus itself all but restates the conflict it would resolve, Wordsworth declares:

> Therefore am I still
> *A lover* of the meadows and the woods,
> And mountains; and of all that we behold
> From this green earth.

(ll. 102–5, emphasis added)

From this perspective abundance is more truly a dearth, a lie practised upon the self by itself as, in the momentary fluctuation of his rhetoric, Wordsworth retreats from sublimation. Against this, *Pauline* deploys Wordsworth's rhetoric to make sublimation irreversible ('A friend that *was* a lover', emphasis added). If Browningesque voice, allusively addressed to Shelley, seems to lose its direction in an engagement with 'Tintern Abbey' it is not without a correspondent gain.

In the second passage for consideration, questions of poetic influence are explicitly thematised:

> And all the influence poets have o'er men!
> 'Tis a fine thing that one, weak as myself,
> Should sit in his lone room, knowing the words
> He utters in his solitude shall move
> Men like a swift wind...

> (ll. 530–4)

Here the denial of poetic power of course denies itself as Browning's text echoes and reverses the Shelleyan figuration of the influential poet in 'Ode to the West Wind':

> Be thou, Spirit fierce,
> My spirit! Be thou me, impetuous one!
>
> Drive my dead thoughts over the universe
> Like withered leaves to quicken a new birth!
> And, by the incantation of this verse,
>
> Scatter, as from an unextinguished hearth
> Ashes and sparks, my words among mankind!

> (ll. 61–7)

Even as the persona might 'know[ ] the words / He utters' to form part of an ironic exchange with Shelley, they come, subsequently, to establish other relations as the passage continues:

> – that tho' he be forgotten,
> Fair eyes shall glisten when his beauteous dreams
> Of love come true in happier frames than his.
> Ay, the still night brought thoughts like these.

> (ll. 534–7)

The forgetting of Shelley might seem in one sense disingenuous but at the same time it is strangely literalised. Browning's language here precisely departs from its Shelleyan point of origin and returns in a recollection of the closing stages of 'Tintern Abbey' and the moment when Dorothy's 'mind' becomes 'a mansion for all lovely forms', her memory 'as a dwelling-place / For all sweet sounds and harmonies', and 'wild eyes' house 'gleams / Of past existence' (ll. 139–42, 148–9). Wordsworth's dominion evidently extends beyond his sister's mansion-mind, into which, at the end of 'Tintern Abbey', he strives to project himself, as his textual 'forms' become lodged in the monument of another poet's language. *Pauline* cannot thus be accommodated to its model of influence as consciously allusive memory, just as the persona is decentred by his text's self-conversion into the allegory of its unattended play.

POETIC BETRAYAL/EROTIC DEFENCE

Pauline's subversive turn toward 'Tintern Abbey' is perhaps to be expected. Despite the election of Shelley as poetic love-object, the earlier poet fails to conform himself to the persona's idealised figuration of their interrelation as *exclusively dyadic* in structure:

> The air seems bright with thy past presence yet,
> But thou art still for me, as thou hast been
> When I have stood with thee, as on a throne
> With all thy dim creations gathered round
> Like mountains, – and I felt of mould like them,
> And creatures of my own were mixed with them,
> Like things half-lived, catching and giving life.

> (ll. 161–7)

If the desire is for a mutual mixing of words – each in the other's purity – its limits are suggested by the linguistic and figurative asymmetry of 'creations' / 'creatures'. They are further confirmed in the recognition that the Shelley whose 'name' the persona 'believed a spell to [him] alone' is also, crucially, as a 'star to men', a 'sacred spring' that turns out to be the 'fountain-head, / Long lost, of some great river' (ll. 169–71, 172, 179–80). It would seem that Shelley is less particular than his admirer in his choice of interlocutors, casting 'life and light' (l. 151) in quarters other to the realms of reciprocity. There is still another side to this disappointing garrulity.

Despite the representation of chooser as chosen, 'first / Caught' and 'set' by Shelley 'as to a sweet task, / To gather every breathing of his songs' (ll. 411–13) the discovery is that:

> woven with them there were words, which seemed
> A key to a new world; the muttering
> Of angels, of some thing unguessed by man.

(ll. 414–16)

Not only addressing themselves to more than one listener, Shelley's 'songs' also open out upon an obscure 'world' of signifying relations 'unguessed' by the 'man' who sings them: Shelley's voice mutters forth the message of its own past entanglements. In this way it becomes clear that the persona's relation to Shelley is only part of a broader network of intertextual exchanges which renders a discrete one-to-one personalism impossible.

One way in which the persona seeks to counteract what might be called a kind of poetic betrayal is through a recourse to the erotic. The decentring experienced with regard to Shelley's position as 'star to men' (promiscuous in his influence) is reworked and overcome in the persona's self-figuration as centre to his beloved, the Pauline who 'Lives strangely on [his] thoughts, and looks, and words' (l. 240). Similarly, Shelley's poetic fickleness is symbolically reversed – yet also indirectly revealed – in the deathly representation of a perpetual erotic constancy:

> I look thro'
> And say, 'E'en at the last I have her still,
> 'With her delicious eyes as clear as heaven,
> 'When rain in a quick shower has beat down mist,
> 'And clouds float white in the sun like broods of swans.'
> How the blood lies upon her cheek, all spread
> As thinned by kisses; only in her lips
> It wells and pulses like a living thing,
> And her neck looks, like marble misted o'er
> With love-breath, a dear thing to kiss and love,
> Standing beneath me – looking out to me,
> As I might kill her and be loved for it.

(ll. 891–902)

Just as the persona's investment in Shelley depends upon the urgent fiction of the exclusivity of their relation, so the loving gaze which eroticises even the gazer's extinction ('looking out to me, / As I might kill her and be loved for it') is purely a projection of the 'I' that claims to behold it. Pauline comes to reciprocate the persona's regard (both gaze and admiration) because she is the product of a series of perceptual similes or mistakings: 'eyes as clear *as* heaven', 'blood . . . all spread / *As* thinned by kisses', 'And her neck *looks, like* marble', 'As I might kill her. . .'. Pauline's murder, then, would only formalise the suspended animation in which she is already caught. Even in the moment before her potential death the beloved is not unlike a statue, with 'marble' neck – a 'living *thing*', a '*dear* thing' (emphases added).

Sole resistance to the persona's mortifying eros is articulated through Pauline's 'lips', where blood – like language – continues to circulate, 'wells and pulses'. This image indeed enacts its own logic, escaping the possession of its present context through an allusive linkage to an earlier moment precisely concerned with the recognition of a life (Shelley's) beyond, or before, the wishful representation of it:

> And I, perchance, half feel a strange regret,
> That I am not what I have been to thee:
> Like a girl one has loved long silently,
> In her first loveliness, in some retreat,
> When first emerged, all gaze and glow to view
> Her fresh eyes, and soft hair, *and lips which bleed*
> Like a mountain berry. Doubtless it is sweet
> To see her thus adored – but there have been
> Moments, when all the world was in his praise,
> Sweeter than all the pride of after hours.

> (ll. 191–200, emphasis added)

Pauline's resisting lips, always implying the capacity for an erotic betrayal ('Love me – love me, Pauline, love nought but me; / Leave me not', ll. 903–4) also bear the traces of an interpoetic one – Shelley's prior engagement or circulation in a pregiven set of textual relations. The irony is that the representation of Pauline, called forth in symbolic defiance of Shelley's poetic inconstancy, is *itself* inconstant, disclosing – through the subtle aperture of those 'lips – that which should remain hidden. As such, it functions against the persona, even as *Pauline's* language works against Shelley, inscribing itself in clandestine dialogue with 'Tintern Abbey'.

ANXIETIES OF BETRAYAL IN 'TINTERN ABBEY'

Pauline's shift toward 'Tintern Abbey' as an alternative ground of address is ultimately not, however, the most propitious means of counteracting a sense of betrayal, poetic or otherwise. For, in the shape of Wordsworth's relation to Dorothy in particular, 'Tintern Abbey' dramatises anxieties analogous to those which the persona of *Pauline* must negotiate with regard to Shelley. Just as (in a curious inversion of temporal and poetic priorities) the persona urges Shelley to 'Remember [him]' (ll. 207, 209, 219) so Wordsworth prescriptively demands that he always be recollected by his sister:

> with what healing thoughts
> Of tender joy wilt thou remember me,
> And these my exhortations!

> (ll. 144–6)

These lines suggest why Dorothy is so regularly 'dear' a friend (ll. 116, 121, 159). On the one hand she is beloved, an enchanting supplement to a 'Nature' from which she is frequently indistinguishable (ll. 108–11, 121–3) and which itself, Wordsworth asserts, 'never did betray / The heart that loved her' (ll. 122–3). On the other hand, Dorothy constitutes a source of *risk* that specifically arises out of the exhortatory mode in which she is addressed. As one critic intriguingly observes, the efficacy of an exhortation (unlike the kind of blessing bestowed by Coleridge upon his son at the end of 'Frost at Midnight', for example) is dependent upon the recipient of it: it is always possible that Dorothy might *not* fulfil the commemorative functions Wordsworth demands of her in the wake of his imagined death (ll. 147–9).[7]

The possibility of Dorothy's departure from or betrayal of her brother's prescriptions enters even into 'Tintern Abbey''s most ostensibly optimistic moments:

> Nor, perchance –
> If I should be where I no more can hear
> Thy voice, nor catch from thy wild eyes these gleams
> Of past existence – wilt thou then forget
> That on the banks of this delightful stream
> We stood together.

> (ll. 146–51)

Wordsworth's discontinuous syntax, dilating the main clause, 'Nor... / ...wilt thou then forget', with the intimation of mortality, 'If I should be where I no more can hear...', enacts the very obliteration he fears in a syntactic shift which transforms affirmation into question: '*wilt* thou then forget'? (emphasis added). In this way the potentially disrupted reciprocity between Wordsworth and his sister in 'Tintern Abbey' is only an ironic mirroring of the treacheries that vex the persona's relation to Shelley in *Pauline*.

'LIFE AND FOOD / FOR FUTURE YEARS': DISREMEMBERING AND THE SELF-REFLEXIVENESS OF ALLUSION IN *PAULINE*

Whether or not Dorothy carries out her brother's injunctions it is clear that in intertextual terms at least Wordsworth is indeed recalled, his text surviving into the revisionary afterlife of Browning's. Yet the irony is that the specific form such recollection takes simultaneously turns it into a kind of forgetting or disremembering. *Pauline* does not simply incorporate the idiom of 'Tintern Abbey' into itself as unconscious echo or allusion but also *transfigures* it into a linguistic material through which it comments upon its own operations: allusion becomes self-allusive, as it were, as the earlier text is co-opted into a process whose effect is to recreate it in the image of the later. In this respect we might say that confession in *Pauline* occurs not so much in relation to the persona's subjectivity as in terms of its *language*, as the letter of Wordsworth's text is conserved while the spirit/consciousness which once animated it re-originates as something other than – and to – itself. These processes can be illustrated through detailed exploration of two passages in Browning's text which might be regarded as paradigmatic of its larger workings. A third passage will also be considered in order to demonstrate that the self-reflexiveness of allusion in *Pauline* can

indeed include other Wordsworthian texts, in this case the 'Intimations' ode. Taken together, all three passages are indicative of *Pauline's* operation as double-critique. On the one hand, their
(inter)textual self-consciousness questions and disrupts the persona's attempted self-containment within an exclusively Shelleyan
dialogue while at the same time proleptically refuting those critics
who choose to read the poem on its own terms.

The first passage occurs at lines 352–6, as the persona describes his
emergence from a time when he had 'first...learned to turn / [His]
mind against itself' (ll. 347–8):

> at length I was restored,
> Yet long the influence remained; and nought
> But the still life I led, apart from all,
> Which left my soul to seek its old delights,
> Could e'er have brought me thus far back to peace.

Self-integration, being 'brought...back to peace' is dependent upon
self-seclusion, 'the still life'. Yet the assertion of autonomy is self-
ironising, linked to a prior scene of self-recuperation through memory in solitude where Wordsworth 'in lonely rooms' had found
'tranquil restoration' through the recollection of *his* 'old delights' –
nature's 'beauteous forms' ('Tintern Abbey', ll. 22–30). In one
respect, *Pauline's* thematic and intertextual levels are here at odds:
the persona's stability and isolation of self are pointedly collocated
with a moment in which Browning's text recalls the language of
another. Equally, however, this passage suggests the precise inter-
relation of those two levels, as the one comes to figure the action at
the other. The restoration of *Pauline's* 'I' simultaneously restores
Wordsworth's text, as one might 'restore' a painting, or 'picture of
the mind' ('Tintern Abbey', l. 61) – into Browning's 'still life' perhaps? Similarly, the persona's conscious pursuit of his 'old delights'
forms a parallel and contrast to how his text *un*consciously finds its
way into an encounter with Wordsworth's, inveterate disturber of
Browning's 'piece'.

In the second passage, the revelatory promise implied by *Pauline's*
confessional status is problematised by the recognition of the limits
of language:

> I but catch
> A hue, a glance of what I sing, so pain

Is linked with pleasure, for I ne'er may tell
The radiant sights which dazzle me; but now
They shall be all my own, and let them fade
Untold – others shall rise as fair, as fast.
And when all's done, the few dim gleams transferred . . .
And when all's done, how vain seems e'en success.

(ll. 516–29)

Aptly, the articulation of failed self-expression enacts its own logic, allegorically expressing, despite itself, the persona's ignorance with regard to the revisionary nature of his own language. Poetry alienates the self ('I feel I but explain to my own loss / These impulses', ll. 682–3) not because of an inherently limited mimetic potential but rather because it is already inscribed with and mediated by unapprehended relations to other texts. Here the specific mediation is the Wordsworthian declaration in 'Tintern Abbey':

And now, with gleams of half-extinguished thought,
With many recognitions dim and faint,
And somewhat of a sad perplexity,
The picture of the mind revives again:
While here I stand, not only with the sense
Of present pleasure, but with pleasing thoughts
That in this moment there is life and food
For future years.

(ll. 58–65)

The persona's inability to 'catch' himself in song not only registers the recession of semantic presence but also the way in which he misses his own text's glancing exchange with Wordsworth's, whose 'gleams' of thought become dimly 'transferred', troped or translated, into a language which glosses its appropriation of them. '[H]alf-extinguished' in 'Tintern Abbey' they are half-rekindled in *Pauline*.

The interplay between Browning's text and 'Tintern Abbey' would seem retrospectively to legitimate the 'present pleasure' of Wordsworth's *bonheur*, as the poet's *textual* 'moment' outlives itself to constitute a kind of revisionary sustenance, 'life and food / For future years'. Yet the 'pleasing thoughts' which such survivals might arouse in Wordsworth as a reader of Browning would be mixed with a certain 'sad perplexity' since it is only 'The *language* of [Words-worth's] former heart' that *Pauline* recalls (l. 117) rather than its informing 'sense'.

This brings us to the third passage for discussion, where *Pauline* intersects with the 'Intimations' ode:

> And of my powers, one springs up to save
> From utter death a soul with such desires
> Confined to clay – which is the only one
> Which marks me – an imagination which
> Has been an angel to me – coming not
> In fitful visions, but beside me ever,
> And never failing me; so tho' my mind
> Forgets not – not a shred of life forgets –
> Yet I can take a secret pride in calling
> The dark past up – to quell it regally.

> (ll. 281–90)

The persona goes on to claim that he '[has] always had one lode-star' (l. 292) – that is, Shelley – from which his imagination is derived. Yet the lines cited above question such a claim, fitfully alluding (syntactically and imagistically) to the fifth stanza of Words-worth's poem:

> Our birth is but a sleep and a forgetting:
> The Soul that rises with us, our life's Star,
>   Hath had elsewhere its setting,
>   And cometh from afar:
>   Not in entire forgetfulness,
>   And not in utter nakedness,
> But trailing clouds of glory do we come
>   From God, who is our home.

> (ll. 58–65)[8]

Browningesque imagination 'springs up' ostensibly, at least, to save the persona's 'soul' from 'utter death'. Yet this vigorous arousal is at the same time somewhat redundant, suspiciously corresponding with and pre-empted by the Wordsworthian 'Soul that rises with us', that divine intimation which rescues the self from the potential embarrassment of its own extinction – 'utter nakedness'. The inter-relation between texts is further substantiated by the fact that the 'Soul' in 'Intimations', subsequently figured as a 'vision splendid' (l. 73), is a trope for imagination – the 'visionary gleam' of line 56. The persona's imagination is activated in *Pauline* only to confront the earlier rising of its veiled Wordsworthian counter-form.

From this perspective *Pauline*'s defensive self-maskings can be discerned. The persona 'Forgets not – not a shred of life forgets' but only by remaining oblivious to his text's recollection of one aspect of its genealogy. Similarly, while he boasts of mastering the past (lines 289–90) the rhythms of its return show themselves to be radically unanswerable to the beck and call of consciousness. Finally, and perhaps most tellingly, he figures imagination as being 'beside [him] ever, / And never failing' at the very point when it seems to be most beside itself, verging perilously upon the lost scene of its precondition (in the double sense of former incarnation and enabling ground). The uncanniness of that scene, we might add, is that it obliquely contains the metaphors for the interplay between *Pauline* and itself. For Browning's persona, creative birth may well turn around memories of Shelley, but it is contingent, equally, upon 'a sleep and a forgetting' – an erasure or repression of Wordsworth's text as the 'elsewhere' in which, in part, his own 'Hath had ... its setting' or initial milieu.

THE RETURN OF THE REPRESSED

At lines 729–31 Browning's persona projects a visionary flight toward self-possession through an absolute relation to the beloved:

> Pauline, come with me – see how I could build
> A home for us, out of the world; in thought –
> I am inspired – come with me, Pauline!

Yet by line 811 such a project has met with negation, a sudden dislocation of consciousness so extreme – 'O God! where does this tend – these struggling aims!' – as temporarily to force the text into arrest, suspended by Pauline's note. While the persona's visionary desires might indeed culminate only in uncertainty with regard to their own telos, the poem's destination becomes progressively clear across the course of this passage. The persona's imagination drives toward 'the very heart of the woods' and the emblematically Shelleyan isolation of 'One pond of water'[9] (ll. 766, 768) yet the language of the text assumes an increasingly Wordsworthian cast, regrounding it, ultimately, in that of 'Tintern Abbey'.

What characterises this passage (ll. 729–811) is unease. No projected place seems adequately to house the narrating imagination as it engages upon a series of penetrative recessions whose momentum is generated by the way in which each of them is resonant with intertextual intimations of Wordsworth. The transition to morning – 'no – we will pass to morning' (l. 740) – is an escape from a 'moonless night' which fashions nature into a figuring of anteriority: the 'woods / Waving and muttering' are likened to 'giant-ghosts, / Looking on earth to know how their sons fare' (ll. 733–4, 736–7). Similarly the subsequent downward thrust to a 'new retreat' (l. 749) – 'shall we stay here / With the wild hawks? – no, ere the hot noon come / Dive we down – safe' (ll. 747–9) – seeks to release the persona from a Wordsworthian landscape, with its 'foam-sheet of the cataract' (l. 746). This sojourn remains temporary in turn, however, because it is 'all round, / Mountain-like, heaped above us' (ll. 766–7), oppressively reminiscent of 'Tintern Abbey' where, prophetically, natural forms 'on a wild secluded scene impress / Thoughts of more deep seclusion' (ll. 6–7). These thoughts resurface in the impulse of Browning's persona to

> leave the old woods:
> See, they part, like a ruined arch, the sky!
> Nothing but sky appears, so close the root
> And grass of the hill-top level with the air.

(ll. 781–4)

Here the age of the 'woods' reverses their previous imaging of earliness, yet the impulse only draws the persona into a textual zone already demarcated as firmly Wordsworthian. What emerges, despite the vision of the all-excluding sky, is a levelling link with 'Tintern Abbey', whose 'lofty cliffs' 'connect / The landscape with the quiet of the sky' (ll. 5, 7–8). Significantly, Browning's image is one of connectivity, as if his text were unconsciously figuring to itself the condition of its own relatedness to Wordsworth's. Every escape deteriorates into entrapment in a process which can only be halted, 'Down the hill – stop...see' (l. 798), when the circularity of its structure becomes evident, along with the recognition that the flight from Wordsworth's text is only a return to (or of) it:

> and all
> The little smoking cots, and fields, and banks,
> And copses, bright in the sun; my spirit wanders.
> Hedge-rows for me – still, living, hedge-rows, where
> The bushes close, and clasp above, and keep
> Thought in – I am concentrated – I feel; –
> But my soul saddens when it looks beyond;
> I cannot be immortal, nor taste all.
> O God! where does this tend – these struggling aims!
>
> (ll. 803–11)

It is the letter rather than the 'spirit' that 'wanders' here, in the direction of another liaison with 'Tintern Abbey', *Pauline*'s Wordsworthian pre-text:

> These plots of cottage-ground, these orchard-tufts,
> Which at this season, with their unripe fruits,
> Are clad in one green hue, and lose themselves
> 'Mid groves and copses. Once again I see
> These hedge-rows, hardly hedge-rows, little lines
> Of sportive wood run wild.
>
> (ll. 11–16)

The persona 'cannot be immortal' because the privilege has been accorded to Wordsworth's text, 'still, living' and literally reiterating itself in Browning's 'Hedge-rows for me...hedge-rows'. The repetitions of syntactic structure in Browning double *Pauline*'s revisionary failure to offer even the illusion of its difference from 'Tintern Abbey' at this point, by means of a defensive figuration of the earlier text, for example. Ironically Wordsworth's language tropes itself, 'hardly hedge-rows, little lines / Of sportive wood run wild', even as it is retrospectively refigured by the later text to become allegorical of the way in which Wordsworth's *poetic* lines stray into

Browning's, disturbingly undercutting the persona's instant of self-composition – 'I am concentrated – I feel'.

The persona's inability to comprehend his poem's 'struggling aims' at this juncture is not lost on Pauline herself, whose note to line 811 begins as follows:

'I am very much afraid that my poor friend will not always be perfectly understood in what remains to be read of this strange fragment, but he is less fitted than anyone else to make clear what from its very nature must always remain a confused dream'.

The persona's limited grasp over his own poem is not confined merely to 'what remains of this strange fragment' but might be said to define his predicament with regard to the poem as a whole. From an intertextual viewpoint, however, such epistemological limits are countered by the poem itself, as we have seen. Perhaps one reason why this text is, in Pauline's words again, 'so singular a production' relates to its uncanny possession of a knowledge which the persona lacks, a certain (inter)textual self-consciousness. *Pauline* not only turns from Shelley to Wordsworth as poetic interlocutor, thus complicating the conscious execution of its apostrophic gestures. It also refashions the Wordsworthian text(s) with which it engages into an idiom through which to remark upon revisionary and allusive affiliations that would otherwise remain unacknowledged. As such, Browning's poem constitutes an example of the way in which literary texts can both deconstruct themselves and, in so doing, offer, in this case, an anticipatory challenge to the critical consensus which comes, subsequently, to surround them.

Notes

1. The quotation in the title to this essay is from Wordsworth's Preface to *Lyrical Ballads* (1802) in *The Poetical Works of William Wordsworth*, ed. E. de Selincourt and Helen Darbishire, 2nd edn, 5 vols (Oxford: Clarendon, 1952), II, 393. This edition is used throughout for all references to and citations of Wordsworth's poetry.

2. Major examples of this approach include Frederick A. Pottle, *Shelley and Browning: A Myth and Some Facts* (Chicago: Pembroke Press, 1923) pp. 34–64; John Maynard, *Browning's Youth* (Cambridge, Mass.: Harvard University Press, 1977) pp. 193–237; Herbert F. Tucker, Jr.,

    Browning's Beginnings: The Art of Disclosure (Minneapolis: University of Minnesota Press, 1980) pp. 30–52; Clyde de L. Ryals, *Becoming Browning: The Poems and Plays of Robert Browning 1833–46* (Columbus: Ohio State University Press, 1983) pp. 9–30 and Loy D. Martin, *Browning's Dramatic Monologues and the Post-Romantic Subject* (Baltimore and London: Johns Hopkins University Press, 1985) pp. 68–78.

3.   This split results, for Bloom, from the fact that authentic manifestations of poetic influence are to be found at the level of relations between texts that are fundamentally repressed or unconscious, rather than openly acknowledged: 'the precursor', as Bloom puts it, 'is absorbed …as part of the id', *The Anxiety of Influence: A Theory of Poetry* (New York: Oxford University Press, 1973) p. 71. The later poet's repression of the precursor's influence relates in turn, in Bloom's heavily Oedipal account, to a desire for self-origination, that he be *'the father of himself'* (*Anxiety of Influence*, p. 64, emphasis in original). For a useful recent analysis and assessment of Bloom's work see Graham Allen, *Harold Bloom: A Poetics of Conflict* (Hemel Hempstead: Harvester, 1994).

4.   *The Poetical Works of Robert Browning*, ed. Ian Jack, Rowena Fowler and Margaret Smith, 4 volumes to date (Oxford: Clarendon, 1983–), I, 54. This edition is used throughout for all references to and citations of *Pauline*. Browning twice revised *Pauline*, in 1868 and 1888, but unless otherwise indicated the text is that of 1833.

5.   *Shelley's Poetry and Prose*, ed. Donald H. Reiman and Sharon B. Powers (New York and London: Norton, 1977) p. 396. This edition is used throughout for all references to and citations of Shelley's poetry.

6.   As noted, for example, by Harold Bloom, *The Visionary Company: A Reading of English Romantic Poetry*, rev. edn (Ithaca and London: Cornell University Press, 1971): 'Certainly [Wordsworth] protests too much, we feel a desperation in his insistence, another presage of waning faith, or faith affirmed more vehemently as it ebbs', p. 135.

7.   See John Michael, 'Emerson's Chagrin: Benediction and Exhortation in "Nature" and "Tintern Abbey"', *Modern Language Notes* 101 (1986) 1067–85. 'An exhortation', Michael writes, 'depends upon its hearer as a benediction does not. The power of a benediction is, as it were, self-contained: the blessing is delivered without needing the consent or even the consciousness of the one blessed. The felicity of an exhortation – the effectiveness of exhorting – rests, by contrast, ultimately with the person to whom the exhortation is addressed. Unlike a benediction, the success or failure of an exhortation depends on the act' reception…whether or not the person to whom the exhortation is addressed is persuaded to do what is demanded', p. 1076.

8.   *Poetical Works of William Wordsworth*, IV, 281.

9.   On the distinctly Shelleyan nature of this locus see Tucker, *Browning' Beginnings*, p. 39.

11

A Rose is a Rose is a Rover
Alistair Walker

For a few weeks in the spring of 1996, Rover cars ran a full-page colour advertisement in some of the Sunday Supplements. This advertisement featured Alma-Tadema's celebrated painting *The Roses of Heliogabalus* (see the jacket of this book). In this painting, the Emperor Heliogabalus with a few of his friends loll over a banquet in a very Victorian-Roman way, idly watching some of the other guests, on a lower level, being showered by clouds of rose petals. At the top of the advertisement were the words, 'If you'd like to know more about how we turn a long journey in a Rover 400 Saloon into a bed of roses, telephone us on...'. Alongside this statement was a small Rover badge with 'Relax, it's a Rover' beneath it. Under the picture, just below the cascading roses, were the words, 'Few places are as comfortable as a Rover 400.'

In fact, Heliogabalus was one of the more disgraceful of the Roman emperors. One of his delights was to invite unsuspecting guests to his palace, and, when the feast was well under way, to release great swags of rose petals on them until they choked to death. Alma-Tadema's picture – or, at least, the part of it shown in the advertisement – shows, not surprisingly, a fairly early stage of this process, when the guests' heads are still above the surface and they seem not be aware of the final outcome.

Several cultural perspectives could be developed on the connections between the subject-matter taken from the late Roman Empire, the highly decorative picture painted in 1888, and the latter's role as an advertisement for Rover 400s; but I would like to concentrate on the nineteenth-century date, the connotations the picture would have had for its first viewers, and the part Alma-Tadema played as a portrayer of the ancient world in late Victorian society. It is here, I believe, that a crucial difference can be found between the reception of a piece of popular, middle-class art in 1888, and the acceptance of the same picture's reproduction as an advertisement for a popular, middle-of-the-range product in 1996, and that this is indicative of

179

one of the differences between the nineteenth and twentieth *fins de siècle*.

Sir Lawrence Alma-Tadema's reputation and success rested on his recreations of the classical world of Egypt, Greece and Rome. Commentators at the time – and since, though not always with the same approval – have concentrated on four aspects of his art: the meticulous use of artefacts and architecture appropriate to the period of the picture in question; the technical skill with which he reproduced, for example, the texture of marble; his expert management of space and perspective; and the way in which the classical scenes and figures, in spite of the accuracy of their portrayal, were somehow, and reassuringly, Victorian. This last quality – or defect – was created partly because his scenes were often domestic: a mother playing with her small child, for example (*An Earthly Paradise*, 1891), a young woman watching for the arrival of her lover or husband (*Expectations*, 1885), or a group listening to a professional reciter (*A Reading from Homer*, 1885). But it also came from something rather difficult to pin down in the features of the characters, something which made them look as though they would suit smart Victorian evening clothes rather better than the togas and stolas they were depicted in. This tendency to familiarise the situations and the characters is easy to mock, but it was an important element of the way Alma-Tadema's public related to his art. Many of the members of the educated English middle and upper classes would have had some knowledge of the classical world and would have recognised a bond between this world and themselves, a bond incorporating differences and similarities which they felt they were well able to assess. This easy recognition was the development of an affinity which had been experienced, of course, long before the nineteenth century; it had adapted itself easily to different phases of neoclassicism, Romanticism and Victorianism, and it had co-existed confidently in the second half of the nineteenth century with the growth of a different kind of affinity with, and interest in, the Middle Ages. To find this bond between their own lives and those of the ancient classical world was gratifying. Alma-Tadema, and painters such as Leighton Poynter and Moore, played their part in creating an aspirational ennobling, reassuring dream world.

To some extent these paintings shared characteristics with the popular portrayals of incidents and characters from English history and from the equally popular depictions of scenes and character from Shakespeare. The former, as Roy Strong illustrates in *And Whe*

Did You Last See Your Father? (1978) showed artists coming back repeatedly to incidents in history which appealed to current pre-occupations – the exploitation of innocence, or the martyrdom of women, for example. The Shakespearean depictions, like the most successful nineteenth-century actors, concentrated on the high emotional moments in his plays: *The Ides of March* (Poynter), *Romeo and Juliet* (Dicksee), *Cordelia's Portion* (Madox Brown). One of the interesting points Strong makes is that the 'popular' characters were not always – as in the case of Mary, Queen of Scots – those to whom the Victorians would have given moral approval if they had tactlessly appeared amongst them in the flesh. In a similar way, to return to Alma-Tadema and the other Olympians,[1] although, as one would expect, they presented a heavily censored version of ancient times and although that, indeed, was part of their success, they also betrayed a certain moral ambiguity in the way in which thoroughly reprehensible episodes were represented. It was the careful, often subtle skill that Alma-Tadema employed in the management of this moral ambiguity that allowed *The Roses of Heliogabalus* (a picture I will discuss in detail later) to appeal to its Victorian buyer and, later, to find itself in an advertisement for a modestly up-market car in 1996.

However dubious and hypocritical the affinity was that the Victorians felt with ancient virtues, they did represent something in which they could believe. They might ignore Roman brutality or Greek slavery and homosexual freedom, but the brilliance with which they practised this willed ignorance created a space for the virtues they were very ready to proclaim. Like the history paintings and the illustrations of Shakespeare, these pictures represented a kind of intellectual and emotional order: in these depictions of the ancient world and of their own past, history could be seen in understandable terms, the violence was manageable, the relationships, even if they were unpleasant, were comprehensible, often melodramatically so. This depiction of the past and its resemblance to the present suggested that their own world was the inheritor of a tradition; there was a continuity with the past that gave confidence. Even if the Goths were at the gate – and despite the apparent and widespread confidence of the 1880s and 1890s there were plenty of assorted Goths shaking the bars – the gate would hold.

Besides, it was not just the subject matter that gave confidence: the resistance to French Impressionism was a factor as well. The scenes that Alma-Tadema, Leighton and the historical artists painted were not concerned with fleeting glimpses of the past. Certainly, they might employ, literally, some of the Impressionists' points of view – Alma-Tadema was especially inventive in his choice of angle from which an incident of classical life could be observed, often offering unexpected glimpses of distant interiors or shafts of light, pillars and corners of buildings frequently making figures incomplete – but those pillars and walls were there to be lingered over, there was no disturbing French instability here, no Paterian sense that the vividness of the momentary impression was its own justification: these were solid recreations that could be confirmed in the paint work and the technical expertise; a lot of *effort* had gone into these, there was nothing slap-dash about them. Alma-Tadema not only used actual archaeological relics, he made them *look* as if they were real: technique and subject-matter bound the Victorians to the solid linear progress of history where lessons relevant to the nineteenth century could be confidently stated.

This feeling of understanding the past and of believing in the classical world as something that had value because it *was* the classical world was one of the factors that sustained the middle classes through the currents of change in the last quarter of the century. Their *fin-de-siècle* worries that we find so recognisable today were real enough and had serious roots in moral, religious and scientific questioning, but although the paintings I am talking about might be scorned by progressives and decadents, aesthetes and prophets of doom, Impressionists, post-Impressionists, modernists and cynics, they still affirmed a core of belief solid enough to make such scorn seem like an aberration. It is surely inadequate for Andrew Graham-Dixon in his recent television series *A History of British Art* to say that the work of the Olympians and of other painters who were not overtly concerned with the modern industrial life around them made him feel that 'they had all just given up'. It is perfectly true, of course, that this was not the way art was reaching into the future, and that to our eyes they are not so *interesting*, but it is also true that the history painters, the Pre-Raphaelites, the creators of an ideal classical world were very relevant to the middle-class Victorian experience.

Besides – and this is the point I want to stress in the rest of this essay – Alma-Tadema was not just being reassuring. I am going to suggest that he was a painter who used a highly stylised but popular form of communication in a way that allowed doubts, and intimations of *fin de siècle*, to cast faint cats' paws of ambiguities upon the smooth blue waters of his classical world, without in the process robbing his public of the feeling that there was enough there to keep the ship steady.

But before looking at one or two of the paintings in more detail to attempt to prove this point, let me recapitulate. The Olympians painted pictures of Ancient Rome, Greece and Egypt which flattered the Victorians by making them believe that they understood the past, and that it was, somehow, theirs; in Alma-Tadema's case, there were enough similarities in some of the situations and characters to make them feel that they were a continuation of great traditions. Those Ancients were like them, and they were like those Ancients; but, because they were Victorians, they had developed an understanding which enabled them to stand apart from and above them: the similarities gave them the feeling that they too were in a golden classical age, but at the same time their own superiority reassured them that they were not going to share the decadence and dissolution of those ancient empires; they knew what had gone wrong and how to avoid its repetition. Darwin, for all the disagreeable aspects of his theories, had surely indicated that a better kind of imperialism could survive; negative Darwinism and reverse colonialism were only nightmares, Jack the Ripper and deviant sexuality were aberrations.

The portrayal of female nudity is a useful introduction to a more detailed discussion of some of Alma-Tadema's paintings. Not only did these apparently sanitised versions of the ancient world soothe, and tell lies, they also sanctioned the depiction of a lot of agreeable female flesh. The mildly pornographic nature of some of this has been commented on at length by feminists, and no doubt it did contribute to their attraction for the mainly male buyers. It was sometimes surprising how few clothes the Ancients seemed to wear, and some of the paintings were probably destined for the male study rather than the drawing-room. Now, it is true that George Du Maurier (in *Trilby*) and Henry James (in, for example, *Roderick Hudson*, *The Tragic Muse*, 'The Real Thing' and 'The Madonna of the Future') in their very different ways made some attempt to portray the lives of painters and their models, but the tantalising and titillating network of relationships between them, between the model and the painting, between the classical nude and the Impressionist naked woman, between husband and wife and mistress, public and private viewing, were not perhaps subjects that

Victorian fiction could deal with in a very satisfactory way. Art, however, had retained some of its ancient licence.

The objectifying of the female body and the possible reactions of female observers of these pictures interests us now and is an intriguing aspect of Alma-Tadema's art. *In the Tepidarium* (1881) is, perhaps, the most straightforward example to choose. It shows a naked young woman lying languorously on a couch, a feather curling discreetly across her body, a strigil held in her other hand. The picture is small – only 9.5 × 13 inches – and perhaps that was the reason that it did not attract a great deal of attention. The classical excuse for the picture seems somewhat threadbare now, but must have been enough for the day. A tepidarium was part of a Roman bathhouse between the hot and cold rooms, and the technical accuracy of the name with its implied knowledge of Roman customs was the licence for this languorous, inviting pose. The feather would have been used for cooling purposes, so its position is mockingly fortuitous, giving rise, perhaps, to the fleeting thought that the painter might equally have chosen another moment before or after to depict it. The phallic strigil, a small curved instrument used for scraping sweat and flaking skin off the body after bathing or exercise, hovers suggestively. As for the model's face: at the risk of making a crass generalisation, surely Roman women didn't look like that? Alma-Tadema is teasing here, not just by being sexually titillating but by bringing the spectator deliberately into an awareness of the double standards being employed, by coming to the brink of asking what the difference is between pornography and art. The smallness of the picture is part of the game. This, I would suggest, is a witty picture, at some distance both from the glum explanation that women were depicted as erotic objects and from the more excitable one that they were terrifying depictions of rampant sexuality, either continually in autoerotic trances or in the contemplation, throes or aftermath of voracious and possibly lethal lust.

It seems that Alma-Tadema plays this kind of game in a broader sense in many of his pictures. He undercuts a reassuring form or message with suggestions, contradictions, disturbing undercurrents which are not enough to deter his buyers, but which show a sensitivity to *fin-de-siècle* fears. At the same time, these fears are contained within a shared moral framework which basically reaffirms a confident core of beliefs about the Victorians' place in history.

Take, for example, *Antony and Cleopatra* (1883). Cleopatra was a deplorable foreign woman, irresponsible and immodest and not at all like the dear Queen. The Victorian theatre dealt with her in its own way.[2] But in Alma-Tadema's portrayal she is punished: she lolls untidily on the barge's throne, her implausibly white body gleaming through muslin. Her sidelong glance and rods of office are pitiful; the servants puffing scented air into her bower deflate Shakespeare's image (the sails 'so perfumed that / The winds were lovesick with them'); on the front legs of the throne, on either side of her, two carved baboons grin smugly. The Christ-like Antony leans forward from his own barge, gazing more compassionately than lustfully at this tawdry figure. And yet she and her barge fill the foreground with colour and warmth: music is playing, the drapes on the barge are luxuriant gold, the leopard skin is lovingly and sensuously painted. These gold drapes colour the shield on Antony's barge, but only fleetingly; beyond are the cold blues and greys of the water, and the soldiers on the right lead the eye to the great hulk of the Roman fighting machine. Behind Antony the might of its empire forges along the Nile; it could crush her barge like matchwood. Cleopatra might be the archetypal Victorian whore, but what is Antony – her victim, a man obsessed, a representative of government, an imperial administrator, or even a pillar of the Church? It could be said that he is protected in this picture, being portrayed as another victim of female wiles, an honest soldier hopelessly led astray; but the extraordinary contrasts and the startling perspectives which open out beyond Cleopatra's barge suggest unresolved sympathies.

A look at two other pictures confirms these characteristics. *A Dedication to Bacchus* (1889), like *The Roses of Heliogabalus*, portrays an event of which the Victorians could hardly have approved. Rites and practices associated with Bacchus or Dionysus encompass all manner of horrors, and the apparent introduction into this celebration of a small child seems a curious choice of subject given the public attitude of the Victorians towards exploitation of children. Would Alma-Tadema's public make any connection between this and W. T. Stead's revelations about child prostitution which had led to his imprisonment this same year? Is it wholly anachronistic to think of the crop of reports in the 1990s of child involvement in satanic rites? It is true that what we have here is a thoroughly cleaned-up depiction. Although there is a touch of abandon in the dancing of the two young women, and a rather obscure animal is being carried in to be sacrificed, the scene seems designed to cause no offence: the marble floor shines immaculately, the groups of participants are decorously grouped; the whole scene, though full of tambourines and, presumably, chanting of some sort, is curiously quiet and still. But again, as with *Antony and Cleopatra*, there seem to be unreconciled oppositions within the picture. How would his female public relate to the women in this picture? This is *their* ceremony, they are in command here, and they are celebrating perhaps the most disruptive god in the Graeco-Roman pantheon. But there's not a footprint on that marble floor, the little riot of pomegranates is contained on its stand, not so much as a shoulder is bared – except on the small, alarmed child, meagrely draped with a diaphanous wisp of material. Is *she* being sacrificed too? Is she being initiated into this cult? And what sort of cult? Will she be asking for the vote in twenty years' time?

Different kinds of women are on display in *The Women of Amphissa* (1887). Dionysus is the spirit hovering over this picture too. A festival dedicated to him used to take place at Amphissa, but in the year 350 BC a foreign army was rampaging through the district, and exhausted bacchantes would have been vulnerable to them. The women of Amphissa, therefore, protected them all night in their town. The picture shows the scene the next morning, with the bacchantes blearily coming to and being looked after in a small town square. The contrast between the worthy women of Amphissa and the bacchantes seems as starkly portrayed as the virgin and the whore of Victorian fiction and melodrama. The beautifully painted architectural features are reinforced by the upright cohort of women, the blatant contrast with the sprawling bacchantes both modified and reinforced by the solicitous concern of some of the 'good' women. But, again, one is aware of something moving in the opposite direction. It is clear from many of his paintings that Alma-Tadema *likes* painting women: he paints them sensuously, affectionately, erotically; in several of his paintings of individual or pairs of women, they seem to have secret thoughts which give them a vividness one does not find, for example, in Leighton's slabs of flesh or Moore's bundles of muslin. So here, the bacchantes, very much in the foreground of the painting, although they are plentifully clothed exude a dreamy, languorous sensuality. And there is a curious, speculative look in the eyes of some of the women of Amphissa as though they were wondering about the experiences their charges had been through.

To return, finally, to *The Roses of Heliogabalus*. What is Alma-Tadema up to here? At first sight, we observe the Emperor and a

few privileged guests lolling, as I mentioned at the start, in a Roman
way at a banquet, looking on the scene slightly below them where
showers of roses are falling on the other guests. We are clearly some
way into the entertainment: there is a good depth of roses already
on the ground, the guests are partly covered. The technical brilliance
of the painting is astonishing; the depiction of the rose petals has a
dazzling effect, it is clearly a picture which would give the purchaser
his money's worth. The conspicuous consumption which the
whole-scale importation of roses by Alma-Tadema implies[3] spills
over into the creation of the overblown decadence of the scene:
here is an artist, a public, an emperor who would spare no expense
in the pursuit of desire. Presumably, however, the knowledgeable
Victorian art dealer/buyer would not assume that the painter shared
Heliogabalus' amoral attitude: Alma-Tadema is depicting a scene
which, however decorative, is deplorable, and the depiction of it
would carry with it an implied condemnation of the event; even the
less knowledgeable would see it as a sign of the excesses of the late
Roman Empire, without necessarily knowing what the exact circumstances were.

Thus far, the painter would be satisfying a spectrum of his pro-
spective buyers. It would seem, however, looking more closely at the
picture, that something more subversive is also being suggested.
The man with the beard on the right of the picture – a part of the
picture, incidentally, that the Rover advertisement omits – is already
alarmed at what is happening. If one looks across the picture
diagonally, one can see that this figure is echoed in the musician
on the dais at the left of the picture; the shape and colour of the
man's beard reflected in her hair. The underlying pattern of reflection between the upper and lower halves of the picture is reinforced
if one looks at the other figures: the half-submerged woman bottom
left, for example, and the female guest third from the right on the
dais. Again it is the hair which forms the visual connection, this time
reinforced by their coronets of white flowers. There are, in fact, the
same number of figures on the dais and on the ground, in each area
we find a fair one, a light red one and six dark ones; the fruit and
bowls for drink are likewise duplicated, and other minor reflections
can be detected in a larger reproduction. What we are seeing here is
a picture which *apparently* shows the melodramatic confrontation of
two factions, the torturers and the tortured, the powerful and the
helpless, the living and the dying. But what is actually here is
something less straightforward. The dazzling impact of the rose

petals' exotic opulence already confuses the issue and it is noticeable that small drifts of them are floating across the Emperor's cronies; the distorted reflections, although they suggest vividly the existing difference between the two groups, also suggest the future engulfing of the tormentors in their own cruelty. Perhaps most interestingly, while the Emperor and his friends are all engrossed in the scene in front of them, three of the guests are looking out of the picture at *us*, engaging us in their fate: everyone is dying here.[4]

This picture was painted in 1888. In 1881 Stevenson had observed in *Virginibus Puerisque* that marriage was not a bed of roses; and in the sour romanticism of late nineteenth-century poetry, roses had indeed lost both the meticulous ambiguity of Blake's and the folk-song directness of their thorns, and they were being scattered with lurid abandon as the *fin de siècle* strained after the ecstasies of guilt. Yeats's Rose of all the World had 'come where the dim tides are hurled / Upon the wharves of sorrow'; Symons' Rose was the face of a woman lit by a cigarette in the dark of a secret assignation; Dowson, trying feverishly to forget, or not to forget, Cynara, had 'gone with the wind, / Flung roses, roses, riotously with the throng'; and Housman's Shropshire Lad mourned where 'The rose-lipt girls are sleeping / In field where roses fade.' Sir Lawrence Alma-Tadema, pillar of the Royal Academy, rich and respected supplier of art to the respectable, is quietly tempting his public into the maelstrom of *fin-de-siècle* distress.

None of this is relevant to the Rover advertisement. And that is the point. There is no tension today between the Alma-Tadema picture and its edited version in the Rover advertisement: firstly because very few people would know the context of the picture; and secondly, even if they did, there would be no sense of outrage, either aesthetic or moral. Postmodernism has seen to it that areas of moral and aesthetic concern are not subject to value judgements of this kind. The incongruity can be shrugged off, appreciated, or easily accepted. In Alma-Tadema's time, however, there would be some awareness of the context of the picture in a general sense, a feeling, say, that there was some connection between English and Roman imperialism; and there would surely be a variety of reactions among those who knew the story behind the picture: a feeling perhaps of superiority (*we* will not go the way of the decadent Romans), a sense of history, a feeling of moral outrage, or a voyeuristic interest. So was Alma-Tadema titillating his public, or delivering a moral lesson? Whatever he was doing, there is a sense that it *mattered* in a way that it does not now: there was a tension which bound the viewer, the picture, the history, the painter, the parallels; a sense that this existed within a framework of shared beliefs, that there was enough of a connection between the subject matter and Victorian life to make a relation possible.

Today we deride the Victorians' hypocrisy, their respect for authority and their ability to shut their eyes to inconvenient injustice, cruelty and double standards. But, whatever evil flowed from these vices, the Victorian middle classes *cared*, they were fervent about their hypocrisy, they did believe in things even if they were half-aware that this belief was self-interested. So the pictures that have been discussed were carefully coded and calculated, and the self-imposed restraints of taste, reputation, and commercial requirements were the creative stimulus all censorship can be in the hands of an inventive artist. Today, such calculations go into purely commercial areas, like advertisements, so the debates concern ultimately trivial issues; at the end of the nineteenth century they were fundamental. As Marlow, brooding about imperialism in *Heart of Darkness*, notoriously said, 'What redeems it is the idea only. An idea at the back of it; not a sentimental pretence but an idea; and an unselfish belief in the idea...'. The idea might be deeply suspect (and even before Marlow reaches the end of that sentence he is beginning to deconstruct it), but, however questionable it was, it touched on matters more important than the sale of a car. The pictures which have been discussed may seem remote from Victorian life but they referred to such ideas and they mattered. The Rover advertisement is, at the best, only a joke.

Notes

1. A useful word, used back in 1952 by William Gaunt in *Victorian Olympus* to describe the late Victorian painters of the ancient world.
2. Ellen Terry's comment on her, made in a lecture *c*. 1911, is interesting to read alongside the picture: 'I believe Shakespeare conceived her as a woman with a shallow nature, and I should like to see her played as such. If she were not idealised in the theatre, it would be clear to us that Shakespeare has done what no other writer, novelist, dramatist or poet has done – told the truth about the wanton ... if she is represented as a great woman with a great and sincere passion for Antony, the part does not hang together.' Quoted in *Shakespeare: Antony and Cleopatra*,

edited by John Russell Brown (Macmillan, Casebook Series, 1968), p. 54.

3.   During the winter months while he was painting this picture he had boxes of them sent to him from the Riviera.

4.   The Rover advertisement covers, roughly, the left-hand half of the original picture, which means it not only omits the bearded guest but also two out of the three guests who gaze at us out of the picture. The third gazer, who should have been in the advertisement's half of the picture, has been removed and replaced by rose-petals.

Also consulted:

Imagining Rome: British Artists and Rome in the Nineteenth Century, edited by M. Liversedge and C. Edwards (Merrell Holberton, 1996).

Alma-Tadema Calendar 1995 (published by Harry N. Abrams Inc., N.Y.).

Sir Lawrence Alma-Tadema by Vern G. Swanson (Ash and Grant, 1977).

12

Haven't I Seen You Somewhere Before? Melodrama, Postmodernism and Victorian Culture

Nadine Holdsworth

Conventional concepts of literary periods – Romantic, Victorian, Modern, Postmodern – may have a descriptive utility and even partial historical validity, their usefulness and truth value appear less and less complete and more and more fictitious when tested against particular texts and paradigms of time as static, circular and repetitious rather than progressive.[1]

Postmodernism is often explained as a way of making sense of and articulating the cultural manifestations of late twentieth-century experience. However, as the above quote indicates, modern notions of historical lineage, temporal sequentiality and logical progression have been challenged by postmodern discourse. Socio-political and cultural observation would seem to corroborate this perspective. Influenced by selective nostalgia, past events and value-systems continually re-emerge to disrupt the forward march of history. The Victorian era regained political and social currency in the 1980s when Margaret Thatcher extolled the virtues of Victorian values; witness also the cultural and commercial imperative of the entertainment industry's current preoccupation with Britain's nineteenth century literary heritage. In turn, it is not hard to find examples of conditions and cultural practices from the past that can usefully be re-examined in relation to postmodern discourse. According to Umberto Eco 'we could say every period has its own postmodernism',[2] or in other words, postmodern concerns are not necessarily new ones.

Whilst acknowledging that the term postmodernism is notoriously difficult to quantify, as it evades definition and disrupts categorisations, it is possible to identify a number of reccurring themes. These themes reference the decline of metanarratives, commodification, the presence of blurred boundaries and the problematic status of reality, authenticity and originality. In turn, these concerns are said to be present in artistic practice through a self-conscious awareness of linguistic and stylistic conventions, apparent through interdisciplinarity, eclecticism, irony, pastiche and self-referentiality.[3] In this essay I want to address how postmodern characteristics become evident through an examination of the Victorian era's dominant form of theatrical entertainment, melodrama. Of melodrama, John Docker suggests that, 'In its theatricality and teasing closeness to self-parody it perhaps joins a postmodern aesthetic, also evident in architecture, of excess, extravagance, flamboyance, extremes'.[4] This discussion will explore how far melodrama can be viewed as exhibiting a postmodern aesthetic. I will concentrate on aspects which have been at the forefront of debates relating postmodernism to performance in recent years, the metatheatrical quality of enactment, inter-textuality, the function of self-conscious cultural signifiers, the status of representation and the construction of the codified body in performance.

The history of melodrama itself is one of a discontinuous narrative, encompassing mass popular appeal, rejection, reassessments, re-workings and appropriations. As it traversed the context of legitimate and illegitimate theatre throughout the nineteenth century, melodrama exhibited an unprecedented popular appeal and achieved a mass audience in much the same way as television today.

> Melodrama contains every possible ingredient of popular appeal: strong emotion, both pathetic and potentially tragic, low comedy, romantic colouring, remarkable events in an exciting and suspenseful plot, physical sensations, sharply delineated stock characters, domestic sentiment, domestic settings, and domestic life, love, joy, suffering, morality, the reward of virtue and the punishment of vice.[5]

Melodrama is wholly reliant on theatrical excess, so with the advent of the society drama and an increased demand for naturalistic forms of representation it was, with an air of embarrassment, consigned to the margins of theatrical history. In terms of dramatic criticism, for the most part of the twentieth century, the genre has been rejected by the high-brow cultural establishment and reduced to the periphery of critical discourse. Critics were content to discard melodrama as a range of constraining stereotypes contained within laughable plots exhibiting over-sentimental platitudes and moral simplifications. In terms of contemporary performance analysis, melodrama has been rescued from the margins and the easy dismissal of critics who found little of dramatic value. Indeed it could be argued that this revaluation of melodrama owes something to the cultural debates of postmodernism which reject traditional value-judgements rooted in the established cultural hierarchies/boundaries of high art and popular culture.

In the 1970s Peter Brooks's *The Melodramatic Imagination*[6] was instrumental in revealing melodrama as a complex theatrical signification system, legitimising its worth as an academic object of study. This retrieval, together with the recognition that the melodramatic is a predominant force of twentieth-century culture, has resulted in melodrama becoming a key site of interdisciplinarity, pursued by those engaged with theatre, film, music, art history and television studies. This is a consequence of the fact that just as melodrama relied on appropriation, it in turn has been appropriated and reconfigured in other media through successive theatre, film and television adaptations and transformations, what Guy Barefoot refers to as 'cross-media intertextuality'.[7] The multi-functional melodramatic narrative can be found competing across time and media, identifiable in various generic categories such as science fiction, soap opera, detective fiction and the Hollywood blockbuster.

As previously stated, one of the defining features of postmodernism is a lack of faith in originality, what Eco refers to as 'the already said',[8] which is demonstrated through a self-conscious referral to the past and an ironic play with conventions and recognisable cultural signs. Melodrama, more than any other theatrical movement before or since, is reliant on a formulaic approach to dramatic construction and thus is characterised by a sense of postmodern re-play. Many melodramas viewed by British audiences were derivative, encompassing reworked novellas or translations of French plays. The reason for this recycling stemmed from a failure to recognise or protect creative originality in the theatre. The absence of copyright laws meant that foreign successes could be bought cheaply and translated for the Victorian stage until the 1886 International Copyright Act. Also, urbanisation throughout the Victorian era created a new market for consumption in much the same way as globalisation has in the contemporary context; hence there was a need to satisfy a consumer-driven market which demanded efficient productivity over and above original craft.

Within the genre there is a thinly disguised lack of originality, 'themes, situations and character types repeat themselves endlessly, and after a while in melodrama there is nothing new under the sun'.[9] Clearly melodrama exhibits postmodern credentials as its self-conscious awareness of its status as a cultural product enables it to continually replicate itself. The audience is faced with a familiar world of reconstituted plots, intertextual references and well-worn characters who, to intensify the sense of imitation, were invariably played by the same stock actor who had performed the villainous scoundrel or virtuous heroine in a previously produced melodrama.

Postmodernism is said to be derived from the epoch of post-modernity which is defined by a diverse range of economic, social and cultural factors undergoing accelerated transformation. Economic and technological changes occurring on the international stage have heralded decentralisation, globalisation, commodification and diversification, resulting in a heightened sense of cultural contradiction. All of these factors are said to be indicative of the period of postmodernity. Similarly the Victorian age was one of social turbulence as British society witnessed rapid change and people were forced to balance a new set of social forces and a shifting political scene influenced by industrial and agrarian revolutions, urbanisation and the population explosion. It was a time of conquests overseas, prestige in terms of trade and industry and economic prosperity. However, this image of Britain was unstable and contradictory, as the impact of industrialisation and the capitalist economy also precipitated a sharp increase in poverty and class conflict as the profit margin dominated. Oppression and repression were rife, countered by a growing band of reformers and the Trade Union, Chartist and Co-operative Movements. It was a time of opposing forces (or cultural contradiction), wealth versus poverty, materialism versus liberalism, religion versus desacrilisation, liberty versus authority and the individual versus the institution.

Whereas postmodern performance signals cultural contradiction through its rampant pluralism, juxtaposition and multiplicity, melodrama attempts to deny cultural contradiction through the use of fixed boundaries and performative rules. The conventional narrative of melodrama has its roots in a series of oppositions: morality/immorality, villainy/honesty, truth/lies, damnation/salvation, all working within the ultimate conflict of good versus evil

The narrative is reliant on polarisation and confrontation which requires heightened emotional responses played out through emphatic physicalisation and grandiose phraseology in order to strengthen the force of juxtaposition. 'What we have is a drama of pure psychic signs – called Father, Daughter, Protector, Persecutor, Judge, Duty, Obedience, Justice – that interest us through their clash, by the dramatic space created through their interplay'.[10] This is reminiscent of Jean-François Lyotard's proposal in *The Post-modern Condition* relating language and communication to the realm of the performative, whereby narratives consist of strategic game-playing, demanding the observation of rules and 'moves'.[11] In melodrama the rules of the game are clearly delineated and pleasure is derived from the playing-out of the narrative or contest.

The melodramatic plot entails the force of evil providing an obstacle to the presence of an ultimately moral universe and closure occurs with the inevitable triumph of virtue. According to Brooks, melodrama's contextual roots in the French Revolution and its after-math is crucial to an understanding of the form.

> This is the epistemological moment which it illustrates and to which it contributes: the moment that symbolically, and really, marks the final liquidation of the traditional Sacred and its repres-entative institutions (Church and Monarch), the shattering of the myth of Christendom, the dissolution of an organic and hierarchically cohesive society.[12]

Brooks argues that in a desacralised age devoid of a wider moral and religious framework, the emphasis is placed on individual morality and that melodrama embodies codes of honour whereby individual conscience prevails. In this reading, Brooks suggests the decline of metanarratives and the stress on localised individuality at the fore-front of postmodern theory. In the contemporary age theorists point to the dissolution of absolutes, fixed meanings and the destabilising of received structures of knowing and identity. As a cultural response to the period in question, melodrama attempts to impose logical solutions and moral order on a disorderly universe, to pro-vide a vision of certainty in an uncertain world. In its adherence to rigid moral structures and monolithic character definition, melo-drama consoles its audience by intimating that the world can be understood. In its literal form 'most melodrama carries with it an assurance of reassurance, of obscurities dispelled, ambiguities resolved, of a vigorously marked binary pattern of coherence'.[13] By placing such a sharp emphasis on the possibility of order and narrative closure in the theatrical arena, the problematic status of stability in the 'real' world is highlighted. There is a sense of teasing the audience with a vision of life which defiantly rejects the complex and contradictory nature of their experience. The fact that this narrative has to be replayed again and again also signifies the irreducible force of evil and a lack of faith in the triumph of virtue.

Although melodramas end with resolution, I would similarly argue that the presence of complexities, ambiguities and inconsistencies in the narrative also point to a departure from the Victorian rhetoric of progress and rational thought. Instead, these qualities imply the contradictory nature and plurality central to postmodern discourse. The ambiguous quality of melodrama is most keenly signalled by the multiple readings of it, the traditional melodrama being viewed as both ideologically reactionary and potentially radical. In just the same way, the rampant pluralism inherent in postmodern theory renders it both radically subversive in its potential liberation from conventional structures of thought and identity, while also reconfirming those very systems of construction in its failure to offer a comprehensive, 'unified' challenge. Within melodrama there is a proliferation of discourses, for example Bratton points to the multiplicity of socio-economic voices which contend on the stage, and to this we could add gendered, racial and age-related voices.[14] The multidimensional nature of the melodramatic mode is also present in the juxtaposition of moments of high pathos with comic interludes. We witness complex familial, sexual and class inter-relationships, the slipperiness of ideals and absolutes and the contradictions inherent between personal and social history. For example, the past continually collides with the present as remembered incidents, personal histories, past lives and hidden relationships creep up on the present, disrupting notions of continuity and linearity as past events have to be acknowledged and retribution made before life can proceed.

By steadfastly presenting one aspect of character, melodrama also implicitly points to the other, suppressed facets which are hidden beneath the mask of virtue or vice. The unreliability of surface appearance, the constant slippage between the 'hidden' and the 'presentational' is revealed in this way and compounded by the thematic preoccupation with (literally) disguised identities.

The stock character types utilised by the genre: hero (protector), heroine (innocent), villain (manipulator), could also be viewed as embodying components of a fractured identity, which when placed together could equate to the multi-dimensionality forwarded by the postmodern rejection of the unified self. Thus, melodrama references the instability of self and the elusivity of accurate representation, as well as the crisis of legitimacy and authenticity at the forefront of the postmodern condition.

An awareness of the physical (re)presentation of melodrama is crucial to an understanding of the form, and it is to this and the performative aspects of the genre that I now turn. In the first instance it is necessary to set the context for the overt consumption of visuality central to the melodramatic mode. Late-twentieth-century society is often characterised as a period dominated by an image-conscious 'designer ideology', whereby a free play of signifiers demand and receive cultural status. However, this preoccupation with style over substance and an emphasis on pleasure through visual excess is not the sole domain of the contemporary age. The Victorian era also heralded a demand for impressive visual spectacle which rejected the principle of utility. This preoccupation with physical presence and display functioned as a celebration of urban development, imperial strength, commercial supremacy and material prosperity. In the cities, extensive construction programmes evolved implementing elaborate architecture and intricate fixtures, and in the home, commodification through ornamentation prevailed. In his study *The Commodity Culture of Victorian England: Advertising and Spectacle, 1851–1914*, Thomas Richards argues that Victorianism heralded the birth of a commodity culture. As evidence of this development, Richards cites the growth of cultural representation, advertising as a respected form in its own right, and one specific event, the Great Exhibition of 1851. 'The Great Exhibition of 1851 was the first outburst of the phantasmagoria of commodity culture'[15] and symbolised the burgeoning global economy as goods from around the world were paraded to potential consumers. Held within the ostentatious Crystal Palace structure, the Exhibition provided a showcase for materiality and the spectacle of commodification, although Richards acknowledges that 'the Victorian taste for luxury, ostentation, and outward show had long been reflected on the stage'.[16]

In terms of theatrical production, these values translate themselves through the consumption of spectacle, pictorialism and verisimilitude. The foregrounding of consummate theatricality is a fundamental aspect of melodrama's dramatic structure and appeal. The extravagant spectacle of the genre dominates the narrative and is achieved through simultaneously operational signification systems such as setting, costuming, properties, tableau and gestural codes. Narratives of extreme situational conflict require appropriate framing and this can be found in scenery offering spectacular illusionism and spine-tingling stage effects. The audience succumbs to the rush of adrenalin achieved through the realistic portrayal of 'natural' disasters caused by fire, sea and snow, as well as the terror associated with 'supernatural' phenomenon such as ghosts and apparitions. The ability to present such sensational scenes is linked to the mechanical innovations of the period and achieved through complex, technologically demanding scenic devices:

> As stage mechanics improved, however, it became possible to produce such scenes more realistically and elaborately. The public demand for greater and greater realism and more and more sensation led to further efforts on the part of playwrights, managers, scene designers, carpenters, property men, and lighting technicians, to give them what they wanted, and the success of a play might well have been ensured by a really good earthquake, train crash, or horse race. As in the early circus spectacles at Astley's the love of sensation and display became an end in itself, and everything was subordinated to it.[17]

The emphasis here is on the privileging of sensation over cognition, the suspense and *frisson* of reception as an end in itself. The overwhelming appeal is to the senses, a bodily response to the action, the tension in muscles, a heightened awareness of blood surging around the body, an electrification of nerve-endings, the rapid drawing of breath and involuntary exclamations. This revelling in bodily thrills, once again, points to the duality of the melodramatic mode. The spectator experiences the juxtaposition of a narrative which encourages clear cognitive appreciation of motives and action, with the irrational physicality of sensation whereby the precarious, unconscious body takes precedence over and defies reason.

Spectacle is often achieved through an advanced pictorialism, a preoccupation evident in the evolution of the picture-frame stage from the proscenium arch. 'The union of stage and painting was publicly and officially consummated when Squire Bancroft had a

2-foot wide picture-frame moulded and gilded right round the proscenium of the Haymarket in 1880'.[18] This compositional device paradoxically signalled the construction of the image by presenting the frame while insisting on the verisimilitude of the content. The panoramas and dioramas used as scenic backdrops to the stage events embodied the visual culture of Victorianism, capturing 'reality' through painstaking illustration which actualised a particular historical or geographical context. In considering this phenomenon in relation to the enquiry of postmodernism, it is necessary to turn to the philosopher Jean Baudrillard's theory of the simulacrum. For Baudrillard, there is no longer any connection between the representation and the 'real', instead we live in a world of signs without origin, whereby the sign itself has its own value without recourse to mediation of an original. 'Baudrillard takes the contemporary condition to be that of the simulacrum, the material imitation, the copy without an original, the "hyperreal"'.[19] Nineteenth-century culture and commodification relied on imitation and reproduction. In *Before Postmodernism*, Daniel T. Rodgers forwards that, 'Inspired by the possibility of mass produced artifacts, middle-class culture revelled in the reproduction of forms and facsimiles, in the capacity of clay, glass, iron, or photographic plate to mimic and multiply the "real thing"'.[20] Even though the Victorians were aware of the original and the referential nature of the copy, commercial value became attached to the simulation for its own sake. This economy of the sign is apparent in a number of theatrical departures, for example in the commodification of theatrical portraiture:

> The point of capturing images of Garrick, Kemble, or Siddons was not to preserve a semblance of their performances for posterity but to suggest the performative simulacrum for commercial purposes in a booming art marketplace.[21]

The tableau, as a stock theatrical convention of melodrama, reaches towards representation which through compositional arrangement and multiple signalling denies ambiguity by capturing the essence of plot and emotional conflict. The pictorial quality of the tableau is unmistakable and was often manipulated during performance as some tableaux emulated paintings of the period. Booth observes that 'an interesting aspect of public taste and the public knowledge of art is the fact that the audience immediately recognised the painting and applauded the resemblance rather than the stage performance'.[22] This phenomenon offers several connections to post-modernism beyond the notion of visual quotation. Concerning postmodern arts, Nigel Wheale asserts that,

> Representation offers the reader/viewer an imitation where the simulacrum stands in the place of the authentic. Because the simulacrum is indistinguishable from the original, all confidence in authenticity and uniqueness of the object has to be abandoned, and what is celebrated is the success of artifice.[23]

The concept of uniqueness and authenticity is destroyed by the reproducibility of the original and the failure to uphold the distinctiveness of art. There is also a rejection of hierarchies of value and a blurring of boundaries caused by the intersection of fine art with the popular cultural formation of melodrama.

The postmodern preoccupation with representativeness and the social construction and signification of the body has an antecedent in the codified melodramatic body. During the Victorian period the emergence of physiognomy and phrenology had a profound impact on acceptable styles of performance, and 'most psychological theories of the time, such as those of Darwin, Herbert Spencer, Alexander Bain and William James, concentrated on the physiological basis of emotion'.[24] It was widely believed that emotion had a homogeneous external manifestation and could be externally legible through emphatic physical signs. A preoccupation with classification and the formulation of defining principles of emotional embodiment had a marked influence on acting technique as every emotion secured a gestural, vocal and facial precedent. The linking of psychology and physiology was confirmed by the influential acting teacher François Delsarte, who developed a mechanistic theory and practice of performance which highlighted the body as a complex, yet competent, signifying system that was able to physically manifest psychological motivations by reference to particular zones and sections of the body. Drawing on these theories and the influence of classical tragic acting, pantomime and the dumbshow, the preoccupation with figurability is apparent in the presentational acting style associated with melodrama's hyperbolic mode. Although acting styles changed throughout the period, responding to societal changes and the increasing demand for realism, the focus remained on an externally manifest, technical performance. The audience engaged with virtuoso displays of individual technique present in points, starts, convulsions and attitudes, rather than character interaction and a responsive attitude to events and characters on stage.

> Strong emotions and intense physical activity marked simple and complex actions alike. Such instructions as 'laughs wildly', 'falls in agony', 'exhibits the most violent agitation', 'trembles violently', 'dreadfully agitated', 'glaring wildly around', and 'significantly exulting' are everywhere in acting editions.[25]

Within melodrama there are competing versions of the body which is designated the site of signification, 'marked or moulded by the structure of causality that determines its existence'[26] and cultural signs are exhibited to confirm socio-economic, gender and racial status. The performer engages in the meta-theatrical adoption of signifying systems, pointing to the elements being referred to whether character, moral disposition or emotion. Highlighting the artifice of production, characters are defined and delineated by surface appearance, the adoption of codified systems of representation, the colour coding of costuming, physical posture, gestural patterning and facial expression. Paradoxically this implies both a faith in the reliability of the body to impart stable meaning and uncertainty as any inconsistency is meticulously denied. There is little room for character idiosyncrasies, for example the conventions of stage villainy are rigorously applied across the genre – the 'evil' machinations are conducted by a figure suitably encoded with black hair, moustache, a deep voice and cape, supported by other sign-systems such as music. Moreover, a recognition of this codification exposes the construction of identity and reveals how meaning is established through structures of difference, constituted through relational performative languages. As in postmodern discourse we can see a concern with the way signs are employed to construct realities signalling a lack of faith in the possibility of objectively representing 'reality'. The signs of melodrama are not replicating reality, they are constituting it, 'each language constructing specific aspects of reality in its own way. The focus is on the linguistic and social construction of reality'.[27]

The important aspect of this constructive process involves the privileging of the sign over the motivation and the iconic status of complex states such as virtue and vice. Moreover, as Brooks recognises, the codification is ultimately inadequate; how can a repertoire of stock responses, looks, sighs and gestures capture the depth of emotional anguish perpetrated by the narrative? The performer cannot fail to highlight the gap between the 'reality' of theatrical presentation and the 'ideal' of authentic emotion. During perform-ance recourse to swooning, guttural noise and inarticulate mutter-ings point to the distance between the 'real' and the 'presentational' – the failings of the codified system. 'For they mark a kind of fault or gap in the code, the space that marks its inadequacies to convey a full freight of emotional meaning'.[28] This observation echoes Lyo-tard's evocation of Kant's notion of the sublime as fundamental to the postmodern aesthetic. For Lyotard the sublime is revealed in the slippage between the 'capacity to conceive and the capacity to pres-ent an object corresponding to the concept'.[29] In short, we have an idea of vice but this cannot be adequately presented. What is pro-duced will always be reductive and distanced from reality, thereby functioning as a critique of the concepts of knowledge and repres-entation.

> The articulation of melodrama's messages in this kind of sign language – and in verbal language which strives toward the status of sign language in its use of a vocabulary of clear, simple, moral and psychological absolutes – suggests the extent to which melo-drama not only employs but is centrally about repeated obfusca-tions and refusals of the message and about the need for repeated clarifications and acknowledgements of the message.[30]

The issue of repetition is fundamental and involves both repetition within a singular performance and multiple representations across performances, denying the uniqueness of situation and emotion, transgressing notions of authenticity. Instead the emphasis is on enactment, 'the act of doubling, and the doubling of action, in imitation, repetition or citation . . . putting it in self-reflexive quota-tion marks'.[31] In the Victorian theatre examples of the stock response for grief, for example, were constantly rearticulated in a sign-language which had previously been employed, compromised and distanced from the 'real'. This can be read in relation to Claude Lévi-Strauss's notion of bricolage, 'that is, an activity that circum-scribes creative expression by making it rely on "a heterogeneous repertoire which, even if extensive, is nevertheless limited"'.[32] The bricoleur, in this case the performer of melodrama, has a limited range of tools at her/his disposal and therefore inevitably fails to capture or embody the original, they can merely refer to it. In many senses this is the nature of all performance as it relies on role-play and this is why, as David George articulates, the language of performance has been appropriated by postmodern theorists drawing on 'terms such as play, game, drama, to describe the new consciousness... the concept of roles, masks, stages: mirrors, doubling'.[33] However, I would argue that melodrama provides the epitome of these elements, the moment in theatre history when this heightened theatrical consciousness was at a premium.

In exploring melodrama it is clear that there are many points of convergence with contemporary issues of postmodern performativity. It is very easy to read Victorian melodrama in the contemporary context and to uncover a sense of ironic 'knowingness', a parody of its own faith in reliable representation and utopian ideals, an awareness of its distance from the 'real' through its insistence on spectacular, self-conscious hyperbole. The departure from postmodernism really resides in how far we are meant to accept the conventions and take the melodramatic seriously. After all, despite the multidimensional character of the narrative, the genre works consistently to support its own myth of stability and moral absolutes through strict adherence to established performative rules, essentialist portrayals and narrative closure. However, this myth is in crisis and this results in the enduring appeal of the form as the spectator can wallow in moral superiority while experiencing the thrill of vice, can engage with cognisable signification systems at the same time as physical excess and bodily sensation, can let the security of inevitable resolution free them to delight in the exhilaration of conflict, contradiction and the possibility of destroyed virtue. In this sense, perhaps the most interesting aspect of the Victorian sensibility's melodramatic mode is its ability to reinvent itself, to engage in metamorphosis, to reappear across time and media, revealing that many current cultural trends and the theoretical discourses evolving to account for them in an ever-decreasing spiral of dependency have, in fact, been seen somewhere before.

Notes

1. Robert Kiely, *Reverse Traditions: Postmodern Fictions and the Nineteenth Century Novel* (Cambridge, Mass.: Harvard University Press, 1993), p. 5.
2. Umberto Eco '"I Love You Madly," He Said Self-Consciously', in Walter Truett Anderson (ed.), *The Fontana Postmodernism Reader* (London: Fontana, 1996), p. 32.
3. See Nick Kaye, *Postmodernism and Performance* (Basingstoke and London: Macmillan, 1994), pp. 5–23; Nigel Wheale (ed.), *The Postmodern Arts* (London: Routledge, 1995), pp. 3–64.
4. John Docker, *Postmodernism and Popular Culture: A Cultural History* (Cambridge: Cambridge University Press, 1994), p. 258.
5. Michael R. Booth, *Theatre in the Victorian Age* (Cambridge: Cambridge University Press, 1991), pp. 150–1.
6. Peter Brooks, *The Melodramatic Imagination* (New Haven: Yale University Press, 1976).
7. Guy Barefoot, 'East Lynne to Gas Light: Hollywood, Melodrama and Twentieth-Century Notions of the Victorian' in Jacky Bratton, Jim Cook and Christine Gledhill (eds), *Melodrama: Stage, Picture, Screen* (London: British Film Institute, 1994), p. 96.
8. See Eco, op. cit., pp. 31–3.
9. Michael R. Booth, *English Melodrama* (London: Herbert Jenkins, 1965), p. 5.
10. Brooks, op. cit., pp. 35–6.
11. See Jean-François Lyotard, *The Postmodern Condition: A Report on Knowledge* (Manchester: Manchester University Press, 1984), pp. 9–11.
12. Brooks, op. cit., pp. 14–15.
13. Martin Meisel, 'Scattered Chiaroscuro: Melodrama as a Matter of Seeing' in Bratton, Cook and Gledhill (eds), op. cit., p. 67.
14. See Jacky Bratton, 'The Contending Discourses of Melodrama' in Bratton, Cook and Gledhill (eds), op. cit., pp. 38–49.
15. Thomas Richards, *The Commodity Culture of Victorian England: Advertising and Spectacle, 1851–1914* (London: Verso, 1991), p. 18.
16. Ibid., p. 21.
17. Booth, *English Melodrama*, p. 165.
18. Michael R. Booth, *Victorian Spectacular Theatre 1850–1910* (London: Routledge, 1981), p. 11.
19. Kaye, op. cit, p. 17.
20. Daniel T. Rodgers, 'Before Postmodernism', *Reviews in American History* 18 (1990), p. 78.
21. Tracy C. Davis, 'Riot, Subversion, and Discontent in New Victorian Theatre Scholarship', *Victorian Studies* (Winter 1994), p. 309.
22. Booth, *Victorian Spectacular Theatre*, p. 10.
23. Wheale, op. cit, p. 51.
24. George Taylor, *Players and Performances in the Victorian Theatre* (Manchester and New York: Manchester University Press, 1989), p. 148.
25. Booth, *English Melodrama*, p. 195.
26. Simon Shephard, 'Pauses of Mutual Agitation' in Bratton, Cook and Gledhill (eds), op. cit., p. 27.

27. Steiner Kvale, 'Themes of Postmodernity' in Walter Truett Anderson (ed.), *The Fontana Postmodernism Reader*, p. 21.
28. Brooks, op. cit. p. 67.
29. Lyotard, op. cit, p. 77.
30. Brooks, op. cit, p. 28.
31. Steven Conner, 'Postmodern Performance' in Patrick Campbell (ed.), *Analysing Performance* (Manchester and New York: Manchester University Press, 1996), p. 108.
32. Claude Lévi-Strauss cited in Richards, op. cit, p. 50.
33. David George, 'On Ambiguity: Towards a Postmodern Performance Theory', *Theatre Research International* 14, 1 (1989), p. 71.

13

'A low born labourer like you': Audience and Victorian Working-Class Melodrama

Darryl Wadsworth

J.P. Burnett's *Jo*, a stage adaptation of Dickens's *Bleak House*, proved one of the great successes of London's 1876 theatre season. This first West End production of *Bleak House* inspired numerous versions in the West End that year and ensured the reputation of its young lead, Jennie Lee. Lee became synonymous with the role of Jo, playing the street-sweeper in revival after revival as late as 1921, and enjoying equal success in Europe, America and Australasia.[1] More striking than the play's success, though, is the lateness of its success. Profitable West End versions of Dickens's earlier novels had followed closely the final number of serial publication, or predated the final number, sometimes even by several months. Yet Burnett's adaptation of *Bleak House* and the numerous other West End versions of the mid-1870s appeared twenty years after the novel. Jo had appeared on stage earlier, however, outside the fashionable West End – that is, outside the area in which theatres gathered together the most socially diverse audiences. Differences in tone between these early productions of *Bleak House* at theatres in working-class areas and Burnett's West End production highlight the necessity of considering audience composition when characterising Victorian melodrama. To ignore audience composition is to misrepresent melodrama; West End melodrama, which includes most of the melodramas to receive critical attention to date, of necessity defuses the potentially explosive issues it raises in socially diverse theatres, while working-class melodrama more openly depicts these concerns as class issues. Such a distinction has implications beyond the generic. Recognising the extent to which the content of melodrama is contigent upon its audience exposes the danger in depicting middle-class Victorian culture as, simply, Victorian culture.

The earliest stage versions of *Bleak House* appeared at the Lord Chamberlain's office for licensing on the week of 31 May 1853, prior to the final five numbers of the novel's serial publication.[2] Numerous events were still to be depicted in the novel, among them Lady Dedlock's flight, the identification of Tulkinghorn's murderer, and the 'resolution' of the Jarndyce Chancery suit. The plotline which had come to a conclusion by the fifteenth number – a conclusion for which the first adaptors were clearly waiting – was the life and death of little Jo. Even those critics of the completed novel who faulted the construction of its plot found its depiction of the street-sweeping urchin praiseworthy;[3] in his *Life of Dickens* Forster quotes Dean Ramsay's judgement that 'nothing in the field of fiction is to be found in English literature surpassing the death of Jo!'[4] Most Victorian stage versions of *Bleak House* attest further to the power of the image of Jo's death by concluding with Jo's death scene, although such a choice diverges considerably from the shape of the completed novel.

The first *Bleak House* adaptation licensed was that of the City of London theatre, an East End theatre that had opened in 1837 with an adaptation of *The Pickwick Papers*. This *Bleak House* was most likely written by John H. Wilkins, dramatist in ordinary at the City of London.[5] Another adaptation was submitted by James W. Elphinstone and Frederick Neale of the Pavilion Theatre in the same week; this version, in fact, may have beaten the City of London's onto the boards.[6] Both the City of London and the Pavilion were located in the East End, and melodrama was a staple of these theatres, as it was of most theatres in working-class areas of London. Both houses were 'minor' theatres; it should be noted, however, that this designation reflects their geographical location rather than their size. With a seating capacity of 2,500 the City of London theatre, for example, was considerably larger than the Adelphi, one of the main houses of melodrama in the West End, with a capacity of 1,500.[7] Size notwithstanding, however, the City of London, the Pavilion, and other 'minor' theatres in working-class areas in the East End and south of the Thames would have been beyond the interest of most middle-class spectators from the West. Michael R. Booth notes that, although the East End entertainment industry was considerable, especially between the 1830s and the 1860s, middle-class critics and audiences knew little about these theatres:

It was the exceptional middle-class critic or writer who made the journey to an East End theatre, usually in search of a colour story, and usually to patronise what he saw. The lack of attention East End theatres received was not merely a matter of geographical remoteness; as an urban entity the whole of the East End was beyond the social and cultural pale for the middle-class Londoner from the West, and his ignorance of it was profound.[8]

This claim is supported by a dearth of critical response to these two early adaptations of *Bleak House*. Possibly such a bias underlies S.J. Adair Fitzgerald's suggestive modifier in his statement, 'I have been unable to trace any adaptation [of *Bleak House*] of any importance until the year 1874...'[9]

The importance of these early adaptations lies in their departures from Dickens, departures which heighten their working-class appeal and mark them as inappropriate for presentation in the West End. Most notably, little Jo in the City of London version appears as an eloquent and outspoken advocate for the poor, in stark contrast to the Jo of Dickens, almost voiceless and completely confounded as to the causes of his suffering. For example, Wilkins's Jo – in an exchange that does not occur in Dickens – lashes out angrily when offered too small a payment for carrying Grandfather Smallweed up a flight of stairs:

> JOE. [*sic*] A penny for lugging you up the stairs, and a 'most throttled by you holding my neck. I won't have it – you may want it yourself. I'm poor in pocket, but I scorn to take nothing from the poor in spirit – I ain't a bloodsucker, for rich blood as that must be pisen.
> OLD S. Impudent rascal – Ah, the pitch of insolence the London poor have come to – I should like to send 'em all to the treadmill.
> JOE. I dare say you would – but poor as they is, they gets their hand in some odd way or another by hard working and making themselves useful, and that's more than I can say, as drives over 'em in their carriages and looks upon ['em] as dogs and dirt under their feet.[10]

Shifting here from 'I' to the class-identifying 'they', this Jo understands his suffering as determined by his class. He suggests a binarism of class identity that poises those who make themselves useful against those with 'rich blood'. Jo's outburst here is clearly pitched towards the audience of the City of London theatre; few spectators in that theatre would drive carriages home.

Jo is drawn into the web of family affiliation in this *Bleak House* through his insistence that his relationship with Esther's father, the deceased Captain Hawdon, or 'Nemo', approaches a familial one; the play implies that all human beings should consider their relationship to the poor as familial. The tightly woven family schema of this melodrama leaves no room for Lady Dedlock's death; indeed she does not even leave the domestic sphere when Esther's parentage is revealed. Sir Leicester here responds with delight to the revelation that his wife is Esther's mother; he accepts Esther as his own daughter without so much as a raised eyebrow: 'Your daughter shall be mine – come to my arms and ever find a father in me' (f. 42). From this declaration follows the announcement of Esther's impending wedding to Woodcourt, then of Rich's to Ada, so that Sir Leicester is left to exclaim, 'By Jove I shall soon have a snug family party' (f. 43). These resolutions, following one after another with little motivation, admittedly show the signs of hasty construction – the City of London's management was apparently competing with that of the Pavilion to have the first *Bleak House* on stage – but their result, the snug family party in which parental bonds are recognised and marriage bonds are proclaimed, is consistent with the ethos of melodrama.

All that remains to interrupt this party is the death of Jo; this death, rather than undermining the existing family relationships and positioning Jo outside of them, suggests his place within the family by emphasising a relationship that takes on a familial significance:

> ESTHER. Joe, you must rouse and recover. Friends are by, and many happy days are yet in store.
> JOE. No, Miss, not for I – for you there be[.] I can see thy father's face in thee and that voice – yes – you be the very spirit of him – but don't come too near me – I've got fever and I wouldn't harm thee for the world. Lay poor Joe in the Pauper churchyard next to him, and put on my tombstone that he – he was very good to me he was. *Dies.*   (ff. 43–4)

In his choice of a grave Jo claims a familial relationship between himself and Nemo. Having no family name, Jo chooses for his tombstone a proclamation of the actions that define a family relationship: 'he was very good to me'. Recognising the visual and vocal affinity between Esther and her father draws Jo, through Nemo, into Esther's intimate family circle – Sir Leicester's 'snug family party'.

In expanding the family circle to include the recipient of charity, this working-class production hints at an ambiguity in Dickens's critique of 'Telescopic Philanthropy'. Dickens both criticises the philanthropic efforts of Mrs Jellyby, who neglects her own (literal) household, and indicts the middle-class reader who might not sympathise with Jo because he is not exotic and therefore not interesting:

> he is not softened by distance and unfamiliarity; he is not a genuine foreign-grown savage; he is the ordinary home-made article.... Homely filth begrimes him, homely parasites devour him, homely sores are in him, homely rags are on him: native ignorance, the growth of English soil and climate, sinks his immortal nature lower than the beasts that perish. Stand forth, Jo, in uncompromising colours! from the sole of thy foot to the crown of thy head, there is nothing interesting about thee.[11]

But these dual attacks exist in an uneasy tension; if Mrs Jellyby were to mind her own home, Jo would still remain outside of that home, would still be without a home. If Dickens's *Bleak House* aims to encourage in its middle-class readership an appropriate domestic economy, where does it place the limits of the domestic?

The emotional force of Wilkins's *Bleak House*, offering Jo an angry voice and the choice of his own burial-place, depends on a direct identification between the working-class audience and Jo. This Jo, then, unlike Dickens's, speaks for himself. While for Dickens's narrator, the task is to point out Jo's humanity *in spite of* his existence at the fringes of human experience – in spite of his inarticulateness, his almost beast-like appearance, his seeming lack of human relationships – Wilkins's play assumes Jo's humanity, and its audience's sympathy with that humanity. The play emphasises both the unfair distribution of wealth – away from those who 'gets their hand in some odd way or another by hard working and making themselves useful' – and the correct moral relation between poor humans and rich humans – 'he was very good to me he was'. Appropriate to the theatre in which it played, in which there was no particular division of audience according to class, this play's conclusion optimistically suggests that the domestic structure can bridge all difference: through marriage, even Sir Leicester joins in the circle of Jo's mourners.

When Jo finally made his stage début in the West End, more than twenty years after the appearance of *Bleak House*, managers seemed unconcerned that their theatres were located in exactly the area through which Jo is made to move in Dickens's novel. Playbills for Burnett's production at the Globe announced that the location of Nemo's graveyard was Russell Court, Drury Lane, and one reviewer remarked that the scenery, 'presenting the places named by the novelist,... has an air of realism which will ensure the popularity of the old story as a new drama.'[12] Not surprisingly, then, this and other West End productions avoid the angry tone of the earlier East End plays; such direct attacks would be unsettling for audiences who would find Jo's brethren still wandering just outside the theatre door. Furthermore, the overt class hostility demonstrated by Wilkins's Jo, while reasonably safe in the East End theatre, could threaten the smooth management of the Globe, where chimney-sweeps slightly better off than Jo sat in the gallery above middle- and upper-class patrons. Bennett, then, not only avoids the angry rhetoric of his East End counterparts, but also carefully excises the indignation of Dickens's narrator. For example, a small addition to Jo's final prayer ensures that Jo's death is a self-contained event that need not disturb the audience beyond a night's entertainment:

BUCKET. (*Very softly.*) Joe, can you say what I say [?]
JOE. (*Very feebly.*) Anything, as you say, Sir –
BUCKET. (*Uncovering. All do the same.*) 'Our Father.'
JOE. 'Our Father' – yes, that's wery good, Sir.
BUCKET. 'Which art in heaven.'
JOE. 'Art in heaven.' – Is the light a 'comin', sir?
BUCKET. It's close at hand.
JOE. (*Moonlight has fallen on his face – he pauses – smiles – mutters gladly.*) I'm movin' on.
(*falls back dead in Bucket's arms.* [Music cue indicated in MS.] *Music swells out forte.*
Slow Drop.)[13]

This version, for the most part following Dickens word for word, adds to Dickens's description moonlight, a smile, and Jo's glad muttering, 'I'm movin' on.' Burnett's ending uses the techniques of the stage – lighting, music, tableau, and curtain – to create from Jo's death a spectacle for the viewer's delight, a cathartic moment which purges the spectator of the need for further responsibility. The viewer's satisfaction in recognising 'Phiz'''s woodcut illustrations 'realised' on stage throughout the production is here matched by the satisfaction of hearing Jo's tag line – 'I'm movin' on' – spoken at the very moment its meaning transforms.

The creation of a cathartic spectacle from Jo's death is precisely the effect which some of Dickens's reviewers had found troubling in the death of little Nell. Such an effect Dickens avoids in *Dombey and Son* by presenting little Paul Dombey's sickness and the moment of his death from Paul's own point of view, and in his *Bleak House* by refusing to describe Jo's dead body, instead emphasising at the moment of Jo's death the continuing presence of death:

> Dead, your Majesty. Dead, my lords and gentlemen. Dead, Right Reverends and Wrong Reverends of every order. Dead, men and women, born with Heavenly compassion in your hearts. And dying thus around us every day.   (572)

Rapidly shifting his attention from Jo's body to the readers who mourn Jo, Dickens's narrator attempts to ensure that the significance of Jo's situation does not end with his death and the reader's tearful response to it. Burnett's adaptation precisely counters such a shift, keeping all eyes on Jo until the curtain falls. This ending leaves no question about the fate of the dying innocent. Burnett further emphasises this fate in a last-minute revision of the manuscript prior to its submission for licensing: striking out the third line of the Lord's Prayer – 'Hallowed be thy Name' – he allows Jo to end his prayer with 'Heaven' rather than 'Name'.[14] Allowing Jo to move on to the afterlife, and with a smile, Burnett relieves the poignancy of his still moving on outside the stage door. The phrase which in the novel denies the possibility of closure here becomes the sign of closure. The novel refuses rest to Jo; this melodramatic version offers it, and includes a musical theme to sing him, and his spectators, to it. Sympathetic identification with Jo here transcends class, is 'above' class – Jo's final moving on is a universal human move from this life to the next, and is thus outside of the considerations of class difference. One need not share a class identity with Jo to share in his suffering and his ultimate reward in this scene; Jo's smile furthermore emphasises his death as rest and reward, and does not implicate the audience in his suffering. While Jo on the streets might continue to be an eyesore, Jo on stage, with his 'brown eyes brimming with tears', led Robert Courtneidge fifty years later to exclaim of Lee's performance: 'I thank God I have been privileged to see it.'[15] Spectators at the Globe, however, need not have been particularly financially privileged to see it; the 6d gallery seats would have been within the purchasing range of many working-class patrons. Presumably, Lee's popular performance, repeated at various venues well into the twentieth century, did not upset the comfortable division of spectators into boxes, stalls, and gallery – the solace of tears, at least, was distributed equally.

The divergence in tone between the East End and West End productions of *Bleak House* highlights the role that class composition of the theatre's audience played in determining what could be presented on stage. Not surprisingly, the largely homogenous audiences of working-class theatres afforded playwrights considerable freedom for the overt expression of class hostility. Wilkins's Jo is just one in a company of angry agricultural labourers, sailors, factory workers and urban poor to decry the system that distributes wealth and power unjustly. While playwrights in the West End described in heightened rhetoric the pathos of the powerless, playwrights in working-class areas as often as not used similarly heightened rhetoric to express the anger of the disenfranchised. Such anger finds its targets beyond a single aristocratic villain, in a corrupt or arbitrary system that places power in the hands of the unworthy. For example, working-class melodramas often display a particular hatred of the law as one element of a corrupt system; the law is an especially useful target for anger because it links the individual villain to the system that makes the villain powerful. While Dickens's *Bleak House* portrays a rapacious but class-blind law, destroying all who become ensnared in its tangles, the law in working-class melodrama distributes power to the wealthy and becomes the most useful tool of the villain.[16] Even the basic melodramatic situation – a wealthy villain uses his financial control over the heroine's family to attempt to seduce her – positions the law on the side of the villain; often one of the villain's underlings is a barrister who comes to seize the heroine's family's goods. The attitude of working-class heroes and heroines to the law further demonstrates their awareness of their position within a class system and of the law as part of that system.

In John T. Haines's *Alice Grey, The Suspected One; or, The Moral Brand*, first presented at the Surrey Theatre south of the Thames in

1839, the law is the most powerful tool of the wealthy in robbing labourers first of the fruits of their labour and finally of the power to labour. Harry Hammerton, the virtuous village smith and Alice Grey's betrothed, reflects on the inequities inherent in the law:

> The law of the land empowers the tyrant, and I bow to the law; it was framed by those who have placed themselves beyond its powers – let their hearts tell them of its justice. It's well to talk of a prison in the green fields – it's well to talk of its high walls and iron bars under the shelter of a title! but to him, who is robbed of the power of earning what would free him – who is stripped of the little he *has* earned, and is thrust hopeless into a dungeon – it is despair, Alice – it is madness![17]

The law is characterised by its power over the labourer, but also by its inability to help the labourer. Alice Grey, wrongly accused of stealing £400 that her uncle has been saving towards the purchase of an inn, loses all social power and earning power in her community, even though the court clears her of the charge. Her inability to conceal the wrongly-applied 'moral brand' gives the villain of this piece, Chrystal Baxter, the Methodist ostler-turned-grocer-turned-landlord, power over her. He offers to marry her to secure her reputation as a respectable woman, then, when she refuses, threatens to seize the goods of the woman with whom she has lived since being disowned by her uncle. Even Harry Hammerton's return after a seven-year absence cannot aid in proving Alice's innocence; tried before the grocer-turned-magistrate David Demure, Alice and Harry are both found guilty. Only the surprise appearance of one of Baxter's accomplices from the inside of a grandfather clock – a literal *Deus Ex Machina* – reveals their innocence and Baxter's guilt.

Similarly, Samuel Atkyns's *Life of a Labourer*, produced at the Royal Albert Saloon in the East End in 1848, shows the law as the tool of the wealthy. Here its use is fraudulent; wealth gives the villain the ability to manipulate the law to his own ends. In this play the angry denouncement of the wealthy reaches its highest pitch as Stephen the labourer attempts to protect his sister from the advances of their landlord, the lascivious Sir Martin Maxwell:

> STEPHEN. Wretch if I were to take you by the throat now (*advancing a step but Ellen interposes*) it would but serve you right. It was

you and your vile lawyer that fraudulently obtained my signature to a paper, which gave you a right to my old heritage.

SIR MARTIN. (*Mockingly*) You see Stephen that I have an eye to business – to extending my possessions – ... when a man with a clear head like me deals with a low born labourer like you, there is little chance for you. I have an idea myself that the over population of the agricultural poor is a crime – and the mothers –

STEPHEN. Silence or I will strangle you – where you stand. Learn that the mothers of the poor are in the eyes of heaven equal to your noblest ladies, that the hardy sons of the soil are its sole and only ornaments, not you, nor your like, who waste in riotous living the produce of *their* labour – and in order to support the extravagance of your panders and your mistresses, you drag to the ground every toiling hand, till he curses the land that bore him as a harsh and cruel stepmother, from whom he may expect no mercy, and never dreams of receiving tenderness.[18]

The threat of violence from the working-class hero is undisguised: twice Stephen threatens to strangle Sir Martin. Hatred for Sir Martin is stirred up by his insult to the mothers – those touchstones of Victorian moral feeling – of an entire class. Sir Martin's fraudulent use of the law destroys the correct domestic relationship between the labourer and his land, transforming the land from a nurturing mother into a cruel stepmother.[19]

In this passage, too, appears the hint of the providential ending of this melodrama, an ending which characteristically rewards the virtuous and powerless, but also threatens to undermine the play's significance for its working-class audience. Sir Martin's lawyer has helped him to rob Stephen of his right to his 'old heritage', so that in this melodrama the resolution of social ills can come about simply by the correct application of the law. And so are these ills resolved; when two officers come on stage to arrest Sir Martin for forgery, reward and punishment are quickly meted out in just measure:

TRUEMAN. Behold the justice of heaven. The wicked man is fallen into his own snare – the poor but honest man rewarded and protected.

STEPHEN. Riches! happiness! new life! –

SIR MARTIN. Detection! misery – transportation! – *Tableau.*   (f. 546)

This happy conclusion, offering a satisfying narrative closure for the protagonists and for the eager spectators, is one of many that ultimately circumscribes the potential of melodrama to advance solutions for the social ills it portrays. Stephen's position as a labourer with an 'old heritage' hints at a solution from the beginning of the play, but this position also distinguishes Stephen from the spectators in the Royal Albert Saloon. Providential endings, including those that yield protagonists rewards beyond what they seem to expect from the start, offer only narrative satisfaction to the spectator, rarely, if ever, pointing to a means for the material resolution of social problems. Sadly, this is no less true for working-class melodrama than for melodrama in the West End, although the implications of such endings differ for East End audiences, imagining themselves as powerless because of social status, and West End audiences, varying widely in status and perceived power to affect social conditions.

What working-class melodrama offers for the contemporary critic of Victorian culture is a conception of the self radically distinct from the dominant Victorian middle-class ideology of self-determination. While *Jane Eyre* and *David Copperfield* present images of middle-class self-made agents acknowledging responsibility and gaining control over environment through self-control, working-class melodrama displays characters with no control over their environment, characters robbed of even the minimal power that labour might afford them, characters whose virtue is rewarded through forces beyond their power: the accomplice hidden in the grandfather clock, the unexpected acceptance of a wealthy stepfather, even an event as seemingly ordinary as the arrival of the police. Such characters may even become most eloquent in moments of least self-control: Jo's angry valorisation of the poor in pocket over the poor in spirit, Harry Hammerton's despair – to the point of 'madness' – about the threat of the dungeon to the worker, Stephen's unconcealed threat of violence as he defends the mothers of the poor.

Such characters, too, exhibit a greater awareness of class as determinative than their counterparts on the middle-class stage. Jo, Harry, and Stephen all speak for the poor as a group, an action that counters images of individual middle-class agents pulling themselves up by their own bootstraps. In working-class melodrama, acknowledging responsibility means not self-control but rather recognition of correct moral relations within and between classes. Wilkins's *Bleak House*, optimistically bringing together different classes into a 'snug family party', is only an extreme example of an ethos that emphasises sympathy and aid across class rather than Smilesian self-help.

The ultimate value in considering Victorian working-class melodrama, then, may lie in correcting a conception of Victorian culture simply as middle-class culture. Such a corrective is particularly useful because the forms that melodrama takes today tend to obscure the group identities and affiliations of their audiences. Once the mainstay of the stage, melodrama today appears predominantly in certain types of film and television.[20] These screen melodramas thus take place in settings which incorporate the largest and most diverse audience possible, but also limit active group identification within those audiences; the pacifying darkness of movie houses and the vastly encompassing but infinitely divided and bounded domestic space of television viewership privilege individual identification over group affiliation. The presentation of today's melodramas, then, often flattens the class differentiation that inheres, both in the audience and on stage, in Victorian melodrama. Nineteenth-century melodramatic playwrights needed to tailor their plays to suit more particular and physically immediate audiences: either the socially diverse audiences of the West End arranged in a spatial hierarchy according to class, or the homogenous audiences of working-class theatres outside the West End. To the contemporary critic who takes these audiences into account, Victorian melodrama offers an alternate image to the middle-class self-made agent. Working-class melodrama, in particular, puts forward this image in its most distinct form, offering anger as self-expression, pointing to class inequities inherent within social institutions, emphasising class position as determinative of life prospects and class identity as self-identity, and extending to relationships beyond the family those bonds of obligation that tie parent to child and husband to wife.

Notes

1. F. Dubrez Fawcett, *Dickens the Dramatist* (London: W. H. Allen, 1952), p. 231.

2. Such an early appearance of a stage adaptation was by no means unusual; Martin Meisel notes in his *Realizations* (Princeton: Princeton University Press, 1983) that, for example, the earliest adaptation of *Nicholas Nickleby* was able to draw on only seven of the twenty parts of the serialised novel. Meisel discusses in detail how playwrights could use the technique of theatrical realisation to lend authenticity to such 'cuckoo fledglings'.

3. See, for example, Henry Fothergill Chorley, anonymous review in the *Atheneum*, 17 September 1853, 1087–8; and George Brimley, unsigned review, *Spectator*, 24 September 1853, 923–5, both quoted in Philip Collins, *Dickens: The Critical Heritage* (London: Routledge and Kegan Paul, 1971).

4. John Forster, *The Life of Charles Dickens*, ed. J. W. T. Ley (London: Cecil Palmer, 1928), p. 563.

5. Malcolm Morley, '*Bleak House* Scene', *Dickensian* XLIX (1953), p. 175. The title page of the play's manuscript in the Lord Chamberlain's collection bears the name of Nelson Lee, probably Richard Nelson Lee, one of the City of London's two managers at the time.

6. See H. Philip Bolton, '*Bleak House* and the Playhouse', *Dickens Studies Annual* XII (New York: AMS, 1983), pp. 81–124, for details of the competing versions at the City of London and the Pavilion. Bolton's invaluable *Dickens Dramatized* (London: Mansell Publishing Ltd, 1987) provides a comprehensive listing of adaptations of Dickens's works.

7. Diana Howard, *London Theatres and Music Halls 1850–1950* (London: Library Association, 1970), pp. 6 and 46.

8. Michael R. Booth, *Theatre in the Victorian Age* (Cambridge: Cambridge University Press, 1991), p. 5.

9. S.J. Adair Fitzgerald, *Dickens and The Drama* (London, 1910), p. 246.

10. John Wilkins, *Bleak House* (1853; British Library Add. MS. 52, 940.K), f. 27.

11. Charles Dickens, *Bleak House*, eds. George Ford and Sylvère Monod (London and New York: W. W. Norton, 1977), p. 564.

12. Anonymous review, Enthoven collection, Theatre Museum, London.

13. J.P. Burnett, *Bleak House* (1876; British Library Add. MS. 53162.B), ff. 88–9.

14. Bolton suggests that the omission of this line of the Lord's Prayer is an attempt to appease the censorship of the Examiner of Plays. Dickens appropriately, given Jo's lack of name and his affiliation with Nemo, has Jo stop speaking just before he can say 'Name'.

15. '*I Was an Actor Once*' (London: Hutchinson & Co. Ltd, 1930), p. 144.

16. Wilkins's *Bleak House*, finding no use for Dickens's conception of a class-blind law, places no thematic emphasis on the law and mentions legal matters only incidentally to drive forward the plot.

17. John T. Haines, *Alice Grey, The Suspected One; or, The Moral Brand* (London: Lacy's Plays No. 646 [Vol. 44], 1850[?]), pp. 10–11.

18. Samuel Atkyns, *Life of a Labourer; or, the Emigrant, The Smuggler, and The Bush-Ranger* (1848; British Library Add. MS. 43, 015 ff. 533–57), f. 540.

19. Paradoxically, although working-class melodrama insists on domestic relationships as the model for the correct moral relationship between people of different classes, it also hints that that domestic relationship only obtains in the very closest 'blood' ties or in the marriage bond. For example, stepmothers, adopted children, orphans, and even uncles and aunts may be designated 'outside' the model family circle, and may be sacrificed in order to uphold the bonds within the circle.

20. In his *English Melodrama* (London: Herbert Jenkins, 1965), Michael Booth offers the Western as the purest form of screen melodrama (p. 189). Many of today's Hollywood action/adventure films, with their emphasis on fast-paced action and special effects, show important characteristics of the genre, although even in these works an atmosphere of moral ambiguity often diverges from the ethos of melodrama.

14

'Victorian Values' and 'Fast Young Ladies': from Madeleine Smith to Ruth Rendell

Nick Rance

Ruskin's 'Of Queens' Gardens' is often invoked as epitomising Victorian male complacency about what was supposed to be an inherent female capacity to discharge the office of 'angel in the house'. However, the text barely testifies to complacency. Not disposed to dispute the maxim that '*La donna e mobile*', Ruskin merely proffers as a bromide his own rose-tinted gloss: her changefulness consists of 'an infinitely variable, because infinitely applicable, modesty of service'.[1] Moreover, a sacred trust of Ruskin's queen is to muster evidence for the continuing participation in earthly affairs of a Providence which, however, apparently is at least bashful, and yet which presumably needs to be invoked as underwriting the essentially feminine nature which Ruskin celebrates and which equips her morally for the task: 'it is for her to trace the hidden equities of divine reward, and catch sight, through the darkness, of the fateful threads of woven fire that connect error with retribution'.[2] If Ruskin is tentative in his address of 1865 to the young ladies of Manchester, one of the incitements would be the trial in 1857 of Madeleine Smith, the prosperous Glaswegian architect's daughter who instigated a torrid affair with a Channel Islander of comparatively paltry means and circumstances, Emile L'Angelier, and then was and is widely presumed to have murdered him by lacing his cocoa with arsenic, though the jury returned the Scottish verdict of 'not proven'.

The Madeleine Smith story seemed to confirm the validity of an abiding male intuition that female sexual impropriety was akin to at least a kind of murder, if not literally of a husband or potential husband, which emerged as a possibility in that particular case then of his bequest. As Fraser Harrison has remarked of the sexual double standard as it was embedded in nineteenth-century divorce law, 'Such a code only sheds its idiotic aspect when it is seen as an expression, in legal terms, of the major social code which dictated the relationship between marriage and property'.[3] The preamble to the Lord Advocate's opening statement at the trial was thus no more than conventionally apocalyptic: 'I shall avoid, as far as possible, travelling into a region which this case affords too great materials for – I mean the almost incredible evidence which it has afforded of disgrace, and sin, and degradation – the dreadful social picture which it has revealed – *the fearful domestic results which must inevitably follow...*' (my emphasis).[4] The implicit concession is that a single instance of nonconformity, or at any rate a notorious one, must be recognised as being lethal to the conception of female nature embodied in the myth of the 'angel in the house'. The floodgates would then be presumed to be opened for Victorian maidens to emulate Madeleine Smith. There ensued at the trial, however, what to some extent was a concerted effort to stem the flow. Both prosecution and defence were avid to cast Emile L'Angelier as Madeleine Smith's dark angel, especially since he lent himself to the purpose so readily by being not merely lower-class, but also not unequivocally British to the point of being virtually French, and might be represented as being equipped with typically French subversive tendencies: 'He goes to the Continent; *he is there during the French Revolution*, and he returns to this country, and is found in Edinburgh again in the year 1851' (my emphasis).[5] Thus one might waste the minimal amount of sympathy on the deceased: moreover, the hypothesis of his being a suicide apart, he might count as having been virtually his own murderer on the assumption that his Red Republican propensities must have rubbed off on the defendant.

The staple tactic of the defence, however, was to presume to retain faith in the validity of the conception of female nature which Madeleine Smith's known behaviour, let alone her suspected behaviour, would seem to have undermined, whether or not she had been led astray. On the other hand, if members of the jury were inclined to scepticism, they might care to note that Providence had been to some pains to equip the case with an element of obscurity, thus appearing as a sponsor of the myth of female innocence, even were it no more than a myth. The implication is that jurymen would be akin to Red Republicans of the desperate stamp of Emile were they not duly to take the hint and restrain their curiosity about what the defendant may or may not have done. The Dean of Faculty elaborated on this eccentric version of the function of a jury by insisting that any such curiosity would inevitably be fruitless: 'Raise not, then, your rash and impotent hands to rend aside the veil in which Providence has been pleased to shroud the circumstances of this mysterious story'.[6] While the Lord-Justice Clerk was to pour cold water on such imprecations, presumably they influenced those to whom they were primarily addressed.

Some elements of the press assumed that the myth of the 'angel in the house' had been scuppered by Madeleine Smith: 'the mystery is unsolved, but enough is known of the unhappy case to invest it with a degree of painful interest *for all time to come*'.[7] *The Saturday Review* thought the case a revelation of 'what may be going on in the inmost core of all that is apparently pure and respectable': irrefutable testimony to the worm in the apple if not in the bud.[8] For journalists, however, as for barristers, there were ways of tempering the alarm. It has been remarked that the majority of English newspapers 'accepted the verdict and either argued Madeleine's innocence or contended that if she were guilty, her victim deserved what he got'.[9]

A prevailing tactic of the less sanguine was to defuse the impact of the case which must have been, according to *The Dublin Review*, 'like an electric shock to the good people of Glasgow', by regarding it merely as a quarry whence to excavate maxims for the copy-book.[10] One way to efface the climactic horror was to shift the focus to what were alleged to be preliminary steps to ruin. Thus was the moral drawn that if women *'grant clandestine interviews* at unseasonable hours, and in questionable places, they enter *upon fearful* perils. If one fall occurs, it leads to another and another'.[11] The preoccupation of *The Dublin Review* was to stress the significance of Scotland's not being a Catholic country, thus simultaneously implying that nothing similar could occur on Irish doorsteps. By a prodigious leap of faith, the journal proceeded on the assumption that Madeleine Smith's expression of shame and remorse in trying to persuade Emile to return her letters was authentic: the tragedy then was that at so propitious a moment, the penitent had no priest to turn to.

Similar defensive quirks occur in a cluster of sensation novels of the 1860s, inspired by the case of Madeleine Smith, though there is also a shift of tone between 1850s' and 1860s' perspectives. Wilkie Collins, the inaugurator of the sensation novel, was absorbed by the case. The trial of Madeleine Smith provided a model for that of the flame-haired temptress, Lydia Gwilt, in *Armadale*, published in 1866. A gentleman present in court had recorded of Madeleine Smith: 'Her smile was ravishing, indeed lighted her somewhat plain countenance...I was compelled again and again to look upon her, so magnetic were her eyes. Her demeanour was both proud and unafraid...I observed many gentlemen near me fascinated by her to the point of open admiration'.[12] One may assume that the jury was likewise fascinated. In *Armadale*, both public gallery and press are entranced by Lydia Gwilt. Unlike Madeleine Smith, she is found guilty of murder (by poison, and indeed of a husband, though an odious character, whose decease has preceded the story proper), but pressure on the Home Secretary induces him to interfere and reverse the verdict: she is then, by way of compromise, tried and convicted on a lesser charge and imprisoned for two years. A further novel by Wilkie Collins, *The Law and the Lady*, published in 1875, tacitly revisits the trial of Madeleine Smith, though the fictional defendant is male rather than female, and the verdict of 'not proven' is returned in the trial of Eustace Macallan, accused of having poisoned his wife.

One reason why the Madeleine Smith case fluttered the imagination of novelists and readers alike would have been as it touched on the teasing issue of the Scottish marriage law. Potentially the most electrifying aspect of the case tends to be effaced from the fiction, though the plausible inference that Madeleine Smith murdered not a mere lover but a husband must have fed into qualms about the security of a possible future spouse of a female poisoner on the loose. Appointed in 1865, the Royal Commission on the Laws of Marriage delivered its Report in 1868. According to Lord Deas, as quoted in the Report, the leading principle of the Scottish marriage law was 'that *consent makes marriage*. No form of ceremony, civil or religious, no notice before or publication after, no consummation or cohabitation, no writing, no witnesses even are essential to the constitution of this, the most important contract which two private parties can enter into...'[13] As Lawrence Stone has detailed, such a state of affairs had prevailed in England, too, prior to the Marriage Act of 1753.[14] Rather more recently in Scotland, a divinity student had formed an attachment to his landlady's daughter, whose surname was Leslie. Having obtained a parish, he then joined the Scottish Ministers' Widows' Fund as a bachelor. There followed forty years of correspondence between Leslie and the clergyman, during which he pleaded lack of funds or lack of furniture as a reason for deferring marriage. The couple did not live together or consummate the relationship: in the letters, however, they addressed each other as husband and wife, and when the clergyman died, Leslie successfully claimed the widow's pension.

Madeleine Smith, likely to have been familiar with the Leslie case, and Emile L'Angelier also had addressed each other in their letters (replete with evidence of sexual intercourse to appease those doubtful whether present consent by itself was enough to constitute marriage) as husband and wife: 'You are my own, my true husband, Emile. No one can or shall prevent us being one. No darling, we are man and wife now, dearest', is a typical concluding flourish of a letter from Madeleine to Emile.[15] Thus the presumed murder of Emile may have been not merely to thwart his threat to send their intimate correspondence to her father, but because she indeed feared that the correspondence supplied grounds for establishing that they were married. A more enticing marital prospect than L'Angelier had been unearthed in the businessman encouraged by her parents, William Minnoch. Nevertheless, had Emile survived, she would have had to live with the qualm that the impending marriage between herself and Minnoch would be liable at any moment to be overturned as bigamous.[16]

The issue was broached only in passing at the trial, where to have pursued it would have been redundant: 'It may be doubted whether they were not man and wife by the law of the land ... There certainly were materials in that correspondence to show that this view might be maintained by L'Angelier had he chosen to do it, and that he considered the prisoner his wife though they had not been married in a regular and respectable manner'.[17] Thus Madeleine Smith in her aspect of murderess conceivably of her lawful husband may have eluded the English public in 1857. Even for that public, however, it would have been a repulsive cloud suspended above the case by 1861. This was the year of the celebrated Yelverton case: the publicity was to be a spur to the appointment of the Royal Commission on the Laws of Marriage, whose Report the case then preoccupied. Maria Theresa Longworth invalidated a regular marriage between Major Charles Yelverton and a Mrs Forbes by successfully claiming a prior irregular marriage between herself and the Major (the judgement was reversed on Major Yelverton's appeal to the House of Lords). The only evidence of the supposed consent, *per verba de praesenti*, 'was that of the landlady of the house, who passing the room one day heard Major Yelverton reading something in a solemn tone to Miss Longworth', who asserted that he had in fact been reading the marriage service.[18]

With the family functioning 'as the ideal model of an *inegalitarian natural institution*', the nuances of the murder by a wife of her husband would have rung all the social alarm bells.[19] Sensation novels whose primary focus is the Madeleine Smith case shirk depicting the murder or even attempted murder of a husband. One of the novels, *Madeleine Graham*, has its character, Camille, an echo of Emile both in name and situation, avowing to the heroine, who like her namesake, Madeleine Smith, will be incited to poison her lover: 'You are my *wife* in the sight of God . . .'[20] Despite Madeleine Graham's Scottish ancestry, however, the story avoids a Scottish setting, so that this remains peripheral rakish sentiment rather than evoking the actual position. In *Man and Wife*, serialised from 1869 to 1870, in which the punctilious bachelor, Wilkie Collins, deplores the Scottish law as 'a trap to catch unmarried men and women, to this day', the trap then induces attempted murder.[21] The fascination of Collins with the Madeleine Smith case notwithstanding, circumspection must have helped to dictate that the murderous character should be male, as the athlete, Geoffrey Delamayn, is forestalled from killing his wife as constituted by Scottish law only by the incursion of a stroke.

The conceivably less ethereal proclivities of the 'angel in the house' were much mooted in sensation fiction. A novel wearing its heart on its sleeve was *Passages in the Life of a Fast Young Lady*, by Elizabeth Caroline Grey (the more sedately prescriptive, 'Mrs Grey', on the title-page), which was published in 1862.

> Oh, that any British maiden should unblushingly, nay, and without the slightest feeling of shame, even glory in such a title! But so it is, in the year 1861.[22]

The Madeleine Smith case served both to focus the moral panic and by no means to diminish it. For the next twenty years or so, events in Glasgow in 1857 seem to have afforded a touchstone for almost any adventure of a 'fast young lady', so that there was scope for G.J. Whyte-Melville's novel, *Black but Comely*, posthumously published in 1879, to be perceived by the author, at least, to be essentially 'about' Madeleine Smith, even though, the heroine's hair-colour and her skittishness apart, the reader is barely nudged towards the specific case.[23] That a heroine should have been wayward and

sensual, at least temporarily, seems to have been sufficient in itself to
evoke Madeleine Smith.

The domination of the literary market-place in the 1860s by sensation novels no doubt owed much to their penchant for 'preaching to
the nerves', as a reviewer who was also Dean of St Paul's Cathedral,
H.L. Mansel, tartly insisted.[24] Presumably, however, the knack was
to invoke anarchistic and revolutionary potentialities only as a prelude to purporting to contain them. Merely to broach the problem of
the 'fast young lady' was liable to recall to the reader female sexual
shenanigans in Glasgow and cocoa laced with arsenic. There was
then scope for sensation novels to stray lavishly from the primary
details, or egregiously to transform them, and yet receive at least
fleeting credit for having dispelled the threat associated with the
name of Madeleine Smith. Thus one of the most queasy aspects of
her case, to which one might have assumed that a sensation novelist
owed allegiance in order to raise her spectre, was that Madeleine
Smith was not so accommodating as to be socially peripheral. She
was the daughter of a wealthy architect, educated in leafy Clapton
by way of banishing her Scottish accent, too abrasive and uncouth
for young ladies. As *The Dublin Review* remarked, with an unexpected dramatic flair which the case tended to elicit:

> It must have been like an electric shock to the good people of
> Glasgow, when they heard that the daughter of one of their most
> respected townsmen, a girl young and gentle, fresh from school,
> and not only accomplished, but, according to the prevalent sys-
> tem, religiously educated, was apprehended on a charge of mur-
> dering her lover! Here all the circumstances of youth, sex, station,
> and education, *seemed* to show the crime impossible.[25]

Nothing abashed, Whyte-Melville created the female protagonist
of *Black but Comely*, Jane Lee, both as anomalous among females and
as an emanation from an underclass, with the latter sufficing to
explain the former. She is 'one of those women, *fortunately rare as
they are dangerous*, who consider they have a prescriptive right to the
homage of all mankind. They seem to believe that the other sex is
created, like the lower animals, for their especial service...' (my
emphasis).[26] Presumably, however, not too much is to be expected
of Gypsy blood. Rather than any male recipient of her impudence, it
is she who is the equivalent of a 'lower animal': 'a *fera naturae* of
some fierce and restless order, such as the leopardess, the wild-cat,

or the lynx'.[27] This was to leave the problem of daughters of the upper-middle class behaving as brazen (not to mention murderous, which Jane Lee is not) hussies where Whyte-Melville found it, however his heroine may have been presumed to evoke Madeleine Smith. If *The Dublin Review* ruefully commented that 'circumstances of youth, sex, station, and education, *seemed* to show the crime impossible', Whyte-Melville's contribution was to insinuate that at any rate in so far as station and education were concerned, miraculously there was no '*seemed*' about it.

The anonymous author of *Such Things Are*, published in 1862, was Matilda Charlotte Houston, who had already caused a splash with *Recommended to Mercy*, one of the more intrepid of sensation novels to focus on the 'woman question' in its mid-Victorian aspect. 'I consider the ceremony of marriage as one of the most absurd inventions ever inflicted on human beings by mortal men', announced the heroine, prompting a reviewer, H.L. Mansel, icily to append: 'the practice of this fair philosopher is in accordance with her theory'.[28] In the preface to *Such Things Are*, while the author punctiliously deplores that 'it is to England that has fallen the unenviable privilege of presenting to the world that baneful type of all that is unnatural and mischievous – yclept "a fast young lady"', the archaism hints that such assumed stern moralism might be regarded as somewhat musty.[29] There is also a whiff of flippancy to the ultra-sensational plotting of *Such Things Are*. For one of a pair of brothers to become embroiled with a female whose career evokes that of Madeleine Smith might be accounted a misfortune: for the other brother's wife to transpire to be a clone of Constance Kent, of the Road Murder case infamy, suggests that carelessness runs in the family.

Formerly the lover of Lord George Annesley, Florence Harley has been smitten by Nemesis in the shape of a pregnancy, not a prospect which seems to have disquieted the resourceful Madeleine Smith. Upper-class seduction of otherwise respectable maidens, however, was a traditional irritation: it was potentially less harrowing than Emile's demonstration of a ready road for foreign-tinged riff-raff with revolutionary connections to become naturalised gentlemen. Moreover, Emile's humble status must have been a crucial factor in deciding that Madeleine should take the lead in promoting the affair, whereas the fictional Florence is more demurely the victim of the wiles of the aristocratic serpent.

As not in the actual case, there are then distinct figures of the lover and the blackmailer. Since only the latter succumbs to being murdered, Florence's preferred cocktail for the irksome involving strychnine rather than Madeleine Smith's arsenic, Florence improves on her prototype in not tactlessly evoking the praying mantis. A typical pattern in some of the more sensational Victorian murder-cases was of a murderer specifically targeting his social inferiors. They would then be assaulted in a fashion designed to stress their distance and remoteness on the hierarchical ladder from the murderer: they were treated as though they were sub-human, to be poisoned apparently at random and whimsically, as Thomas Neill Cream disposed of prostitutes, or to be slashed and anatomised in a manner to evoke the abbatoir, the hallmark of Jack the Ripper (widely believed, of course, to be a gentleman). Such a pattern would be an index of contemporary tensions and anxieties not confined to psychopaths. *Mutatis mutandis,* Madeleine Smith's stratagem of arsenic in the cocoa might have appealed as demonstrating an appropriately short way with underlings (Cream's idiosyncratic sense of satire seems to have persuaded him to model himself on the stereotype of the murderess as reinforced by her example). Her inherent subversiveness as a murderess apart, however, Madeleine Smith could do no more than evoke the idea of a chasm between herself and Emile which her conduct had precisely belied: her shadow in *Such Things Are,* on the other hand, Florence Harley, merely dispatches a common pest.

The brother of Florence's admiring clergyman has married Isabel Forbes, with cause to travel under a pseudonym, that of Olive Redfern. The notoriety of Isabel Forbes springs from the Bogden Murder case, alluding in detail as perhaps in designation to the actual Road Murder case, and the undiluted suspicion in 1863 that the sixteen-year-old Constance Kent had murdered her three-year-old half-brother, Francis Saville Kent, prior to wedging the corpse between the splashboard and back wall of an outside privy. Constance Kent was arrested, but not charged with the crime for lack of evidence, in 1860, the year of the murder: she confessed in 1865. Eight years earlier, she had purloined copies of *The Times* from her parents to devour accounts of the trial of Madeleine Smith. Commentators on the case remain divided between those assuming Constance Kent to have been guilty of murder, and those maintaining her innocence, despite her confession. A detail which seems to have been overlooked, however, is that in 1860 the bloody knife was wiped with a copy of *The Times,* subsequently to be casually discarded, reporting the penultimate day of Madeleine Smith's trial: this apparent tribute to a role model cannot be in Constance Kent's favour.[30] Having quoted from *The Saturday Review*'s commentary on the case in 1865 – 'That a little infant should be murdered at all, still more that it should be murdered by its sister, still more that the sister should be herself all that was young, pure, innocent and engaging, is a monstrous solecism in nature and mind' – Janet Trodd stresses the affinity with what had been the keynote of the defence of Madeleine Smith in 1857.[31] The extremities of the case, however, as duly noted by *The Saturday Review* – that of a murder within the family rather than of an intrusive and lower-class lover – make the judgement consonant with the rather more quizzical attitude in relation to Madeleine Smith to be traced in the sensation fiction of the mid-1860s.

Once Florence has resorted to murder to silence the blackmailer, her clergyman is poised on the brink of the catastrophe which might have enveloped William Minnoch. Clayton Bernard's brother, Gerald, has already provided a hint of one kind of future which may be in store, belatedly having received intelligence that his wife is reputed to be the Bogden murderer. Even though as a chronically depressed invalid, Gerald survives; the impact of the news is akin to another murder: 'a loud scream broke from his parted lips, and falling heavily to the ground, he was in a moment bathed in the life-blood which rushed in torrents from his mouth, and spread in hideous streams along the floor on which he lay'.[32] For either brother to be suspended in a state of ignorance of his wife's or potential wife's promiscuous or lethal impulses, or both, would scarcely promise to result in bliss. At this point, however, a bizarre ploy to abort the narrative marks the limits of what is conceivable or at least marketable, and the reader bids adieu, or, as was tricksily insinuated, perhaps merely au revoir, to Florence, 'paler than the orange-wreath that decked her head, and whiter than her bridal veil', on her wedding-morning.[33] As for what happened next, the reader was left to concoct her or his scenario if she or more particularly he were up to it. 'Circumstances, as unforeseen as they were impossible to contend against, have interfered with the immediate conclusion of this story.'[34] Nor was the sequel promised were there deemed to be sufficient public interest to merit one forthcoming.

Another novel inspired by the Madeleine Smith case was the brazenly entitled *Madeleine Graham*, published anonymously in 1864, but whose author was Emma Robinson. (In the only slightly more veiled *Such Things Are*, one character owns a yacht, the *Madelina*, which to her credit fails to live up to her name: 'she is not a fast

sailor – she was built for safety – not speed; and these two qualities
don't go together in yachts or anything else'.)[35] Presumably partly
by way of compensation for such audacity, there was a cornucopia
of extenuating circumstances so far as the fictional Madeleine was
concerned, belying the innuendo that she was the heroine of a work
of 'faction'. There had been scope in the actual case to suggest that
baneful foreign influences were the root of all evil, so that Madeleine
Smith might be presented as being essentially the victim of her
defunct lover, 'a kind of gasconading, boasting man, such as a Jersey
man might be...'[36] In *Madeleine Graham*, such influences are not
only stressed but multiplied.

Under the pernicious yoke of a French teacher, Mademoiselle
Loriot, Madeleine is introduced to the fiction of Loriot's native
country. In the 'domestic sagas', as they had been termed, the fiction
dominating the literary market in England from the end of the 1840s
and through the 1850s, for a character to read French novels had
been to solicit catastrophe. In her turn, too, Madeleine Graham
encounters 'a species of heroine, bare allusion to whose social existence and position would have emptied a drawing-room full of our
grandmothers'.[37] Predictably, Madeleine pays back her teacher by
appropriating the affections of her compatriot and lover, Camille,
whose reputation echoes Emile's: 'a vain insolent strutter, altogether
unworthy of any sensible Englishwoman's preference'.[38] French
teacher, French novels, French lover: however heinous the crime
which the fictional Madeleine is ascertained beyond rational or even
whimsical doubt to have committed, France would seem to have
plenty to answer for. Thus the conundrum propounded by *The
Dublin Review* – 'Here all the circumstances of youth, sex, station,
and education, *seemed* to show the crime impossible' – again met
with a kind of solution: albeit one which pre-empted one of the
more equivocal ploys of an Agatha Christie novel, wherein the
murderer, if English, at least would be liable to be sufficiently tactful
to use an intrinsically foreign dagger.

Like Emile, Camille is the recipient of 'such letters as, perhaps,
were never written before by woman to man!'[39] He further echoes
his prototype in becoming redundant so soon as his Madeleine
encounters her rich man. Nothing would suggest, however, that
Madeleine Smith had other than an exclusively erotic hankering
after Emile, or that she was so moved by William Minnoch as to be
averse to him rather than merely indifferent. On the other hand, the
fictional Madeleine seems born to discover that she 'had consigned

to a death of enormous suffering a man she loved, in order that she might marry a man she disliked, for his riches!'[40] The most brazen of detours from actual events in Glasgow is that the fictional lover recovers: Madeleine Graham's tribulation as a consumer (sensation novels of the blander sort specialised in being consumer-conscious) is that her arsenic has 'been wonderfully adulterated by a large admixture of pulverized lime...'[41] Not only is Madeleine Smith metamorphosed into a relatively milk-and-water Madeleine Graham, but Camille's survival allows for an ironic retribution both for her licentiousness and her homicidal bent. The price of a cover-up of the latter is that Madeleine must be wedded to her intended victim, and thus precluded from being a loose cannon on the marriage-market. A benefit of conceding that Madeleine Smith's fictional epigones were at least somewhat guilty was that they could be punished and contained, whereas the strategy actually adopted, of insisting on the young lady as innocent *per se*, necessarily was high-risk.

The notion of female nature as being angelic flourished especially in the years from 1840 to 1860, so that while the period includes the trial of Madeleine Smith, the sensation fiction responding to the case falls narrowly outside, as does Ruskin's 'Of Queens' Gardens'. In 1857, the fervour with which the myth is sustained is not much diminished by local variations: from the defence's claim that it was impossible that a young lady should be guilty of murder, to the actual verdict of 'not proven', and the opinion of most of the English press that either Madeleine Smith was innocent, or at least if she were not, Emile brought his death upon himself. While it would have been untenable to claim that Madeleine Smith's sexual misdemeanours were 'not proven', to reject the idea that she was a murderess did more than merely constitute her as a relatively less heinous exception to the rule of female nature as witnessed by the 'angel in the house'. Such licentiousness was robbed of its aura: it ceased to seem to be ratified as a lethal assault in embryo on the system of private property and inheritance, not to mention the standard male sense of identity, which depended on a certain confidence about the ineluctable femininity of the female identity. By 1865, however, Ruskin himself seems to recommend the creed primarily as a necessary pledge of faith, while in the sensation novels of the 1860s, whose sensational effects often derived from contravening sexual stereotypes, the harsher details of the story are merely mitigated (Madeleine Smith's fictional clone murders a blackmailer, or botches an attempt to murder a lover devoid of any claim to be a potential husband), or there is even the odd hint of pandering to the suscept-ibilities of the readership in not drawing to an awful conclusion.

Contemporary commentators on the Madeleine Smith case had not presumed that an exception proved the rule: on the contrary, which was why potentially the case was invested 'with a degree of painful interest for all time to come'. At least from as early as the rise of the 'New Woman', however, it became impossible to avoid acknowledging that some women must be conceded to outer dark-ness. Bram Stoker's *Dracula* was published in 1897, and from the 1890s, without necessarily invoking vampires, the resort was liable to be at least to Ruskin's dictum in the face of those female char-acters in Shakespeare's plays who were less than immaculate, Lady Macbeth, Goneril and Regan, that 'they are felt at once to be fright-ful exceptions to the ordinary laws of life'.[42] An example may be picked not from the Victorian period but rather from the 1980s, heyday of a revival of 'Victorian values', if evoking to the sceptical commentator Marx's qualification of Hegel's observation 'that all facts and personages of great importance in world history occur, as it were, twice' – 'He forgot to add: the first time as tragedy, the second as farce'.[43] For the more perspicacious of late Victorians, 'Victorian values', or at least those of a Smilesian hue, had been exploded within their own era, perhaps from 1889, when Charles Booth's *Life and Labour of the People in London* began appearing, demolishing the middle-class myth that poverty resulted from per-sonal failure, vice or improvidence.

Like the batch of subsequently knighted editors of newspapers, detective novelists of the 1980s were less inclined to sneer. In an interview published in 1983, P.D. James insisted on an affinity between revived 'Victorian values' and detective fiction. A char-acteristic of detective novels was to:

> provide a puzzle ... which is solved by human ingenuity and by logical deduction, in other words, by the human brain. I am sure that this is part of their appeal in a world in which we are increasingly coming to believe that so many of our social prob-lems are literally beyond our capacity to solve and that we are at the mercy of vast impersonal forces, social and economic, against which we are absolutely powerless.[44]

Moreover, detective fiction of the 1980s seems avidly to collaborate with Margaret Thatcher and Norman Tebbit in belabouring the

1960s, so that motives for murder are often derived from the 'permissiveness' of the earlier and vilified period. The main plot of Ruth Rendell's *An Unkindness of Ravens*, published in 1985, is preoccupied with a volatile and intermittently lethal league of feminists (compounding elements of St Trinian's and the Angry Brigade, ARRIA is named after Arria Paeta, a Roman matron of inexorable disposition, but is also an acronym for 'Action for the Radical Reform of Intersexual Attitudes'). The murder of Rodney Williams by his daughter, Sara, a member of ARRIA, in collusion with her recently discovered half-sister, is apparently in retaliation for her father's sexual abuse. However, 'Freud's "seduction theory" as expressed in the famous paper of 1896' ('The Aetiology of Hysteria'), is invoked to provide a twist to the tale, especially for readers innocent of a knowledge of Freud.[45] Rodney Williams has not committed incest with his daughter. Instead, as Detective Chief Inspector Wexford sums up, 'Sara had a daughter's fantasy about her father'.[46]

Freud's authority has its uses in initiating the rebuff to mutinous women: Sara's accusation of her father, however, turns out to have been maliciously rather than unconsciously inspired. The final twist has seemed to be that Sara, rather than having been paternally seduced, has merely projected her own fantasy of having sex with her father, and Wexford must remind his torpid auxiliary, Burden, that a fantasist is not to be equated with a liar, since the fantasist believes that the fantasy is true. But then when Burden puts the apparently redundant question, 'Did Sara convince herself?', the answer is an equivocal, 'Yes and no'.[47] To the extent that the answer is 'no', we may dispense with Freud. 'She had a motive all right, and as calculated and cold-blooded a motive as any poisoner polishing off an old relation for his money.'[48] Sara's wish to be a medical student has been thwarted by her father ('Perhaps he sensed in that daughter of his... traits in her character that were abnormal, that were destructive'), whose salary is too high for her to be eligible for any but a minimal grant, while she has no hope of the makeweight of a parental contribution: thus there is a provocation to be rid alike of her father and the impediment of his salary.[49]

The reputation of Sara Williams is inexorably corroded: first the idea of her being a victim is mooted, then of her merely being deluded that she is a victim, until finally she is presented as a cold-blooded criminal. Combining being a psychopath with membership of ARRIA, the fictional exemplar of the feminism of the 1980s evidently may be claimed to constitute an exception 'to the ordinary laws of life'. As for the presumed murderess in actuality, however, Madeleine Smith, occupying the heyday of the 'angel in the house', there could be no such insidious concession as that the odd apparent angel was a psychopath under the skin. Necessarily, the lady was for turning.

Notes

1. E.T. Cook and Alexander Wedderburn (ed.), *Sesame and Lilies* in *The Works of John Ruskin*, vol. XVIII (London: George Allen, 1905), p. 123. *The Angel in the House* (1855–6) was Coventry Patmore's long poetic celebration of married love.
2. Ibid., p. 126.
3. Fraser Harrison, *The Dark Angel: Aspects of Victorian Sexuality* (London: Sheldon Press, 1977), p. 11.
4. F. Tennyson Jesse (ed.), *The Trial of Madeleine Smith* (London, Edinburgh, Glasgow: William Hodge, 1927), p. 180. In equivalent English terms, the Lord Advocate is counsel for the prosecution; the Dean of Faculty is counsel for the defence; the Lord-Justice Clerk is the judge.
5. Ibid., p. 234.
6. Ibid., p. 273.
7. *The Press*, quoted in W.F. Finlason (anonymously), 'Madeleine Smith and Scottish Jurisprudence', *The Dublin Review*, XLIII (September 1857), p. 129.
8. Quoted ibid., p. 131.
9. Mary S. Hartman, *Victorian Murderesses* (1977; London: Robson Books, 1985), p. 281.
10. 'Madeleine Smith and Scottish Jurisprudence', p. 128.
11. A 'shrewd and sensible contemporary', quoted ibid., p. 143.
12. Quoted in Nigel Morland, *That Nice Miss Smith* (1957; London: Souvenir Press, 1988), p. 157.
13. *Report of the Royal Commission on the Laws of Marriage* (Shannon: Irish University Press, 1969), p. xvi.
14. Lawrence Stone, *Road to Divorce: England 1530–1987* (Oxford: Oxford University Press, 1990).
15. *The Trial of Madeleine Smith*, p. 202.
16. Morland, *That Nice Miss Smith*, pp. 199–203, argues that Madeleine Smith was thus motivated.
17. *The Trial of Madeleine Smith*, p. 202.
18. *Report of the Royal Commission on the Laws of Marriage*, p. 74.
19. The phrase is appropriated from Michel Foucault (ed.), *I, Pierre Riviere...* (London: Bison Books, 1982), p. 222.
20. Emma Robinson (anonymously), *Madeleine Graham* (London: John Maxwell & Co., 1864), vol. III, p. 65.

21. Wilkie Collins, *Man and Wife* (Oxford: Oxford University Press, 1995), p. 132.
22. Mrs (Elizabeth Caroline) Grey, *Passages in the Life of a Fast Young Lady* (London: Hurst & Blackett, 1862), vol. III, p. 304.
23. Henry Blyth, *Madeleine Smith: A famous Victorian murder trial* (London: Duckworth, 1975), p. 19.
24. H.L. Mansel (anonymously), 'Sensation Novels', *Quarterly Review* CXIII (April 1863), p. 482. Mansel's batch of sensation novels includes *Such Things Are*: he demurs about the borrowings from the careers of Madeleine Smith and Constance Kent that 'Crimes of this horrible individuality are the very last from which any one will draw a general moral: they are the crimes of their perpetrators, and of no one else'.
25. 'Madeleine Smith and Scottish Jurisprudence', p. 128.
26. G.J. Whyte-Melville, *Black but Comely: or the Adventures of Jane Lee* (London: Chapman and Hall, 1879), vol. I, pp. 293–4.
27. Ibid., p. 112.
28. 'Sensation Novels', p. 494.
29. Matilda Charlotte Houston (anonymously), *Such Things Are* (London: Saunders, Otley, 1863). This is the second edition; the now elusive first edition appeared in 1862.
30. Bernard Taylor, *Cruelly Murdered: Constance Kent and the Killing at Road Hill House* (London: Souvenir Press, 1979), records both Constance Kent's enthusiasm for Madeleine Smith, and the date of the newspaper, but without connecting the two.
31. Janet Trodd, *Domestic Crime in the Victorian Novel* (London: Macmillan, 1989), p. 21.
32. *Such Things Are*, vol. III, pp. 164–5.
33. Ibid., p. 332.
34. Ibid., p. 334.
35. Ibid., vol. II, p. 263.
36. *The Trial of Madeleine Smith*, p. 228.
37. *Madeleine Graham*, vol. I, p. 40.
38. Ibid., vol. II, p. 327.
39. Ibid., vol. III, p. 66.
40. Ibid., p. 234.
41. Ibid., p. 267.
42. *The Works of John Ruskin*, vol. XVIII, p. 114.
43. Christopher Norris, *What's Wrong with Postmodernism: Critical Theory and the Ends of Philosophy* (London: Harvester, 1990), p. 30.
44. Diana Cooper-Clark, *Designs of Darkness: Interviews with Detective Novelists* (Bowling Green: Bowling Green University Popular Press, 1983), p. 19.
45. Ruth Rendell, *An Unkindness of Ravens* (1985; London: Arrow, 1986), p. 260.
46. Ibid.
47. Ibid., p. 262.
48. Ibid., p. 263.
49. Ibid., p. 268.

15

Vampires and Victorians: Count Dracula and the Return of the Repressive Hypothesis

Robert Mighall

What is peculiar to modern societies, in fact, is not that they consigned sex to a shadow existence, but that they dedicated themselves to speaking of it *ad infinitum*, while exploiting it as *the* secret.

Michel Foucault, *History of Sexuality*[1]

The [vampire] myth is loaded with sexual excitement; yet there is no mention of sexuality.

James Twitchell, 'The Vampire Myth'[2]

This essay is not a reading of Bram Stoker's *Dracula* (1897). It is an examination of the myths and assumptions which operate when modern culture approaches this text, and the way it represents its central figure, the undead Transylvanian count. It proposes to historicise that which often forgets that it has a history: the 'sexuality' which Count Dracula supposedly embodies. It is a commonplace in contemporary critical and cinematic discourse that vampirism has an erotic 'meaning'. However, what for many critics is 'simple, evident, unavoidable',[3] will perhaps appear less obvious when history is brought to an assumption that reveals more about the myths and desires of 'modernity', than it does about Stoker's text or the folklore of vampirism. This essay will approach this subject from three perspectives: the history of cinematic and critical representations of Dracula; the history of sexuality; and what could be called the erotic history of the vampire. The former will be dealt with first. To do this it is necessary to go back to where it all began; not to the

Transylvania or London of the 1890s, but to Bray in Berkshire and 1958, the year Hammer studios released its first *Dracula* movie.

I. THE GOTHIC HISTORY OF THE VAMPIRE

In 1958, when Hammer resurrected Stoker's vampire count, he had fallen on hard times. Indeed, that such a small company could use him at all testifies to the fact that Universal Studios who owned the exclusive rights to his name had written him off as unprofitable. Universal struck a deal with Hammer, and the English company brought *Dracula* back to the screen. The film, which featured Christopher Lee in the title role, was an immediate, astounding and highly profitable success. But why did Hammer succeed where Universal had failed? Or, as David Pirie puts it: 'how could a modern audience, saturated in the material anxieties of the post-war period, respond to what was basically an outmoded superstition?'[4] Hammer's innovation was their use of a nineteenth-century setting for the drama, a detail which, Pirie asserts, 'had never been considered remotely necessary in low-budget horror before'.[5] The Victorian setting proved a winning formula, to which Hammer would return obsessively (and not just for vampire films) for the next fifteen years. But why should the Victorian setting alter the fact that vampirism is, after all, an 'outmoded superstition'? The short answer is that through this emphasis Hammer replaced an 'outmoded' superstition or myth with a more current one – the myth of sexual 'repression'. For as David Pirie observes, Dracula represents 'the great submerged force of Victorian libido breaking out to punish the repressive society which had imprisoned it'.[6] But whilst this statement accurately describes the Hammer *mise-en-scène*, it is a somewhat problematic reading of Stoker's text, to which his comments in this case apply. Pirie's reading from 1973 is bound up within the same 'liberatory' ideology which informed the Hammer Dracula cycle. Pirie reads Stoker through Hammer, and, as will be seen, he is not alone in this. Pirie implies that Hammer's return to the Victorian setting is a move towards textual authenticity, and that Lee's highly eroticised portrayal restores the psycho-sexual 'truth' at the heart of Stoker's text or the myth of vampirism. However, Hammer's Dracula cycle, far from constituting a return to authenticity, actually distorts the text's original motivation. And furthermore, this distortion reveals more about the historical context in which the films were produced than the erotic 'essence' that Lee's portrayal supposedly uncovers.

Pirie's reference to vampirism being an 'outmoded superstition' unwittingly testifies to something that is fundamental to the Gothic. The 'outmoded', the anachronistic and the atavistic are prerequisites of Gothic horror. Vampirism was an outmoded superstition when Stoker's novel utilised it; and therein lay its appeal. Stoker took great pains to establish the modernity of the context into which his medieval monster intrudes. As Jonathan Harker records in his journal, having witnessed Count Dracula crawling lizard-like down a castle wall, 'It is [the] nineteenth century up-to-date with a vengeance. And yet, unless my senses deceive me, the old centuries had, and have, powers of their own which mere "modernity" cannot kill'.[7] It is this clash between 'modernity' (established by the narrative's reliance on and reference to technological innovations) and the anachronistic that gave the text its terrifying power. Such a conflict, as Chris Baldick explains, is essential to the Gothic:

> typically a Gothic tale will invoke the tyranny of the past (a family curse, the survival of archaic forms of despotism and superstition)...
>
> It is a middle-class tradition, and its anxiety may be characterized briefly as a fear of historical reversion; that is, of the nagging possibility that the despotisms buried by the modern age may prove to be yet undead.[8]

By depicting the terrible scenario of the past re-visiting the present, Stoker's *Dracula* is a development on the earlier Gothic of the late eighteenth century. The first Gothic novels, the romances of Horace Walpole, Ann Radcliffe and 'Monk' Lewis, had evoked anachronism by typically projecting a 'modern' sensibility back into the benighted past. The heroes and heroines of these novels were the readers' eighteenth-century counterparts, made to suffer at the hands of despotic and rapacious aristocrats and scheming ecclesiastics. Gothic history is Whig history *par excellence*. It depicts the triumph of modern virtues over the delusions and iniquities of a (mythical) social order that momentarily imperils them. Literary Gothic, as Baldick points out, 'is really anti-Gothic'.[9]

Stoker's late-Victorian Gothic therefore reverses this original scenario, but retains the essential emphasis on anachronism. In *Dracula*, instead of a modern sensibility being projected into the past (the

Radcliffian scenario), the Gothic past of vampiric superstition and aristocratic power which the Count embodies visits the modern urban context. Therefore, whilst Universal's *Dracula* retained Stoker's emphasis, bringing the Count to a contemporary 1930s setting, Hammer's Victorian Dracula cycle actually distorts, rather than restores, the text's original motivation. Nevertheless, it is still effective as Gothic horror, and for the very same reason that Radcliffe's Gothic and Stoker's Gothic were effective in their own specific contexts. Hammer does not drop the emphasis on anachronism, but adapts it according to its own mythic historiography. In short, Hammer's Dracula cycle from its first *Dracula* (1958) to *Taste the Blood of Dracula* (1969) worked as Gothic horror because the Victorian context (that which signified modernity for Stoker) had become Gothic in its own right.

The Hammer house of Victorian horror is a world of Gothic delusion. But its 'outmoded' beliefs are not associated with the magic and superstition that had troubled the earlier Gothicists; quite the contrary, this was the age of science, industry and progress. Rather, the 'Gothic' (that is archaic and oppressive) character of this world is premised entirely on its attitude to sexuality – the basis of our own 'enlightenment'. It is sexuality – its manifest absence in the 'typical' Victorians who people these films, and its overbearing presence in the vampire and those whose libidos he liberates – that informs Hammer's reversal of the oppositions operating in Stoker's text. Hammer's Count Dracula is still an anachronism, but by virtue of his *modernity* not his atavism: it is his Victorian antagonists who now represent the Gothic past and all its repressive follies.

Lee's Dracula is a far cry from the hairy-palmed, bad-breathed, pointed-eared, 'criminal type' which Stoker describes: he is suave, sophisticated and above all, sexy. Gone is the Eastern European, old-world, melodramatic staginess of Lugosi's performance. Lee's Dracula moves through such films as *Dracula Prince of Darkness* (1965), and *Taste the Blood of Dracula* (1969), like libido incarnate, bending erstwhile straitlaced Victorian virgins to his irresistible will. What Dracula represented was increasingly spelt out as the cycle developed. How up-tight, virtuous and asexual these maidens were before their vampirisation stood in direct correlation to how ravenous and alluring they became when his orgasm-inducing bite liberated the sexuality that their repressive culture had denied them.

This (Gothic) scenario of Victorian repression vanquished by vampiric liberation clearly informs Hammer's fourth Dracula film, *Taste the Blood of Dracula* (1969). Its plot is explicitly organised around a conflict between the hypocrisy of Victorian patriarchal and repressive sexual codes, and a younger generation liberated into rebellion by Dracula. Typical 'Victorian values' are represented in the film by a trio of paterfamilias who inhibit their children's sexual maturity by denying it its 'natural' gratification in romance and marriage. However, the fathers themselves indulge in clandestine orgies in an East End brothel (under the cover of philanthropy), and even flirt with a little black magic. The message is clear: the dictates of respectability and duty pervert the natural expression of sexual desire and lead to their own destruction. Their nemesis comes in the form of Dracula, whom they resurrect with the help of a debauched aristocrat in a black mass ceremony. Once brought back to Victorian England, Dracula sets about seducing the children of these hypocrites to avenge the death of his servant, the aristocrat whom they had attacked at the climax of the ceremony. However, what is really avenged is the tyrannical repression which these representatives of Victorianism had imposed upon their children. These youthful characters, with their taste for parties, romance and freedom which they display on the rare occasions when they escape their domestic prisons, are clearly the audience's contemporaries, misplaced in the nineteenth century. It is Dracula who enables their rebellion. He is the catalyst of their modernity, who, by seducing the young, gives them the wherewithal to rise up against their oppressors. This is explicitly portrayed when Alice, the most oppressed of all the young characters, is encouraged by Dracula to attack her father with a shovel. The basis of her parricide is unambiguous, and could even be regarded as justifiable self-defence. Her drunken, whip-brandishing father was intent on punishing her for going to a party with her lover against his expressed prohibition. Vampirism is therefore in this case less an 'outmoded superstition' than the agent of necessary change and enlightened action. Dracula is eventually destroyed, but not before he has performed his task of vanquishing Victorianism. Alice, who is not punished for her 'justifiable' parricide, is now free to marry her lover. The film's final scene depicts the young lovers walking arm in arm from the old church where Dracula had been resurrected and finally destroyed. They turn and take one last glance at the ruin (the hair that in her inhibited days had been held fast in a bun and caged within a bonnet, now falls about her shoulders in care-free late-'60s abandon), emphasising that the Victorian past is now behind them. The dawn into which they walk marks the bright future of modernity, the future enjoyed by the teenagers who now leave the cinema.

The fact that it is the Victorians who are the real villains of the Hammer Dracula cycle is evidenced by the relative failure of the last two films of the series, *Dracula AD 1972* (1972) and *The Satanic Rites of Dracula* (1973). The former, whose American title was *Dracula Today*, delivers exactly what its title suggests. Like Stoker's original it brings the Count to modern London, a world of Chelsea coffee-bars and youth culture, where teenagers indulge in drugs, rock music and making love. In pursuit of 'kicks', the youths take part in a black mass ceremony (complete with psychedelic music and half-naked 'chicks'), which once more resurrects the vampiric lord of the undead. It is logical that Dracula should have his entrée into modern London through its youth culture. After all, as *Taste the Blood* had demonstrated, the vampire, despite his great age, is on the side of 'the kids'. Once resurrected he sets about vampirising these youngsters. The question is why? The youths he seduces are liberated enough, and there are no Victorian tyrants to avenge. *Dracula AD 1972* fails where the earlier Hammer films succeeded because it omits the anachronistic dimension. Even Dracula's cape is no more out of place than some of the bizarre garb worn by the habitués of the King's Road 'Cavern'. It is a Gothic text without monsters. To reject the Victorian context is to undermine the purpose of the vampire's liberating agency.

With their Victorian formula Hammer films revitalised vampirism. According to Alain Silver and James Ursini, 'Ninety percent of the vampire films produced to date throughout the world have been made since the Hammer *Dracula*, and its influence continues to be felt both creatively and economically'.[10] They might have added, critically. Critical interest in Stoker's text coincides historically with Hammer's (eroticised) resurrection of the vampire. From Maurice Richardson's 'The Psychoanalysis of Ghost Stories' (1959), to Ken Gelder's *Reading the Vampire* (1994), academic critics have 'discovered' the sexuality at the heart of Stoker's text. Encouraged by the obviously 'libidinal' and 'liberating' force of the vampire which Lee's portrayal suggests, *Dracula* criticism generally endorses Hammer's version of vampirism. Within this discourse, the vampire is still an erotic force which disrupts the repressive society into which it intrudes. Consequently it is the vampire with whom the critics identify, and the Victorians who are the (Gothicised) villains of the piece. Thus for Robin Wood, 'It is not far-fetched to claim that Count Dracula offers himself as a privileged focus for any inquiry into the possibilities of liberation within western civilization'.[11] The liberation which the vampire promises is, of course, sexual liberation – the basis of our modernity and enlightenment. For Wood, Stoker's atavistic, blood-sucking, medieval aristocrat represents 'promiscuity or sexual freedom'.[12] Similarly, for Burton Hatlen Dracula embodies 'the sexuality that Victorian England denied, more specifically a sado-masochistic sexuality that recognizes no limits and that no social order can accept'.[13] For him Stoker's text testifies to 'our desire (by "our" I mean middle-class whites)... to be... sexually violated by the "dark," "foul-smelling" outsider'.[14]

But why this insistence? Why this need to submit ourselves to the vampire, and denigrate his 'pallid, prissy, asexual' antagonists?[15] Because our 'modernity' depends upon it. The more we identify with the vampire the more we distance ourselves from his (and our) Victorian antitheses. Critical comment, I would argue, perpetuates the Gothic plot initiated by Hammer's Dracula cycle. Pirie is right; modern audiences are no longer afraid of the 'outmoded superstition' that is vampirism. Whilst we may not fear vampires, however, we do fear Victorians.

II. WE OTHER VICTORIANS

The notion that the Victorians were fundamentally 'repressed' and refused to acknowledge their sexuality has of recent years undergone a revision. This is, in part, a consequence of Michel Foucault's *History of Sexuality* (1976), the first volume of which calls for a rejection of this 'repressive hypothesis'. For Foucault, the nineteenth century witnessed not the suppression of sexuality, but its increasing deployment and proliferation in a number of *specific* discourses and institutions (mainly in the spheres of medicine, psychiatry and pedagogy). In Foucault's reading of this process, 'sexuality' is not a universal fact or biological imperative. Rather, it is a discursive construct which has a history; a history in which we with our myths of 'repression' and 'liberation' are still implicated.

But whilst Foucault's ideas have been highly influential in certain spheres, initiating a re-examination of discourses on sexuality, and its *historical* construction,[16] *Dracula* criticism, a field obsessed with the erotic, has largely resisted the implications of Foucault's critique. For example, his name does not appear in the index of Margaret L. Carter's *Dracula: The Vampire and the Critics* (1988), whilst Ken Gelder's theoretically inclined *Reading the Vampire* (1994) mentions him only once. Although *Dracula* criticism has not engaged with Foucault, it actually serves to illustrate and validate his thesis. As will be seen, by applying his theories about the historical construction of sexuality, and his critique of its 'liberatory' or revolutionary potential, to this field the Gothic oppositions outlined above are unsettled.

Foucault rejects the popular view that sexuality is a natural universal human drive which was distorted by the Victorians, and gradually reclaimed in the twentieth century. This latter view of sexuality informs *Taste the Blood of Dracula*. Hammer's film suggests that the Victorians had a sexuality which was identical to our own, only they repressed and perverted it with disastrous consequences. In the adult males this lead to sexual perversion, and in the children it meant the frustration of their 'natural' sexual inclinations. Foucault's view is directly opposed to this universal view of human sexuality. He proposes instead a model which makes us both less like and more like the Victorians than the popular view suggests. We are less like our Victorian ancestors because their 'sexuality' was not a repressed version of our own 'true' liberated one. Rather, Victorian sexuality was represented in different terms, and was the object of discourses different from the ones which represent 'sexuality' today. The 'domain' of sexuality was predominantly the fields of medicine, psychiatry and sexology, which concentrated primarily on its perverse and pathological forms. As Foucault observes:

> The legitimate couple, with its regular sexuality, had a right to more discretion. It tended to function as a norm, one that was stricter, perhaps, but quieter. On the other hand, what came under scrutiny was the sexuality of children, mad men and women, and criminals; the sensuality of those who did not like the opposite sex...and if regular sexuality happened to be questioned once again, it was through a reflux movement, originating in these peripheral sexualities.   (*HS*, pp. 38–9)

In the nineteenth century, 'regular' sexuality (the sexuality which through Freud, Reich and Kinsey, the twentieth century increasingly focused upon) was rarely the object of non-medical, public or novelistic discourse. But this does not signify repression so much as a differential deployment of this concept. Because the twentieth century failed to find in the Victorian age a version of its own ostentatious sexuality (now the domain of novels, films, journalism and popular science), it deduced that it had been silenced and repressed. It is, however, by virtue of this 'reflux movement' (the popular 're-discovery' of normal sexuality) that Foucault's critique implicates his modern readers in the process which his historical study maps out. This emphasis also makes us more like the Victorians than we are perhaps ready to admit. Hailing his readers as 'We "other Victorians"', Foucault undermines the basis of twentieth-century sexual liberation. He does this by historicising the process by which this liberation was supposedly achieved, placing on the same historical continuum Freud's 'revolutionary' theories, and the practices of the Victorians from whom Freud and the sexologists supposedly wrested our imprisoned sexuality. Foucault's thesis suggests that Freud's theories were part of, rather than a break with, the same mechanism which had supposedly 'repressed' sexuality, but had in fact invoked it as an object of knowledge. For Foucault, the desire to believe that sex was once, or still is, repressed *is part of the process which equates sex with truth and which serves power*. The twentieth century did not discover sex, but it discovered repression. As Foucault prophesies:

> People will wonder what could have made us so presumptuous; they will look for the reasons that might explain why we prided ourselves on being the first to grant sex the importance we say it is due and how we came to congratulate ourselves for finally – in the twentieth century – having broken free of a long period of harsh repression ... And what we now perceive as the chronicle of a censorship and a difficult struggle to remove it will be seen rather as the centuries-long rise of a complex deployment for compelling sex to speak ... for getting us to believe in the sovereignty of its law when in fact we were moved by the power mechanisms of sexuality. (*HS*, p. 158)

If Foucault is correct, this must radically affect critical comment on *Dracula*. However, as stated above, this critical field has been reluctant to admit Foucault. As a consequence, implications of repression and vampiric sexual liberation still inhere within *Dracula* criticism, a discourse which continues to dwell in the crumbling house that Hammer built, with Freud as its undead sovereign lord.[17]

III.   THE EROTIC HISTORY OF THE VAMPIRE

In Hammer's Dracula films it is the vampire who brings sexual liberation to the repressed Victorians. But when a modern critic approaches Stoker's text it is his or her turn to act as liberator – liberating the sexual secret which lies at the heart of this 'quintessentially Victorian' text.[18] For whilst *Dracula* is 'obviously' sexual, its erotic content is still nonetheless 'disguised' as vampirism. Or as Ken Gelder puts it: '*Dracula* overcodes sexuality at the level of performance, but undercodes it at the level of utterance. Critical analysis intervenes at this point enabling these deafening silences to "speak".'[19] What vampirism speaks, or is made to speak, is always tautologically erotic. However the sexuality which the critic discovers reveals less about the text or the cultural context which produced it than about the theoretical or ideological agenda of the respective critic, and his or her desire to equate (the text's) truth with sex. Thus we find references to the 'charming innocence' of the Victorian reviewers for failing 'to pick up on the erotic content of *Dracula*', but concentrating instead on it 'ghoulish' elements.[20] They made the mistake of believing it to be a horror story, not the 'quasi-pornography' we know it to be.[21] As one critic states: 'however we are to interpret blood-sucking it is clearly other than "normal" copulation, for the Victorians, the only legitimate *method* of sexuality'.[22] That a vampire might only be a vampire and that blood-sucking is merely blood-sucking rarely enters critical debate on *Dracula*. The desire to pursue 'the dark shimmer of sex' (*HS*, p. 157) which the text holds for the critical analyst so often precludes other considerations. Indeed, in a number of critical accounts the metaphorical relationship between vampirism and sexuality has been lost sight of. There are references to Dracula's 'peculiar sex tastes',[23] and statements about how 'the vampire consumption of blood... *is* simultaneously and complexly a sexual act'.[24] One critic has even provided an anthropological study of 'vampiric sexuality', and its own peculiar 'incest taboo[s]' based on Stoker's text;[25] while another observes how *Dracula*, 'releases a sexuality so mobile and polymorphic that Dracula may be best represented as bat or wolf or floating dust'.[26] It would appear that within this critical discourse the erotic nature of vampirism has become an (un)dead metaphor, with sex serving as a 'unique signifier and... a universal signified' (*HS*, p. 154).

However, there is nothing *essentially* erotic about vampirism, and there is nothing essentially subversive about sex. Both assumptions have a history, and are the products of a process which equates truth with sex. Furthermore, the desire to punish the Victorians through the agency of the vampire's sexuality paradoxically closes the gap between 'Victorianism' and 'modernity' which so many critics insist upon. For if Foucault's historical theories are brought to some of the statements encountered above, these oppositions start to appear problematic. The more the critic asserts that the 'truth' of *Dracula* is erotic, and that the vampire represents sexual liberation, the more he or she presents his or her 'Victorian' credentials.

This 'sexual fix' does not 'subvert' power, nor does it help us to escape from our Victorian ancestors. Even our eroticisation of the vampire does not escape the 'taint' of Victorianism. The erotic history of the vampire is also bound up in the process – the 'reflux movement' – which Foucault describes. As explained above, in the nineteenth century the monogamous, heterosexual couple tended to operate as an unstated norm, it was not until the twentieth century that it was increasingly placed centre stage by sexual evangelists and 'revolutionaries'. Victorian discourse on sexuality concentrated primarily on its perverse and dysfunctional incarnations. And one of these was 'sexual vampirism'. If the work of Stoker's contemporary, the sexologist Richard Von Krafft-Ebing, is consulted, a number of cases of 'vampirism' are encountered. The most explicit comments on this phenomenon found in his *Psychopathia Sexualis* (1886, English translation 1892), refer to female vampirism, a manifestation of 'sadism'.

> A married man presented himself with numerous scars on his arms. He told their origin as follows: when he wished to approach his wife . . . he first had to make a cut in his arm. Then she would suck the wound and during the act become violently excited sexually.
> The case recalls the widespread legend of the vampires, the origin of which may perhaps be referred to such sadistic facts.[27]

Most modern critics would agree with this Victorian doctor. However, what this reveals is that it did not require Freud, Ernest Jones, or even Christopher Lee, to 'discover' sexual vampirism, to liberate the vampire's sexuality from 'the all-obscuring cloak that once shrouded the Count's nocturnal adventures in a delicate obscurity'.[28] The nineteenth century produced the erotic 'meaning' of vampirism, a discovery we delight in claiming as our own. For Victorian sexologists, the vampire was a 'pervert' or the pervert was a vampire. But then, for many modern critics, the 'polymorphous perversity' of the vampire guarantees its 'subversiveness', and therefore its (and our) non-Victorian liberatory/liberated status. The poles are reversed: we merely celebrate what they denigrated, and the 'Queer' vampire becomes its latest incarnation.[29] What the twentieth century discovers in, or projects onto, its, analytic, cinematic and critical representations of the vampire are versions of its own sexuality. However, the fascination which the vampire continues to hold for us derives not its embodiment of some deep, universal, suprahistorical 'truth' about our sexual selves. Ultimately it serves to establish what we have in common with our much-maligned Victorian ancestors.

In conclusion, to apply history – the history of the vampire and the history of sexuality – to that which appears obvious and self-evident is to unsettle one of the most persistent myths of modern culture. The twentieth century started its love affair with the vampire, not when it discovered sexuality, but when it discovered repression. Hammer Studios did not invent the myth of repression, but by taking it up and dramatising it, they made it the organising principle of what was to prove to be a highly influential narrative. Because this myth still operates in our culture, Hammer's version of Dracula continues to exert its influence. But this is understandable, for without this Gothic myth of Victorian repression we lose the basis of our own 'modernity'. Our desire to see our own faces in the vampire's mirror is really our refusal to recognise our true counterparts in his Victorian antagonists.

Notes

1. Michel Foucault, *La Volonté de Savoir*, translated by Robert Hurley as *The History of Sexuality: An Introduction* (1976; Harmondsworth: Penguin Books, 1984), p. 35. Hereafter indicated as *HS*, with page references given in the text.
2. Twitchell, 'The Vampire Myth', first published in 1980, reproduced in Margaret L. Carter (ed.), *Dracula: The Vampire and the Critics* (Ann Arbor and London: UMI Research Press, 1988), pp. 109–16; p. 112.
3. The phrase is Christopher Craft's, and refers to the application of Freud's 'Primal Horde' theory to Stoker's Text, Craft, ' "Kiss Me With Those Red Lips": Gender and Inversion in Bram Stoker's *Dracula*', in

248 Varieties of Victorianism

Elaine Showalter (ed.), *Speaking of Gender* (New York: Routledge, 1989), pp. 216–42; p. 225.

4. David Pirie, *The Vampire Cinema* (London: Hamlyn, 1977), p. 67.
5. Ibid., p. 74.
6. David Pirie, *A Heritage of Horror: The English Gothic Cinema 1946–1972* (London: Gordon Fraser, 1973), p. 84.
7. Bram Stoker, *Dracula*, edited by Maurice Hindle (1897; Harmondsworth: Penguin Books, 1993), p. 51.
8. Chris Baldick, 'Introduction' to *The Oxford Book of Gothic Tales* (Oxford: Oxford University Press, 1993), pp. xix, xxi.
9. Baldick, p. xiii.
10. Alain Silver and James Ursini, *The Vampire Film: From "Nosferatu" to "Bram Stoker's Dracula"* (New York: Limelight Editions, 1993), p. 123.
11. Robin Wood, 'Burying the Undead: The Use and Obsolescence of Count Dracula', *Mosaic* 16 (1983), pp. 175–87; p. 175.
12. Wood, p. 180.
13. Hatlen, 'The Return of the Repressed/Oppressed in Bram Stoker's *Dracula*', first published in 1980, reproduced in Carter (ed.), *Dracula*, pp. 117–35; p. 120.
14. Hatlen, p. 133.
15. Hatlen, p. 130.
16. For example see Thomas Laquer, *Making Sex: Body and Gender From the Greeks to Freud* (Cambridge, Mass. and London: Harvard University Press, 1990); Jeffrey Weeks, *Against Nature* (London: Rivers Oram Press, 1991); Ed Cohen, *Talk on the Wilde Side: Toward a Genealogy of a Discourse on Male Sexualities* (London and New York: Routledge, 1993); Joseph Bristow, *Sexuality* (London and New York: Routledge, 1997).
17. Foucault's absence from the index of Ken Gelder's *Reading the Vampire* (London and New York: Routledge, 1994) is revealingly matched by the preponderance of Freud. Freud appears fifteen times, with Lacan enjoying a ten-page spread.
18. Gail B. Griffin, '"Your Girls That You Love are Mine": *Dracula* and the Victorian Male Sexual Imagination', first published in 1980, reproduced in Carter (ed.), pp. 137–48; p. 148.
19. Gelder, p. 67.
20. Roxana Stuart, 'The Eroticism of Evil: The Vampire in Nineteenth-Century Melodrama', in James Redmond (ed.), *Melodrama* (Cambridge: Cambridge University Press, 1992), pp. 223–44; p. 238.
21. C.F. Bentley, 'The Monster in the Bedroom: Sexual Symbolism in Bram Stoker's *Dracula*', *Literature and Psychology* 22 (1972), pp. 27–35; p. 27.
22. Robin Wood, 'Burying the Undead', p. 181.
23. Burton Hatlen, 'Return', p. 129.
24. Jennifer Wicke, 'Vampiric Typewriting: *Dracula* and its Media', *ELH* 59 (1992), pp. 467–93; p. 479.
25. John Allen Stevenson, 'A Vampire in the Mirror: The Sexuality of *Dracula*', *PMLA* 103 (1988), pp. 139–49; p. 143.
26. Christopher Craft, '"Kiss Me"', p. 220.

27. Richard Von Krafft-Ebing, *Psychopathia Sexualis. With Especial Reference to the Antipathic Sexual Instinct: A Medico-Legal Study*, 7th German edn, first English translation (1886; London: F.A. Davis & Co., 1892), p. 87. For a 'Krafft-Ebian' reading of *Dracula* which expands on these points see my 'Sex, History and the Vampire', in William Hughes and Andrew Smith (eds), *Bram Stoker: History, Psychoanalysis and the Gothic* (London: Macmillan, forthcoming).
28. David Pirie, *The Vampire Cinema*, p. 9.
29. See Craft ' "Kiss Me" '; Sue-Ellen Case, 'Tracking the Vampire', *Differences* 3 (1991), pp. 1–20; Gelder, pp. 61–3, 69–76; Ellis Hanson, 'Undead', in Diana Fuss, *Inside/Out: Lesbian Theories, Gay Theories* (New York and London: Routledge, 1991), pp. 324–40.

16

Of Elephants and Men: the Freak as Victorian and Contemporary Spectacle[1]

Jonathan Skinner

'Look at the nigger!...Mama, a Negro!...Hell, he's getting mad....Take no notice, sir, he does not know that you are as civilised as we...'

Frantz Fanon[2]

INTRODUCTION

Queen Victoria's lifespan (1819–1901) just manages to link two centuries, one renowned for Britain's industrial and imperial might, strict values and moral codes, the other, a century which posterity may record as a period of British decline and decadence, of devolution from the international stage and fragmentation within the queendom. Further juxtapositions – between the years of Queen Victoria's reign (1837–1901) and the final bi-centennial years of the twentieth century – reveal more substantial contrasts. Historically, Britain's part in the European 'Scramble for Africa' (1880s) can be contrasted directly with African decolonisation eighty years later. Economically, Britain emerged from the Industrial Revolution with a strong production-base and colonial distribution network, whereas now, post-structuralists and postmodernists claim that Britain has entered a post-industrial age of computers and information technology where knowledge is (industrial) power.[3] Sociologically, British society now no longer reflects the working/leisured class divisions which the Marxist historian E.P. Thompson once chronicled,[4] for all members of the public can now work towards becoming politicians and archbishops, bankers, and officers in the armed forces – traditionally the blue-blooded pursuits of the aristocratic. The Victorian 'Zeitgeist', if you will, is modern and progressive, despite harping back to the civilising ideas and ideals of the Enlightenment: the Aquarian Zeitgeist, in contrast, is postmodern, characterised by a New Age barbarity and Jean-François Lyotard's terse 'incredulity toward metanarratives'.[5]

The aim of this chapter, however, is not to contrast general perceptions about the end of a particular century with those held at the end of a certain millennium. Rather, my aim is to highlight several unexpected correspondences between the Victorian era and what will be known as Britain's second Elizabethan era. I take as my example the dispossessed, the marginalised, an example of performative 'othering' and distancing which occurs on the sides of society – the cast from the side-show. For my example I conjure up from the back of the mind, sawdust and the secrets of the circus; shadows in the folds of the tent; side-shows, shows from 'The Fringe' – the ostracised; the oddity; the freak; the bizarre; the curio; the alien; the inhuman. I do this by juxtaposing the sad Victorian case-history of Joseph 'The Elephant Man' Merrick (1860–90) with my contemporary observations of characters belonging to The Jim Rose Circus Side-show in the 1990s, both bizarre accounts of extra-ordinary (in)humanity. Initial contrasts between the 'unnatural' Victorian freak, and the monstrous postmodern stage troupe of freaks, give way to some tentative correspondences between the two epochs, particularly in the way that 'the freak' is socially constructed.

A REPULSIVE ATTRACTION

It was an unwritten tradition that, during the early years of Queen Victoria's reign, leisure time and leisure activities were segregated by breeding. Tracing the development of the English seaside resort, John Walton notes that Blackpool encouraged a seasonal and physical 'social zoning' system to preserve the peace between the hordes of working class weekend excursionists and the select few upper class seasonal residents: the city corporation used picture posters to attract the working class between mid-July and early September, leaving Blackpool quiet for Easter and the rest of the year; and they developed a fee-paying 'select lounge' on the North Pier (1862), allowing the Central Pier (1868) to cater for the working class with the cheap attraction of open-air dancing.[6] Elsewhere, entertainment was often divided between those who joined in with the music-hall songs, participated in the magician's show, egged on the local prize-fighter, or watched amazed at the circus acts; and those who sat quietly listening to an Italian opera, a Viennese orchestra, or the Russian ballet. According to Hugh Cunningham's report into class and leisure in mid-Victorian England, the managers of Covent Garden opera house and Drury Lane theatre caused a great scandal when they first allowed horses, lions and elephants onto their hallowed stages.[7] High culture should not be seen to be mixing with low culture, with 'popular' culture – what Cunningham refers to as the culture 'of the people'.[8] The suggestion, here, being that popular culture was – and perhaps still is – ordinary, lacking in quality, and monolithic – regardless of the gender or ethnicity or background of the performers and the audience.[9]

The annual street fairs, travelling circuses and public holidays celebrated across all of Victorian Britain were, no doubt, the leftovers from a bygone era when Britain was a pre-industrial society and the population lived and worked in tune with the rhythm of the seasons. These events occur as the vestiges of a carnival cycle of festivity, Rabelaisian flashes which function, according to Emile Durkheim, as sacred high points in the yearly cycle of an individual's profane working life.[10] Bartholomew Fair was one such carnival moment which opened each year on 23 August and lasted for two weeks. At this fair, and many others, giants, dwarfs, and hermaphrodites were exhibited. In fact, there was such a great public fascination with the exotic, the unusual, with what we would retrospectively refer to as 'the exceptional', that several permanent exhibition halls were established in London. One of them, the Egyptian Hall in Piccadilly, claimed to have 'upwards of Fifteen Thousand Natural and Foreign Curiosities, antiquities and Productions of the Fine Arts'.[11] It was there, in 1844, that Phineas Barnum, the renowned American side-show entrepreneur, displayed all two feet eleven inches of General Tom Thumb.[12] Participating in a similar human display, but at a less prestigious London showroom, was Joseph Merrick.

The most detailed records of Joseph Merrick come from the published reminiscences of Sir Frederick Treves, a surgeon based in London.[13] In 1884 Treves visited a run-down shop in Whitechapel Road where he saw 'the most disgusting specimen of humanity' that he had ever seen.[14] Before him was The Elephant Man, a man, twenty-four years old, with a twisted body and an effeminate left hand and arm, but a right hand, in Merrick's own words, 'almost the size and shape of an Elephant's fore-leg, measuring 12 inches round the wrist and 5 inches round one of the fingers'.[15] In addition, parts of Merrick's torso were covered in pendulous growths of skin. However, Merrick was named and known for his head: it was the circumference of a man's waist (36 inches); it was misshapen and covered in cauliflower-like growths of skin; there was a bony bulge across his forehead the shape of a loaf of bread extending down to his right eye-brow, a growth down the right-hand side of his face, and a compression of skin about the lower half of the face which forced his lips back into trunk-like folds. Billed as The Elephant Man, Merrick had spent most of his life as a professional freak, first for his fellow Leicester-man Sam Torr – a music-hall showman and liquor merchant – and then for Tom Norman, an exhibitor of freaks and novelties.

Showmen and audiences naturally assumed that because Merrick could barely speak or communicate, he had to be an imbecile. Subsequent to his visit to see The Elephant Man, Treves called him for a medical examination so that he might record Merrick's abominable infliction. Merrick returned to his stage and his trade of attracting Norman's audience so that they might then be repulsed by him. His showman toured him around England and over to the Continent. In every place, the gross nature of his charge forced Norman to move on. Eventually, Norman grew tired and discouraged by the incessant movement of his show. He split up with Merrick in Brussels, leaving him enough money to pay for his passage back to London.

According to Treves's story, The Elephant Man succeeded in his travels by hiding himself under a large cloak – a particularly poignant image which was spotlighted in Bernard Pomerance's *The Elephant Man* play (first produced at the 1977 Edinburgh Festival).[16] Back in London in 1846, The Elephant Man was destitute, penniless and a physical cause for alarm on the streets. As chance would have it, Treves declared that his calling-card was still in Merrick's possession, and so the police turned him over to the capable hands of the surgeon healer. Intrigued by the case of The Elephant Man, Treves allocated Merrick an attic room in his London Hospital. There Merrick stayed, under the medical gaze, until he died in 1890. During this time, Treves exhibited Merrick to his peers as a medical case at the Pathological Society of London,[17] published scholarly notes about Merrick's condition,[18] arranged for a public trust fund to cater for Merrick's expenses, and encouraged members of the leisured class such as Victoria's son Edward, Prince of Wales, to visit and befriend him.

Merrick was visited by members of high society who did not have to pay a showman to see him. Instead, they brought gifts: the ladies often brought signed photographs of themselves, the gentlemen walking-sticks; Merrick often received silver-backed brushes and razors which he could not use; and occasionally they even booked a private box at the theatre for Merrick to watch shows whilst remaining in his abominable privacy. Such attentions beg the unanswerable question as to whether or not they saw him as Joseph Merrick, or as The Elephant Man? Certainly, the visitors to the hospital attic were more hospitable to the man/elephant than the visitors to the exhibition rooms and tents of his earlier years. But to what extent were these new relationships social as opposed to economic? Perhaps Merrick's new visitors came to him to show their sympathy, or because of the guilt which they felt, thankful that they did not have his terrible affliction. Treves encouraged all the noble visitors to Merrick's quarters, once he realised – to his horror – that Merrick was not an imbecile but an intelligent and sensitive Caliban of the city. With the advantage of hindsight, it is all too tempting to declare that Treves was courting the upper class by exploiting a vulnerable member of the working class, whilst also furthering his own literary and medical careers; despite even the presumed close relationship between Treves and Merrick, it was Treves who performed Merrick's autopsy. Pomerance, however, prefers to suggest in his play that it was The Elephant Man who was the exploiter, a man making the most of his affliction. Just as it has been difficult to diagnose Merrick's medical condition (now thought to have been multiple neurofibromatosis), it is difficult to ascertain the complex nature of Merrick's relationships with the working-class audiences at the fairs and side-shows, the medical professionals of an educated middle class, and the casual visitors from amongst the upper class. Whichever the interpretation of events, I would like to suggest that Merrick was constructed as a freak by himself and society around him, especially when he was packaged and sold by showmen such as Norman and presented as a medical specimen by Treves. In the next section I will further exemplify the social construction of the freak with a contemporary ethnography of a freak show. I now turn to the more immediate – and possibly more socially constructed – Jim Rose Circus Side-show.

GUTS AND GORE (AND A WHOLE LOT MORE)[19]

One of my visits to The Jim Rose Circus Side-show was whilst it was playing at the Edinburgh Festival Fringe from Monday 16 August to Saturday 4 September 1993.[20] They performed alongside the likes of the Scottish folk-rock band Capercaillie, the singer Howard Jones, Russian clowns, the Peking Opera circus, Nicholas Parsons and Tony Slattery. The circus side-show's venue was a 300-capacity tent on a hill overlooking the centre of metropolitan Edinburgh. Sponsored by Jacob Staudier Exportbier, they 'played', performed and shocked their youthful audience for $1\frac{1}{4}$ hours every night.

The hill which The Jim Rose Circus Side-show performed upon is called the Acropolis because of a folly of false ruins built there to infer links between sophisticated and acculturated Scots and their traditional, classical education. It provided the most ironic backdrop for a show which tested the limits of visual performance and pushed at the boundaries of acceptable culture. It was precisely this Graeco-Roman heritage which Conservative Councillor of Culture Moira Knox was appealing to in her calls for the show to be banned from her capital.[21] Yet why would Edinburgh entertain and plunder classical themes and images from the exotic Mediterranean but maintain an aloof distance from the exotic, alien, modern-day freak show from Seattle, home to grunge and Jim Rose? Let me spend some time exploring the nature of the show itself, the learned routines of the volunteer stage characters Jim and Bebe Rose, The Torture King, The Human Enigma, The Amazing Mr Lifto and Matt 'the Tube' Crowley.

Throughout the show, Jim Rose – a spry renegade figure, impresario, side-show master and showman – enthused and expounded over the scientific beauty of each character's presentation, which lasted approximately two to three minutes before rotating with another. Mr Rose not only praised the range of abilities of the human body which can endure repeated pain, torture and masochism, but he also shocked and amazed the youthful audience. Jim had successfully desensitised his body to withstand darts thrown into his back, his face trampled into shards of a ground-up light-bulb, and juggling razor blades in his throat without tripping the gag reflex. Such abuse of his body did not appear to discomfort him, nor did he or the other showmen appear to be disabled by their acts; rather, the audience seemed the more affected by the visual and verbal abuse than the characters' activities upon themselves.

The Torture King – a ponytailed hippie – worked with swords and nails. He swallowed swords as far down as his intestines and walked up a ladder of swords, balancing on their blades. The Torture King lay down on a bed of swords and had a breeze-block smashed upon his chest with a sledgehammer. He then went on to push nails into his chest, through his arms, eyelids, cheeks and nostrils before passing high-voltage electricity through his body. Again, as in Jim Rose's painful-looking acts, no permanent injury was done and there was no bleeding.

On entering the Fringe tent, a caged, automated figure wearing a top-hat and cloak – like a robotic Phantom of the Opera – was playing a synthesiser. He revealed himself to be The Human Enigma, a bald, stocky youth playing a sub-human animal, creature, *üntermensch*. The Human Enigma was led by his, or its, dog-collar to the front of the stage where he was stripped of his clothes, bar loincloth, and displayed, cowering like an urban Caliban in front of the audience. His own personal trait was not just his behaviour but also his appearance: The Human Enigma has been cleverly tattooed in his entirety, with jig-saw shapes all interlocking bar the occasional black space of a missing piece. This accounted for his aptly named stage persona – The Enigma – with the ironic prefix – Human. Once revealed, The Human Enigma was fed a nutritious assortment of live grubs and insects such as maggots and grasshoppers, before he left for back stage to help prepare the other acts.

From sub-human to super-human, *üntermensch* to superman, the side-show contrasted The Human Enigma with the hulk-like figure Matt 'the Tube' Crowley. Matt put on typical circus strongman acts: inflating and blowing up a hot-water bottle and a condom stretched over his head; lighting cigarettes from the sparks of a metal grinder; extinguishing a blow-torch in his mouth; supergluing a bowling-ball to his fingertips and, after raising and lowering it, ripping most of the flesh on his fingers off on the ball. Lastly – and most spectacularly – Matt 'the Tube' revealed to the audience, like The Human Enigma, the reason for his stage name. The climactic act of the entire show occurred when he passed some plastic tubing through his nose right down into his stomach. Some beer was poured down into Matt's stomach whereupon it was sucked back up into the cylinder of the pump. Ketchup, mustard and milk of magnesia were added to the concoction which was again pumped down into Matt's stomach. After a 'suitable' pause, the pump drew back up the liquids which had mixed with each other and turned into a thick oozing potion with the addition of Matt's stomach bile.

What was the audience reaction to this act? Most spectators and observers felt both a revulsion and fascination throughout the entire side-show performance; many had come prepared to be shocked and had been forewarned and even attracted to the show by the international publicity which the show had received and encouraged. At this stage in Matt's bilious act, most of the audience were intrigued by his regurgitations. The presentation of all the acts consisted of treating them as an historical display or as scientific experiments exhibiting the conditioning abilities of the human body. In this way, the audience were drawn into the show, intrigued, aroused, shocked, and eventually relieved. It was in such a manner that when the contents of Matt's stomach was poured into pint glasses, there were many volunteers keen to drink the brew.

The final character, actor and curio to behold was Mr Lifto, an anaemic, frail and effeminate man with pierced ears, nipples, tongue and penis. Mr Lifto, with his ambiguous and confusing gender, contrasted himself with the apparent normality of Jim Rose, the superhuman qualities of Matt 'the Tube' and the inhuman nature of The Human Enigma. With effeminate postures and gestures Mr Lifto dangled irons from his ears, tongue, nipples and penis, causing women to fold their arms across their chests and men to cross their legs – all with expressions of hurt concern across their faces. Unfortunately, the heavy, masochistic atmosphere was broken by Councillor Knox's final puritanical attempt at cultural censorship – the constraint of having one iron swung beneath a lengthy mass of shaving foam.

As I have stated earlier, the side-show participants – namely Jim Rose and his assistant Bebe Rose, The Torture King, The Human Enigma, the Amazing Mr Lifto and Matt 'the Tube' Crowley – left the show neither harmed nor maimed. And the audience dispersed with pints of beer and bile in hand, refreshed by such a cathartic journey through aesthetics, contortions, perversions, pain, sadism and masochism; a journey which was presented in a positive light as a harmless side-show pageant after which the audience could buy the T-shirt[22] and buy drinks for the real people living up to their fictional stage personas; an escapism removed, recast and suspended by distance from the cultural proprieties and bustle of Edinburgh proper and her Festival.

NATURAL AND SELF-MADE FREAKS

The five Jim Rose Circus Side-show characters which I have outlined are 'self-made freaks'. They fit into Robert Bogdan's category of '"authentic" fabrications – people who worked within legitimate freak roles with a long history in the amusement industry.'[23] Unlike The Elephant Man, sword-swallowers, tattoo artists, wild men, supermen, Jim Rose and Mr Lifto are people not born with any abnormality; they are people who have learned to do unusual, entertaining acts, which are presented in an exotic and aggrandised form. The Jim Rose Circus Side-show's voluntary social misfits do not exploit any abnormalities from birth: they are not dwarfs – people under four feet ten inches; they do not have microcephaly – a condition associated with mental retardation and characterised by very small, pointed pin-like heads; they have not 'lost' any limbs, nor have they 'gained' a twin who might be joined at the hip. In this respect, contemporary side-show players such as Matt 'the Tube' and The Human Enigma might appear to have no authentic claim to similarity with the likes of General Tom Thumb; Tik Tak the Aztec Pinhead; the tandem cycling pair – armless Charles Tripp and legless Eli Bowen, or the inseparable Hilton Sisters.[24] Yet whenever or whatever the act – Victorian or contemporary, natural or self-made freak – Bogdan maintains that freaks are socially constructed. '"Freak" is a frame of mind, a set of practices, a way of thinking about and presenting people. It is the enactment of a tradition, the performance of a stylized presentation.'[25] I concur with his statement, even in the case of The Elephant Man. Both types of freak physically transcend what Erving Goffman refers to as our 'normative expectations' of humankind.[26]

These side-show routines – whether presented as circus entertainment, as in the case of The Jim Rose Circus Side-show, or shock horror as with the exploitation of Mr Joseph 'The Elephant Man' Merrick – deliberately make themselves the object of inquiry and scrutiny, separating and distancing themselves from the immediacy of daily life. The social construction of the freak even occurs in the hospital attic and in the lecture room of the Pathological Society.[27] Either directly (Jim Rose) or indirectly (Joseph Merrick), side-show characters distinguish, reiterate, challenge and demarcate the boundaries and limitations of normal appearance and behaviour vis-à-vis the audience.

Whether in Victorian or contemporary times, this occurs in much the same way that different nations obtain a construction of 'self', defining 'us' by constructing 'you', frequently deforming 'the other' in the process: here is civilisation, there is barbarity. On a more local level, describing his fieldwork in the Yorkshire Dales, the anthropologist Nigel Rapport compares the position of the Anglican vicar in Wanet with that of the Anglican vicar, Mr Beebe, in Forster's *A Room With a View*.[28] In both examples, one real and the other fictional, the vicars fail to cross a boundary between outsiders and insiders in the community; in fact, the vicar is used to identify where precisely that boundary lies. In the same way, side-show characters establish boundaries between the performance and the audience, the decent and the indecent, the socially accepted and the properly unacceptable. But Rapport does more than identify the otherness of the church, he mentions the persistent and idiosyncratic distancing and social alienation with occurs in everyday circumstances. In Wanet,

> any number of very different distinctions can come to the fore: updale (Wanet village) versus downdale (Thurn); Methodists versus Church of England; those who support the Women's Institute, the Choir, the Thurn Thespians, versus those who keep to themselves; those who work the land versus those who do not; those highly capitalised farmers in the 'big league' versus those just getting by on crowded, rented plots; those in business who profit from the tourists versus those who do not; the young drinkers of the Mitre versus the old hands of the Eagle; Tetley beer drinkers versus Courage drinkers; beer drinkers versus larger drinkers; weekend drinkers versus regular drinkers. And so on.[29]

Rapport demonstrates that not only is it always possible and very easy to distance someone or turn them into an other – just as my discipline, anthropology, constructs its anthropological object – but that this process is all pervasive. Consider Jenny Sharpe's brutal example of the British soldiers during the 1857 Indian Mutiny who were inspired into battle with the belief that Indian men have a pathological lust for white women.[30] This is an historical fiction with a deadly reality effect; a canny use of rape as a master trope to other and alienate the Indian.

CONCLUSION

In this essay I have concentrated upon the social construction of the freak. I have used examples from the life of Joseph Merrick and the work of Jim Rose to show a particular correspondence between Victorian and contemporary times. These examples from the fringe raise some other interesting questions which I have not been able to address. Do the Hilton sisters, with their two brains and minds united in the one body, substantiate Foucault and Lyotard's supposition that the concept of 'man' is a short-lived product of the process of evolution? Is the individual a relatively contemporary cultural construct? These questions remain unanswered, but what I have done at the end of this essay is to move from an examination of the social construction of natural and self-made freaks to a more general discussion of the process of social alienation which occurs in both real and literary life.

Of additional interest in Jim Rose's show is the fact that he desensitises his audience, so that some go on to participate in the show and perform acts such as drinking Matt's stomach contents, breaking light-bulbs and grinding Jim's face into the shards. Jim's success at desensitising the audience – showing that his 'freaks' are his 'friends', normal people with a skill at performance – changes the audience's attitude to the socially constructed inhuman other. This process turns into something more than mere shock and horror entertainment, it becomes a reversal of army basic training – the activity which dehumanises the enemy thereby allowing men to perpetrate atrocities in the name of their civilised society. Perhaps, then, Jim Rose's technique is a useful way of confronting and dispelling the audiences' unthinking prejudices and animosities, a pseudo-anthropological method of making the strange familiar. When Edmund Leach declared his anthropological ambitions – 'to understand alien societies from the inside rather than from the outside',[31] to become the marginal native and so break down the barriers between the constructed self and the constructed other – I am sure that he did not expect the realisation of such intentions on the level ground of Edinburgh's Acropolis.

Notes

1. I gratefully acknowledge the thoughts and suggestions made by Gary Day, Nigel Rapport and Holly Gray whilst I was writing this chapter.
2. Frantz Fanon, *Black Skin, White Masks* (London: Pluto Press, 1991), p. 113.
3. Madan Sarup, *An Introductory Guide to Post-Structuralism and Post-modernism* (Hemel Hempstead: Harvester Wheatsheaf, 1993), p. 133.
4. E.P. Thompson, *The Making of the English Working Class* (London: Victor Gollancz Ltd, 1963).
5. Jean-François Lyotard, *The Postmodern Condition: A Report on Knowledge* (Manchester: Manchester University Press, 1992), p. xxiv.
6. John Walton, 'Residential amenity, respectable morality and the rise of the entertainment industry: the case of Blackpool, 1860–1914' in Bernard Waites, Tony Bennett and Graham Martin (eds), *Popular Culture: Past and Present* (London: The Open University Press, 1982), pp. 133–45; p. 138.
7. Hugh Cunningham, 'Class and Leisure in mid-Victorian England' in Waites, Bennett and Martin (eds), *Popular Culture*, pp. 66–91, especially p. 67.
8. Ibid., p. 68.
9. See Tim Harris, 'Problematising Popular Culture' in Tim Harris (ed.), *Popular Culture in England c. 1500–1850* (London: Macmillan Press Ltd, 1995), pp. 1–27. This article is a damning critique of the bi-polar 'high/low culture' model. By extension, it can also be applied to Thompson's bi-polar 'working/leisured class' model.
10. See 'The functions of ritual' in Anthony Giddens (ed.), *Emile Durkheim: Selected Writings* (Cambridge: Cambridge University Press, 1990), pp. 232–8.
11. Michael Howell and Peter Ford, *The True History of the Elephant Man* (Harmondsworth: Penguin Books, 1981), p. 14.
12. Ibid.; see also Robert Bogdan, *Freak Show: Presenting Human Oddities for Amusement and Profit* (Chicago: University of Chicago Press, 1988), p. 150.
13. Sir Frederick Treves, *The Elephant Man and other reminiscences* (London: Cassell & Company Ltd, 1928). Though critical of several inaccuracies in Treves's account of his meeting with Merrick, Howell and Ford have reprinted the relevant chapter in full (1981, pp. 190–210). Though I quote directly from Treves's original account, I have relied, largely, upon Howell and Ford's corrected version in writing this chapter.
14. Treves, op. cit., p. 11.
15. Appendix One, 'The Autobiography of Joseph Carey Merrick' in Howell and Ford, op. cit., pp. 182–9.
16. Bernard Pomerance, *The Elephant Man* (London: Faber & Faber, 1980).
17. One such presentation took place on 2 December 1884.
18. See, for instance, Frederick Treves, 'A Case of Congential Deformity' in *Transactions of the Pathological Society of London* XXXVI (1885), pp. 494–8.
19. This is the catch phrase on the show's promotion labels.

20. I have witnessed several performances of The Jim Rose Sideshow over the years. Though some of the characters change from year to year, much of the show remains the same. My account of The Jim Rose Circus Sideshow in this chapter refers mainly to their August 1993 visit to the Edinburgh Festival Fringe. For another account of the sideshow performance see Robert Grant, 'I did it for you' in the *Times Literary Supplement*, 27 August 1993, p. 20.

21. Michael Paterson, 'Councillor freaks out at Calton Hill circus showdown' in *The Scotsman*, 17 August 1993, p. 1.

22. On a black setting, the T-shirt portrays the characters and their gory acts in vivid colours.

23. Bogdan, op. cit., p. 235.

24. Ibid., p. 149, p. 132, p. 220, p. 166.

25. Ibid., p. 3.

26. Erving Goffman, *Stigma – Notes on the Management of Spoiled Identity* (Harmondsworth: Penguin Books, 1990), p. 12.

27. See Peter Berger and Thomas Luckmann, *The Social Construction of Reality* (Harmondsworth: Penguin Books, 1971), where they argue that even the nature of reality is socially constructed.

28. Nigel Rapport, *The Prose and the Passion – Anthropology, literature and the writing of E.M. Forster* (Manchester: Manchester University Press, 1994), p. 98. See also E.M. Forster, *A Room with a View* (Harmondsworth: Penguin, 1983).

29. Rapport, op. cit., p. 74.

30. Jenny Sharpe, 'The Unspeakable Limits of Rape: Colonial Violence and Counter-Insurgency' in Patrick Williams and Laura Chrisman (eds), *Colonial Discourse and Post-colonial Theory – A reader* (Hemel Hempstead: Harvester Wheatsheaf, 1993), pp. 221–44.

31. Edmund Leach, *Social Anthropology* (Glasgow: Fontana Press, 1982), p. 161.

Index

Romanticism, 112–13, 119
Ronell, Avital, 77, 79n
Rosen, David, 141n
Ruskin, John, 3, 45, 61n, 220, 231,
  235n
Ryals, Clyde, de L., 178n

Said, Edward, 87
Samuel, Raphael, 21n
Sarup, Madan, 261n
Saturday Review, The, 229
Schopenhauer, Arthur, 121–2
Schwarz, Bill, 24n
Scott, Gilbert, 60
Scott, Sir Walter, 83
Seddon, Mark, 23n
self, 11–16, 130–3, 147, 149, 151–2,
  171–2, 197, 260
self help, 1, 7–20, 217
Selincourt, E. de., 177n
sensation novels, 222–31, 235n
sexuality, 183, 236–47, 247n, 248n,
  249n
Sharp, Granville, 8
Sharpe, Jenny, 259, 262n
Shelley, Percy Bysshe, 161–77, 177n,
  178n; 'Adonais', 162; 'Ode to the
  West Wind', 165
Shephard, Simon, 204n
Sheridan, Alan, 96n
Shiman, Lillian Lewis, 144, 158n
Showalter, Elaine, 248n
Shyllon, Folarin, 140n
Sibthorpe, Colonel, 48–52, 54–5
Silver, Alain, 241, 248n
Simmel, Georg, 63–4, 75, 77n
Skidelsky, Robert, 23n
slavery, 128
Smiles, Samuel, 1, 7–20, 217; *Self
  Help*, 1, 7–20, 23n
Smith, Andrew, 249n
Smith, James and Horace, 83
Smith, Madeleine, 20, 220–34, 234n,
  235n
Smith, Margaret, 178n
Smout, T.C., 21n
society, 2, 8–11, 98–9, 103–5, 118–24,
  147, 149, 152–7
soldiers, 27–8

Southey, Robert, 83; 'The Old Man's
  Comforts', 83–4, 95n
spectacle, 197–8, 212
Spencer, Herbert, 13, 115, 200
Spivak, Gayatri, 34, 39n
Stanley, A.P., 28, 32, 35–6
Stead, W. T., 185
Stevenson, Robert Louis, *Virginibus
  Puerisque*, 188
Stevenson, John Allen, 248n
Stivale, Charles, 96n
Stoker, Bram, *Dracula*, 133, 232,
  236–47, 247n, 248n, 249n;
  adaptations of: 20, 236–47, 248n
Stone, Lawrence, 223, 234n
Strachey, James, 79n
Strong, Roy, 180–1
Struik, Dirk J., 79n
Stuart, Roxana, 248n
subjectivity, 17, 88–91
Sully, James, 125n
Susman, Warren, 23n
Sutherland, John, 134, 139n, 140n
Swanson, Vern G., 190n
Swift, Jonathan, *Gulliver's Travels*, 55
Sydenham Palace, 44, 61n

Tawney, R.H., 24n
Taylor, Bernard, 235n
Taylor, George, 204n
Tebbit, Norman, 232
technological development, 43, 46,
  48
Tennyson, Alfred, Lord, *Idylls of the
  King*, 3; 'The Lotos Eaters', 13
Tennyson Jesse, F., 234n
Terry, Ellen, 189n
Thackeray, William Makepeace, 6,
  83, 139n, 140n, 141n, 159n; *The
  Adventures of Philip*, 19, 126–39,
  139n, 140n; *The Four Georges*, 138;
  The Newcomes, 132, 137, 144;
  'Novels by Eminent Hands', 83;
  Pendennis, 127; *Vanity Fair*, 127,
  144; *The Virginians*, 128, 140n
Thale, Jerome, 124n
Thatcher, Margaret, 1, 21n, 23n, 118,
  125n, 191, 232
theatre, 192–203, 204n, 206–17, 218n